UNDERSTANDING AND USING COMMUNICATION IN BUSINESS

Satellite texts to accompany
UNDERSTANDING AND USING COMMUNICATION IN BUSINESS:

Available now
Techniques of Job Search

Future titles
Writing Skills
How to Write
Business Letters
Reports
Small Groups
The Nature of Communication
Reading and Listening
Nonverbal Communication
Oral Communication
Interpersonal Communication
Formal Presentations
Organizational Communication

CANFIELD PRESS • SAN FRANCISCO

HARPER & ROW, PUBLISHERS
New York Hagerstown Philadelphia San Francisco London

UNDERSTANDING AND USING COMMUNICATION IN BUSINESS

JOEL P. BOWMAN, Ph.D.
BERNADINE P. BRANCHAW, Ed.D.
WESTERN MICHIGAN UNIVERSITY

Production Editor:
Thomas E. Dorsaneo

Interior and cover design, chapter opening art:
John Patrick Sullivan

Copy editor:
Patrick J. Foley

Understanding and Using Communication in Business

Library of Congress Cataloging in Publication Data
Bowman, Joel P.
Understanding and using communication in business.

Includes index.
1. Communication in management. I. Branchaw, Bernadine P., joint author. II. Title.
HF5718.B68 658.4′5 76-54907
ISBN 0-06-453709-9

77 78 79 10 9 8 7 6 5 4 3 2 1

CONTENTS

ABOUT THE AUTHORS

Drs. Joel P. Bowman and Bernadine P. Branchaw combined their professional experience and expertise in the area of effective communication to write *Understanding and Using Communication in Business.* Their ability to demonstrate the interrelationship of topics create this unique and comprehensive examination of communication skills and techniques. Because Bowman and Branchaw are concerned with how to communicate effectively, they think students should know practical aspects of all major communication systems, including written, oral, nonverbal messages or a combination of these.

Dr. Joel P. Bowman is Assistant Professor in the Department of Business Education and Administrative Services at Western Michigan University. His more than ten years of experience in developing and teaching introductory and advanced business communication courses and his work as consultant for leaders in business, industry, and government give him a professional base and understanding of the application of effective communication. He contributes regularly to professional journals and was Review Editor for *The Journal of Business Communication* the summer of 1975. As a lecturer he has brought the best aspects of the traditional and modern styles of communication to national, regional, and state conventions. Bowman is a member of American Business Communication Association, Phi Kappa Phi, Pi Omega Pi, and National Business Education Association.

Dr. Bernadine Branchaw worked five years as a secretary in Illinois and has fifteen years teaching experience in high schools, junior college, and universities in Illinois, Ohio, and Michigan. She is at present Assistant Professor in the Department of Business Education and Administrative Services at Western Michigan University.

Dr. Branchaw keeps abreast of developments in areas of communication as she lectures to businesses, industries, and government agencies. She proctors the Certified Secretary Examinations, chairs annual secretarial seminars sponsored by her department and writes articles for business educational journals. She is listed in *Leaders in Education, The World's Who's Who of Women,* and is active in National Business Education Association, Michigan Business Education Association, American Business Communication Association, and Delta Pi Epsilon. As a teacher she focuses on practical application of communication skills. Her awareness and access to problems and solutions in the area of business communication make her contribution invaluable.

In addition to their separate accomplishments, Drs. Bowman and Branchaw team teach secretarial and communication seminars for business, industry, school districts, and government agencies. The informal sense of teamwork that they have developed is evident in *Understanding and Using Communication in Business*. The knowledge of communication problems and solutions gleaned from these seminars is also evident in these pages. The combination of their skills is unusually effective.

Through the contribution of these two authors, *Understanding and Using Communication in Business* offers a total picture of the communication process: writing skills, letters, reports, writing problems (grammar, vocabulary, logic) organizational communication and presentations for small groups or formal meetings. Bowman and Branchaw are currently hard at work in their next book for Canfield Press on business letters.

PREFACE

Our goal in writing *Understanding and Using Communication in Business* was to present between the covers of one book as much information as we could about why and how certain messages communicate and other messages don't. We have tried to do so in a way that combines the advantages of the numerous "practical" communication texts with the advantages of the also numerous communication theory books.

Our own teaching experience and the results of a nationwide survey of business communication teachers conducted by Canfield Press indicated that this is the kind of book that can best meet the needs of business communication students — both in and out of college.

Because we believe that it is more important for most students to understand general theoretical principles than it is for them to know the results of field and laboratory studies that support the principles, our focus is on the practical use of principles. We have deliberately avoided the so-called "cookbook" approach to business communication. Because no two business problems will ever call for exactly the same solution, we believe that students of business communication need to understand enough of the theory behind communication principles to be able to adapt specific skills to a variety of situations without having to look up a "recipe" for a particular message type.

From Chapter One to Chapter Twelve, you will — we think — find this book readable, instructive, and useful. Each chapter begins with specific, measurable objectives. Each chapter concludes with questions and exercises which will enable your students to test themselves to see how much of the material has been mastered. The problems and exercises are relevant to the needs of the person in business and are the practical kinds of examples to which students can respond.

In Chapter One, "The Nature of Communication," we present the general principles and purposes of communication and relate these principles and purposes to specific methods of application.

In Chapters Two, Three, and Four, we discuss written communication, including basic skills, letters, and reports. In Chapter Five we present some simple techniques to help improve reading and listening skills. In Chapters Six, Seven, and Eight, we discuss the basic principles involved in face-to-face communication situations, including nonverbal and oral techniques of communicating and the psychological principles of formal and informal interpersonal relationships. In Chapter Nine we discuss communication behavior in small groups, and in Chapter Ten we discuss formal presentations.

Chapter Eleven, "Organizational Communication," shows how the information we've presented in the first ten chapters is combined to coordinate activity in organizational life.

Chapter Twelve, "The Job Search," shows the student how to use what you've learned about communication to find and obtain the job of their choice.

Understanding and Using Communication in Business can be used alone in courses that cover business communication in one semester or quarter, or it can be used in combination with one or more books treating a specific topic in depth. The forthcoming satellite publications for the Canfield Press business communication core/satellite series are designed to meet the need for special area emphasis, and the series will provide current and complete information in paperback form to supplement each of the twelve topics covered in this text.

We have avoided footnoting, but the suggested readings listed at the end of each chapter will help students pursue the specific details and the results of communication studies which may be of interest. To make it easy to find and use other materials, we've deliberately selected readily available books.

Although we have restricted documentation to the lists of suggested readings, we have not written this book in a vacuum. We have learned a great deal from the field and laboratory studies of others, and we have benefited from the writings of and conversations with many business communication authorities. We owe special thanks to Francis W. Weeks of the University of Illinois, C. W. Wilkinson of the University of Alabama, and many others in the American Business Communication Association. We also appreciate the advice and assistance given by James E. Freel, Cynthia A. Newell, and Thomas Dorsaneo of Canfield Press and Lucian Spataro of Ohio University. We also thank Mary Ann Bowman for her careful proofreading of the manuscript.

Good reading.

Joel P. Bowman
Bernadine P. Branchaw

1

THE NATURE OF COMMUNICATION

After you have read this chapter, you should be able to

1. **Define communication.**
2. **List eight communication variables.**
3. **Use models to illustrate the communication process.**
4. **List and explain barriers to communication.**
5. **Explain how communication systems help organizations to achieve definite objectives.**

THE NATURE OF COMMUNICATION

Purposes:
Principles
Practice
Problem Solving

This book is designed to help you understand communication principles and to show you how to use these principles effectively. Our goal for you is primarily practical: we want you to become a successful communicator. Most of this book deals with the practical uses of communication to solve typical interpersonal and business problems.

This first chapter, however, is theoretical. Because we want you to understand the *why* as well as the *how* of communication, we shall first present the theoretical framework of communication. But even when we are presenting the principles, our approach and goals are practical.

Because business will require you to communicate effectively but will not require you to pass exams on communication theory, we think it more important for you to know the principles that govern communication than it is for you to learn the results of specific studies. In this book, we are more concerned with *how* than with *why*. At the end of each chapter we provide a short bibliography that will enable you to find out more about the studies that support the theory if you desire. We hope that you will become sufficiently interested that you will want to read more than this one book, but we will have accomplished our purpose if reading this book makes you an effective communicator. We think it will.

In addition to defining and explaining the communication process, in this first chapter we present communication theory, relate it to communication and organizational objectives, define communication effectiveness, and identify the major communication systems in business organizations.

Although we will concentrate on how communication functions in business, most of what we say applies just as well to other kinds of communication. Business communication differs from all other forms of communication primarily in the environment in which it takes place. Much, but not all, business communication has a specific, practical purpose; that element isn't always present in other communication situations. But as a rule, what works well with your business associates will also work well with your family, friends, and others with whom you communicate.

Whether you recognize it or not, you have no choice but to communicate. If you try to avoid communicating by not replying to messages, you send a message anyway. When you don't say yes, you say no by default. The only choice you can make about communication is whether you are going to attempt to communicate effectively.

Language, like any other tool, can either be used or misused. You can use it to pursue ethical or unethical goals. Unprincipled or misguided persons can use communication to mislead others — just as Hitler used his skills as an orator to convince Germans that they were destined to rule the world. Once you've learned effective communication techniques, however, you will be able to prevent misunderstandings between people because you will know how to send clear messages and to interpret correctly the messages you receive. You will also learn how to avoid being manipulated — hustled — by someone who would mislead you. And, by knowing when someone is trying to manipulate you, you will be in a position to help prevent the manipulation of others.

COMMUNICATION PROBLEMS AND PROCESS

Importance of Communication

In the past 20 years or so, the business community has become increasingly aware that many of its problems are directly related to communication. The need for improved communication skills is evidenced by the demand for professional seminars on communication, the increasing number of "communication" jobs in business and industry, and the increasing number of colleges across the country with required communication courses.

Communication Can Be a Problem

What is it about communication that makes it a problem? Communication is such a standard, common occurrence in our lives that we tend to take it for granted. We talk to people; they answer. We write letters; we receive replies. We read books, take tests, and write papers. Almost everything we do requires some kind of communication activity. Information is going in and out all the time. (Some of it even makes sense!)

As is the case with other "automatic" activities such as walking, we communicate so much that most of us consider ourselves experts. When we don't understand or cannot make ourselves understood, we usually blame the other person. Most of the time, however, we are understood — or at least we think we are. And usually we are able to understand the other person — or at least we think we do. So it's only natural for us to consider ourselves experts. Most of the time we use communication fairly well. We're polite and friendly. We get along well with most of the people we know.

Communication Is Essential

Communication is essential for all human relations; it makes civilized, cooperative life possible. Our ability to build and shape our environment depends on our communication skills. To a certain degree, communication skills distinguish human beings from other animals. Without communication skills, we would have only the physical power of our individual bodies to control our environment. Without communication skills, our ancestors would have been no match for the many animals that were faster, stronger, and larger than they were. They undoubtedly communicated to survive.

We also communicate to make our lives better. We use communication skills to try to make our lives what we wish them to be. Building a city requires more communication than concrete. That civilization exists is testimony to our combined communication skills.

Unfortunately, the problems of civilization are also testimony to our skills as communicators. Even with those we know and love best, we have misunderstandings. With those we neither know nor like very much, communication is frequently difficult and sometimes impossible.

Communication Is Deceptive

Communication is deceptive. On the surface it seems easy to understand and achieve by using common sense. And much of our current knowledge about communication is based on a common-sense approach to communication problems. Often, however, common sense is not enough. Skilled communicators draw on an extensive and complex body of knowledge, including not only semantics — the study of language — but also aspects of psychology, sociology, and the graphic arts.

Because communication seems so simple, we tend to forget that it is a process involving a number of complex variables, and that for each of these variables, a number of things can go wrong.

COMMUNICATION VARIABLES

What Is Communication?

What is communication? We can begin with a simple definition. Communication can be broadly defined as the transmission of a message. Because this book is about human communication, we'll limit our discussion to the transmission of messages from one person to another — but we recognize that other animals, and perhaps even plants, are also capable of certain kinds of communication.

Although some writers discuss what they call "internal" or "intrapersonal" communication (a mental talking to yourself), it is generally more useful to limit the term communication to the transfer of meaning between and among people. Communication begins with a perception in the mind of a sender. This perception is the impetus for a message for which the sender selects a channel that will convey the message to a receiver. The goal of this process is the transfer of meaning. Several factors influence the communication process:

Communication Variables

1. Perception
2. Sender
3. Message
4. Channel
5. Audience (Receiver)
6. Transfer of meaning
7. Feedback
8. Noise

Perception

What Is Perception?

The first factor in the process, perception, is responsible for all of the others. To paraphrase René Descartes, we know that we exist because we perceive. Perception is the act of using the senses to become aware of the environment. Although we all live in the same *objective* world, each of us has a different *subjective* view of the world. We see the world with different eyes. No matter how similar two people may be, no two of us are exactly alike, and so each of us perceives the world and events differently.

Communication Is an Effort to Be More Comfortable

Human perception is a complicated subject, and we have space to deal with only a small part of it. Our perceptions begin in a simple way, however. Infants perceive themselves as either comfortable or uncomfortable. When they are uncomfortable, they communicate. The survival of the infant depends on the success of that communication.

At first, infants do not perceive themselves as separate beings. When they finally do perceive that they are separate from their mothers and the rest of their environment, the complexity of perception — and of the communication process — greatly increases.

In addition to expressing the relatively flat emotions of comfort and discomfort, infants begin to express gratitude, fear, anger, and even rage. Infants wish to control their mothers to ensure continued gratification of their needs; infants want their mothers to perceive the world of their needs with the full intensity with which they perceive it. The infant insists: "My hunger is your hunger; my pain is your pain."

As we grow older, we cease to expect such a total sharing; but because humanity's survival has for so long depended on making others share our perceptions, the mental health of each of us depends on our ability to share our perceptions with others. If it were not for our different perceptions, we would not have the need to communicate.

Sender

Who Is the Sender?

Another important factor in the communication process is the sender. The sender is responsible for formulating a message that will convey the meaning the perception has created. This book attempts to help you improve your communication skills by showing how you, as a sender of messages, can control the communication process by the way you present yourself and your message.

Credibility

As a message source, you must be concerned with your believability or credibility. Your credibility and that of your messages greatly influence the kind of reception your messages will receive. Your credibility will depend on how well you convey trustworthiness and professional competence, but you can't convey these qualities by skilled communication alone — you'll have to earn them.

Message

Messages Are Symbolic

The third major factor in the communication process, messages, is *what* we communicate. Messages consist of verbal or nonverbal symbols containing information, meaning, or intelligence. Each message is an attempt to define and share with our intended receiver some aspect of our perception of the world — what we see, hear, feel, taste, smell, or think — and what that perception means to us.

Of course messages can vary greatly in complexity from the infant's cry announcing discomfort to the complicated language of détente. When people's perceptions are similar, simple messages serve; as perceptions become increasingly dissimilar, the complexity of messages must also increase. You know from experience how much easier it is to communicate with your friends than with strangers whose age, occupation, or nationality differs markedly from your own. Messages, then, may be placed on a continuum according to their complexity, with simple messages on one end and complex messages on the other.

Simple Messages

Simple messages contain few components requiring interpretation. In American culture, a sign stating "No Smoking" would be an example. Our shared perceptions — including the common language, the widespread acceptance of definitions for "no" and "smoking," the brevity of the message, and our previous experience with this and similar messages — contribute to our ability to understand the message without having to struggle with interpretations.

Complex Messages

Complex messages, on the other hand, contain many components that must be interpreted before the message can be understood. If we say, for example, "Broad diversification rules out extraordinary losses relative to the whole market; it also, by definition, rules out extraordinary gains," we have three principal terms for which a wide range of interpretations is possible. If we choose to send that message to someone we are probably safe in assuming on the basis of shared culture that the other words in the message would be relatively clear; but we would need to make sure that our receiver knew exactly what we meant by "diversification," "extraordinary," and "market," or miscommunication would result. Such a message is extremely simple, however, when compared to the messages required for building a bridge or selecting a site for a new motel.

Channel

Channels: Written Nonverbal Oral

Communication channels include written, nonverbal, oral, and electronic methods. Because electronic channels (ranging from teletype to television to computer meetings) serve primarily as transducers — converting one form of energy to another — for written and oral communication channels, we will focus on the traditional channels for conveying messages.

Each of these channels has certain characteristics which can either help or hinder the transfer of meaning, depending on the circumstances, message, and audience involved. Chapters Two, Three, and Four deal with the effective use of written channels; Chapter Six discusses the nonverbal channel, and Chapters Seven, Eight, Nine, and Ten deal with the effective use of oral channels.

Audience

Audience:
Size
Familiarity
Attitude
Relationship

Like the other factors in the communication process, the audience can vary in several ways. Its size, its familiarity with the content of the message, its attitude toward the subject, and its previous relationship with and attitude toward the sender of the message are all important. The audience's distance — both physical and emotional — from the sender also has an important influence on the transfer of meaning. The greater the distance becomes, the more difficult it is to communicate. As we said previously, it's easier to communicate with friends than with strangers or enemies.

Transfer of Meaning

What Is Transfer of Meaning?

The next factor, the transfer of meaning, is the goal of all communication activity. Some kind of information is transferred from the sender to the receiver. But because the message selected by the sender may not adequately express the intended message, and because the message represents a new perception for the receiver, the meaning transferred to the receiver may be quite different from the sender's original perception. To illustrate some of the problems involved in the process, communication experts say: "I know that you believe you understand what you think I said, but I am not sure you realize that what you heard is not what I meant."

Feedback

What Is Feedback?

Feedback is not so much a part of the original process of communication as it is an entirely new message from a new sender, prompted by a new perception. Feedback is, however, related to the original message in that it indicates the transfer of meaning in that message. It lets the sender know that *some* transfer has taken place, that a message — if not an accurate conception of the original perception — has been received. Feedback can be as simple as a nod of the head, a brief yes or no, or a quick question; or it can be as complex as a lengthy written response. Feedback is important because we use it to evaluate the effectiveness of the messages we send. Companies judge the effectiveness of their advertising, for example, by measuring the increase in name recognition and sales.

Noise

What Is Noise?

Noise, a term borrowed from the vocabulary of electronic communication, is a factor in the communication process because the process is imperfect. Noise refers to any interference with the clear transfer of meaning. If we're delivering a speech while a band practices in the next room, we have a noise problem. If we put greasy fingerprints all over a letter, we have a noise problem. If we're trying to communicate with people from another culture, we probably have a noise problem. *Anything* that interferes with the accurate transfer of meaning is noise. When we communicate, we attempt to eliminate all known possibilities for noise to enter the system. The unknown sources of noise will cause enough trouble.

MODELS

Define Models

Because the communication process is complicated, people interested in communication and communication problems try to simplify the process by isolating factors for separate study. One way of doing this is to use models. *Models are simplified, symbolic representations.* Models help us understand complicated subjects because we can examine parts independently, rearrange them, and see how each contributes to the whole.

Until a few years ago, models of the communication process were essentially sequential, based on a psychological model derived from Pavlov's S-R (Stimulus-Response) model, illustrated by Figure 1-1.

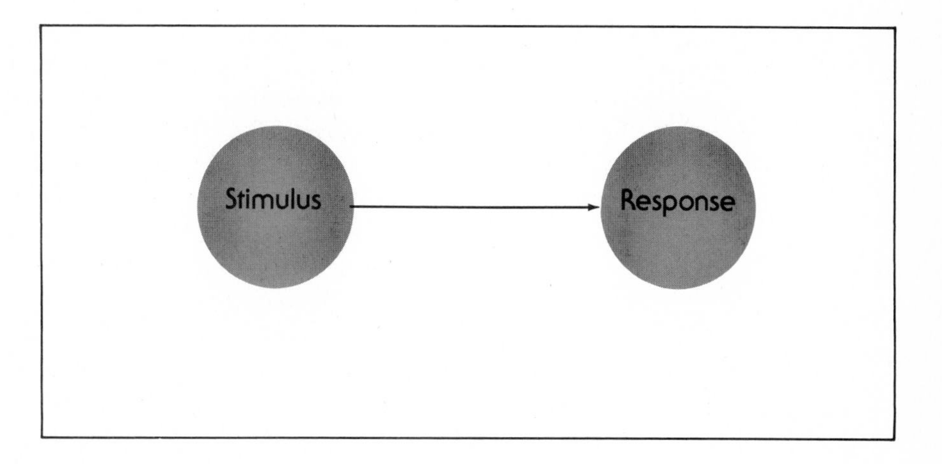

Figure 1-1. The stimulus-response model.

For communication purposes, the model became Sender-Message-Receiver, as shown in Figure 1-2.

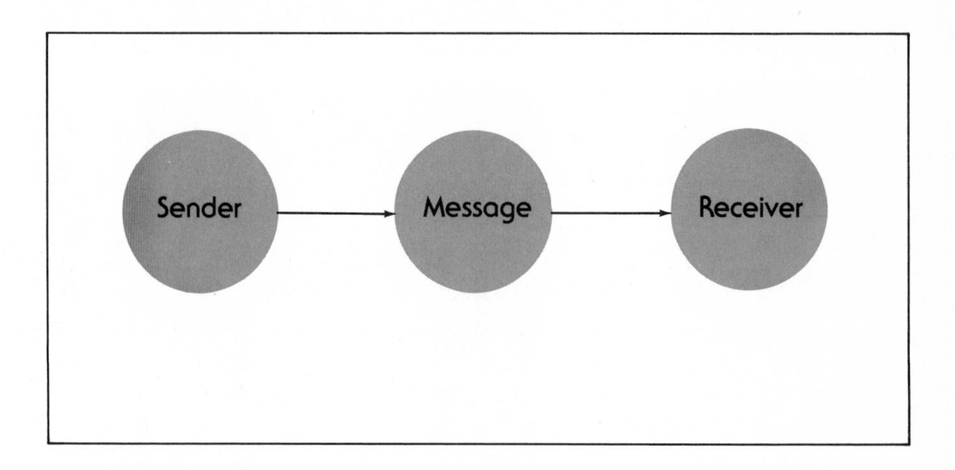

Figure 1-2. The sender-message-receiver model.

Refinements were added to this basic model, as shown in Figure 1-3. The *sender* first has a *perception,* which he or she then formulates into a *message* to send to a *receiver.* The receiver sends *feedback* to the original sender to acknowledge receipt of the message. Some *noise* enters the communication system at each step in the sequence.

Sequential models serve a useful purpose, but they don't fully capture either the speed or the complexity of the process. Especially as we learn more about the importance of nonverbal communication, models based on the sequencing of perceptions and messages become increasingly inadequate.

Unlike the electronic equipment that helped refine our concepts of sequential models, the human organism sends and receives at the same time. Communication specialists have developed several models that attempt to illustrate the simultaneous sending of messages and receiving of feedback. Figure 1-4 is one example.

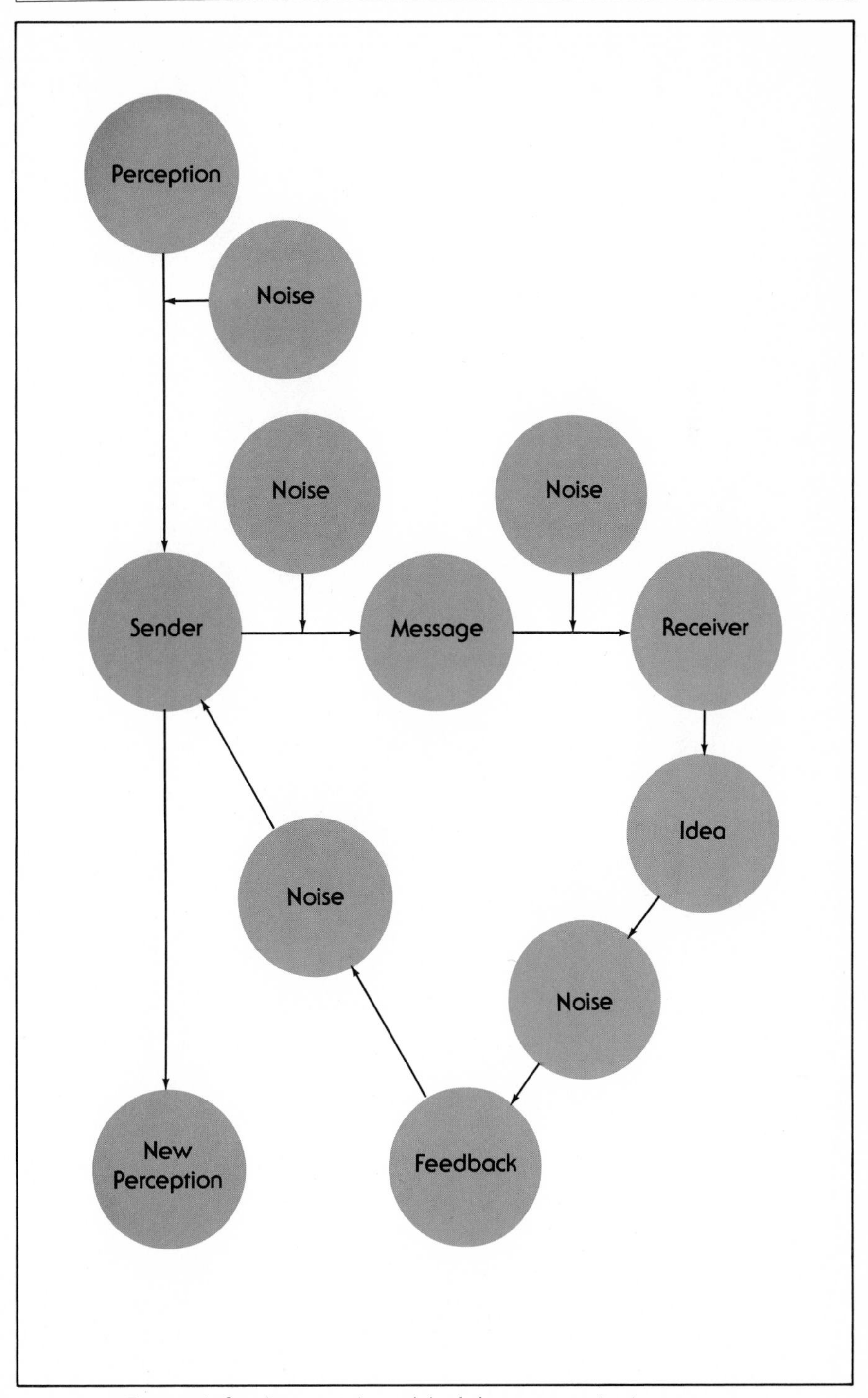

Figure 1-3. Sequential model of the communication process.

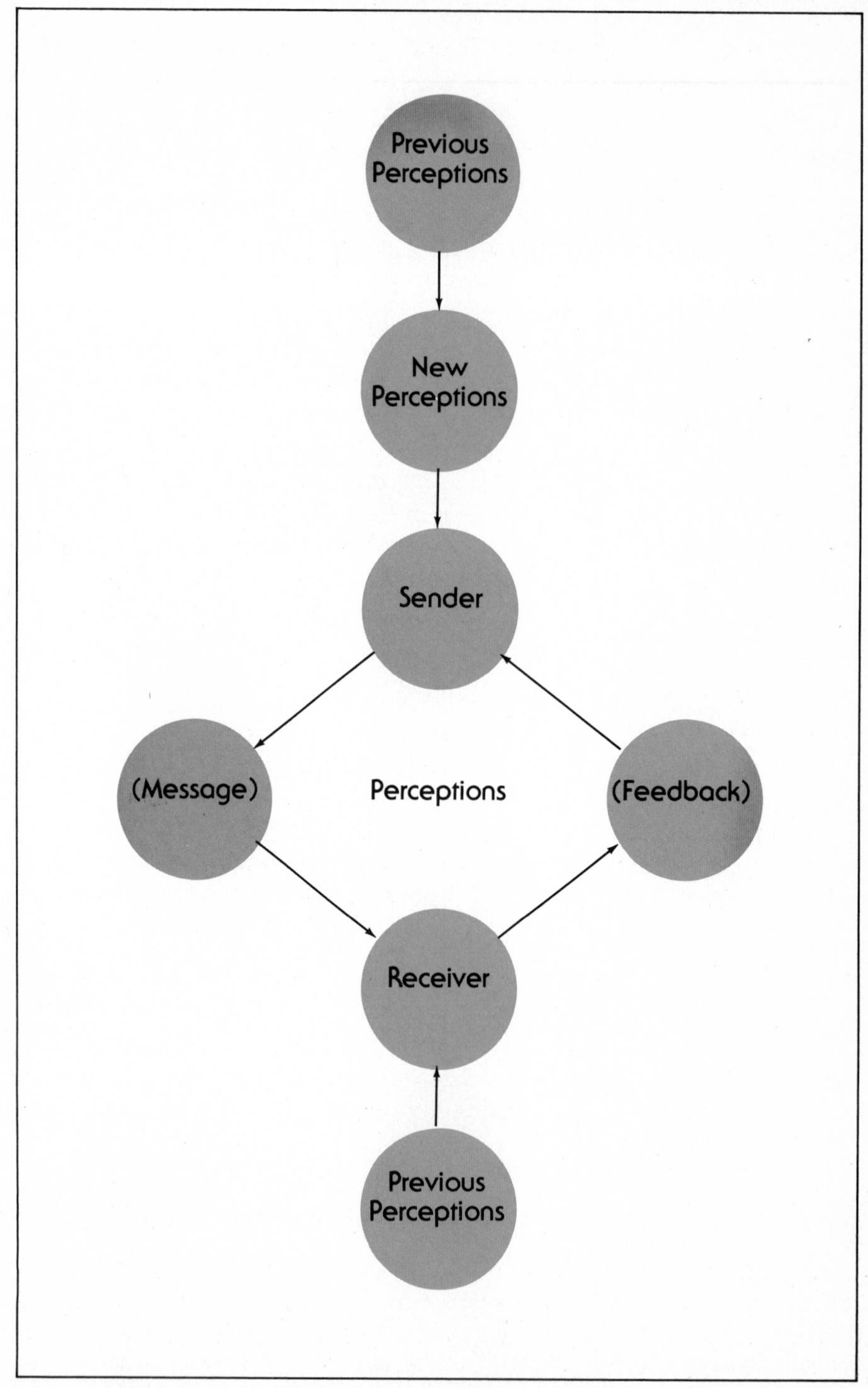

Figure 1-4. Simultaneous model of the communication process.

According to this model, our previous perceptions influence our current perceptions; we send a message to a receiver who interprets our message according to a different set of previous perceptions; and we receive some kind of feedback indicating receipt, understanding, and approval or disapproval of our message.

The main problem with this model and others that try to represent simultaneous activities is that, in trying to capture the complexity of the communication process, they can themselves become so complex that their usefulness is diminished. In spite of such problems, models help us to identify important variables in the communication process so we can begin to understand how each contributes to a complex whole.

Our earlier description of the communication process represents what might be a useful model for understanding communication variables — a verbal model. It reads: Communication begins with a perception in the mind of a sender. This perception is the impetus for a message for which the sender selects a channel that will convey the message to a receiver. The goal of this process is the transfer of meaning. As simple and as brief as the foregoing is, we can further reduce it:

Verbal Model of the Communication Process

I perceive something;
I begin to think about it;
I decide to share this perception with you;
I formulate a message;
I select a channel;
I send a message;
I study you, searching for indications that you are receiving, understanding, and perhaps approving of my message.

The model identifies the variables in the communication process but does not indicate the complexity of each. It also omits the fact that at each step, noise enters the process. To be effective, communicators must watch for sources of noise that may become barriers to communication.

BARRIERS TO COMMUNICATION

Communication Barriers: Perception Semantics Mechanics

Because communication is so complex, each variable involved presents barriers which must be overcome if accurate transfer of meaning is to take place. These barriers fall into three broad, overlapping categories — problems involving (1) *perception,* (2) *semantics,* (3) *mechanics*. Perceptual and semantic problems are the more difficult to control and correct because they are internal, or mental, rather than external. Thus they are neither readily observable nor specific.

Problems with Perception

Definition: Primary Mediation

Problems with perception include all aspects of the sender and receiver that interfere with accurate perception of the world. Perceptual problems may be primary, if the deficiency is physical, or secondary, if it is mental. Physical deficiencies occur during primary mediation. Primary mediation is the act of perceiving the environment with our physical senses: seeing, hearing, touching, tasting, and smelling. If you are myopic and you remove your glasses, for example, you will be unable to report distant visual perceptions accurately because you cannot observe them accurately. If you have a hearing impairment, you will have difficulty perceiving oral messages accurately.

Definition: Secondary Mediation

Deficiencies of this sort are usually obvious and correctable. Other perceptual barriers, however, are more subtle. Our perceptions are influenced not only by the powers and limitations of our senses but also by our previous experiences, attitudes, beliefs, and expectations. Our minds select from and alter the information (stimuli) our senses perceive. This influence is called *secondary mediation.*

The Mind as a Filter

We never perceive anything in its entirety. We select or abstract from the whole those things that seem important to us; our minds work like a filter, refusing to recognize that which seems unimportant. An example of this point is the story of the six old, blind wise men who each tried to describe an elephant after examining only one part:

After examining the elephant's tusk, one said that the elephant was like a spear.

After examining the elephant's knee, one said that the elephant was like a tree.

After examining the elephant's side, one said that the elephant was like a wall.

After examining the elephant's trunk, one said the elephant was like a snake.

After examining the elephant's tail, one said the elephant was like a rope.

After examining the elephant's ear, one said the elephant was like a fan.

Definition: Projection

Because our perceptions seem so obviously correct to us, we are inclined to believe that others perceive the world in the same way that we do. We attribute similar perceptions to others. This psychological principle is known as projection.

But because no two people are alike, each person's mental filter — based on experiences, attitudes, and expectations — selects different aspects of the environment. It is frequently difficult to remember that our own perceptions may not be complete and that they may not constitute the whole story. *The other person's perceptions are also part of the truth.* Everyone's perceptions are partially correct — sometimes we may think that the other person's portion of truth is awfully small, but we must still acknowledge that portion, regardless of its size.

We must also understand that we have a natural tendency to resist perceptions we find unpleasant. We find it difficult to accept ideas that do not agree with what we already think, believe, or feel. In days of old, bearers of bad tidings were frequently put to death. Even today, our inclination is to reject unpleasant messages *and* their senders. For example, if we hear from a stranger that a friend of ours can't be trusted, we will probably not believe the message — *and* we will dislike the person saying it.

Problems with Semantics

Semantics — the way we use language — can also cause communication difficulties. Because language, like mathematics, is a symbol system, *language has meaning only in the minds of its users.* Semanticists are fond of saying that the map is not the territory. Just as the map is not the territory but merely represents it, the words we use represent or symbolize our view of reality. We run into difficulty when we forget that our words and the words of others are symbolic rather than "real." Problems with semantics are as much a matter of faulty thinking as they are of faulty communicating. We forget that just thinking something is true doesn't make it so. The following guidelines can help us focus on the symbolic nature of language.

1. **No statement tells the whole story.** We cannot perceive totally or with complete accuracy; therefore we cannot make statements that are totally or completely accurate. By the time we've made a statement, we are twice removed from the actual event. When we think we are telling the whole story, or when we accept an account of something as the whole story, we are committing the Allness Fallacy. Consider, for example, any simple object around you — your desk, a chair, or the floor. How many readily

observable facts can you think of that apply to that object? Consider its uses, its measurements, its physical and chemical properties, its history, its evolution, its manufacturing process, its marketing, and even its future. Effective communicators need to remember that nothing is as simple as it seems.

2. **No two things are identical.** The human mind works by a process of generalization and differentiation. When things are similar, we tend to class them together. We divide the world into groups of things by pigeonholing and stereotyping. These groupings are useful. But we run into difficulties when we forget that each thing in any group is different from every other thing in the group. The human mind tends to overlook small differences. We need to remember that because nothing is simple, the smallest differences between things may well be significant. A very small pinhole makes a ping-pong ball unusable — and unsalable.

Definitions:
Fact
Observation
Assumption
Inference

3. **Observations, assumptions, and opinions are not the same.** You've heard the phrase "jumping to conclusions," and you know that it's something to avoid. A **fact** or **observation** is something that has been verified by some form of measurement or sense data (keep in mind that perception is selective and our sense data may not be entirely accurate). **Assumptions** or **inferences** are conclusions based on certain observations. The more relevant observations we make, the greater the chances that our assumptions will prove correct. For example, our assumption that the sun will come up tomorrow has an excellent chance of being correct. If, on the other hand, we assume that it will not rain tomorrow because it did not rain today, we have jumped to a conclusion. **Opinions** are based on observations and assumptions, but they are **value judgments** unrelated to fact. Opinions, value judgments, are feelings or beliefs not substantiated by knowledge or proof. You may have observed in the past that you did not like Kool Kola. That is a fact. You may assume that you still do not like Kool Kola. That is an inference. But when you say, "Kool Kola tastes awful," that's an opinion. Your opinion has to do with you, not with Kool Kola.

Definitions:
Opinion
Value Judgment

4. **Few things are either-or.** Most things are matters of degree rather than absolutes. One example often used to illustrate this point is the term "slightly pregnant." Pregnancy is one of life's few absolutes. Every day, science reduces the number of things that can be considered **mutually exclusive.** Life and death were once considered absolutes; now scientists are not so sure. Recent

medical discoveries have made it difficult to draw a definite line between the two. We must remember that most things are relative. A person is tall only in comparison with someone or something else; a person is intelligent only in comparison with someone else; a decision is only good in comparison with another decision.

5. **Time changes all things — especially people.** You are not the same person today as you were yesterday. The changes in you from yesterday to today may not be dramatic or even significant, but you *have* changed. And the further back in time you go for your point of comparison, the more you have changed. Each day's perceptions give you new experiences against which to evaluate each new perception. But people aren't the only things that change: laws, interest rates, institutions, and even solid rock are subject to the influence of time.

Problems with Mechanics

Mechanical Barriers

Even if communicators are fully aware of the communication problems that can be caused by perceptual and semantic difficulties, mechanical difficulties can cause communication barriers. The best-known example of a mechanical barrier is "noise" in electronic communication channels. Mechanical barriers are those that are superimposed on the communication. The following are just a few examples:

In oral communication:
- bad acoustics
- poor sound system
- outside disturbances
- cars
- sirens
- people
- doors
- phones

In written communication:
- poor quality paper
- greasy thumbprints
- carbon smudges
- faded ribbon
- dirty typewriter keys
- color of paper
- water or coffee spots
- poor typing corrections

ORGANIZATIONAL OBJECTIVES AND COMMUNICATION

Most theories, including the foregoing, are useless until we have specific goals in mind. On a personal level, for example, we may wish to reduce the level of conflict we experience with a certain person. If we remember that individual perceptions vary and that language is symbolic, we may be able to listen for what that person *means* rather than to what that person *says* the next time conflict arises. On a personal level our main objectives are to understand and be understood — and liked — by other people.

Communication Is a Tool of Management

Even though understanding and being understood are still the most important of organizational communication objectives, the communication objectives of organizations are more complex. We must remember that organizational objectives are *not* the same as communication objectives. Communication is a tool that management uses to define, clarify, transmit, and achieve other objectives. Communication objectives contribute to organizational objectives. For example, the organizational goal of selling has a corresponding communication goal, persuading. It's obvious that to make a profit an organization must sell its goods or services; and to sell, the organization must have a specific goal of selling so many units or services. The corresponding communication goal is persuading a given audience to purchase the product or service. The goal of selling cannot be achieved without communication.

Task Goals
Maintenance Goals
Human Goals

Organizational objectives can be divided into three general categories — task, maintenance, and human — for the purpose of analyzing the way communication influences organizational behavior. Task objectives are established to achieve definite goals (sell 5,000 units by 1 May). Maintenance goals regulate the sustenance of the organization (set prices to ensure long-range profitability). Human goals foster improved interpersonal relationships and high morale (offer sales incentives, health-care programs, and special vacation plans).

Communication can be classed as task, maintenance, or human as it helps an organization achieve those objectives. Because organizations cannot achieve those objectives without related communication, the people involved must understand the role communication plays in achieving those goals. The main role of communication is coordination. Communication brings a sender and a receiver together, focusing their attention on mutual interests and objectives. The company wants to sell a product or service, so it communicates — through advertising — to receivers who must at least have an interest in the product or service before they can receive the company's communication.

When we begin to study the ways organizations use communication to help achieve general task, maintenance, and human objectives, it's helpful to divide the communication process into categories or systems and look at each system independently. Organizational communication systems consist of three overlapping, practical aspects of communication:

Communication Systems

Communication Channel: nonverbal, oral, written
System Size: interpersonal, small group, public
System Behavior: formal, informal

These systems define the manner of the communication, the size of the group involved, and the attitude of the people involved. For example, most organizations require that formal written reports be submitted to the small group that constitutes upper management. Likewise, most organizations have—some would say *require*—informal, oral communication networks. The latter system is usually called the "grapevine."

Channel

Size

Formality

All communication requires at least one element from each of the three communication systems. All communication requires a channel and is expressed in nonverbal, oral, or written form or by a combination of these forms. All communication takes place between a sender or senders and an audience. And all communication has a degree of formality.

Because each item of communication is likely to contain several components, the most useful way to analyze messages and communication systems is to examine their ability to achieve specific job-related goals and their effectiveness in establishing and maintaining good human relations. The specific objective of a communication is the answer to the question, "What do I want this message to do?" After determining this objective, the sender of the message must then ask, "Who is my audience?" The sender next needs to consider, "What is the best way of sending this message to my intended audience?" Although this may not be the order that naturally occurs to us, we must consider the following factors:

1. Communication objectives
2. The audience's expectations
3. The communication systems
   a. Channel
   b. Size
   c. Formality

COMMUNICATION OBJECTIVES

Each communication system influences organizational behavior in specific ways; in later chapters we will discuss the practical aspects of each system in detail. We will now show you very briefly how each of these systems fits into the organizational whole, so that as you read each later chapter you'll have a better understanding of the way that one part fits into organizational communication systems.

Purpose

Purpose

In addition to the general organizational goals of performing task, maintenance, and human functions, each message has a definite, practical goal of its own that can and should be considered apart from the theoretical roles of communication in business. For example, knowing that a particular message is a task message is not very helpful when you need to write an invited sales letter.

The **specific business-related objectives of messages** can be divided into three general categories: to inquire, to inform, and to persuade. A fourth objective of messages, to entertain, is not specifically an organizational objective, though it may help a sender achieve one of the more practical goals. We will concentrate on the first three.

To Inquire. Inquiries include messages designed to obtain information, goods, or services: asking questions, placing orders, and making *simple* requests.

To Inform. Informative messages are designed to convey positive, neutral, or negative messages to an audience. Information is positive if the receiver will welcome it. If the receiver has no special interest in the information, it's neutral. The information is negative if it will hurt the receiver's feelings or make the receiver angry or resentful.

To Persuade. Persuasive messages attempt to alter an audience's behavior. Typical sales messages, of course, are persuasive. In addition, any message that would be resisted by the receiver for any reason needs to be persuasive. If, for example, you are inviting someone to speak at an event but you can't meet that person's expected compensation, you will need to send a persuasive request rather than a simple request.

Organizations measure the effectiveness of communication by whether the communication achieves its particular objective in an economical way. Correctness, technique, and form may contribute to communication effectiveness, but the important test is whether the audience adopts the suggested behavior.

AUDIENCE'S EXPECTATIONS

In formulating your message, you need to consider two other practical objectives. Both concern your audience's expectations.

1. Your message must satisfy your receiver's emotional needs.
2. Your message must satisfy your receiver's logical expectations.

Emotional Needs

It is, of course, perfectly possible to understand perceptual and semantic barriers to communication fully and still not be an effective communicator. Your receiver may understand exactly what you mean but pay absolutely no attention to your message. You can prevent this from happening by including something to satisfy your receiver's emotional needs in each important message you send. The following emotional characteristics have the greatest influence on the effectiveness of communication:

1. **People are self-centered.** Receivers always want to know what a message will do for them. A receiver's first question is, "How will this message benefit me?" A successful communicator answers that question by specifying the kind of satisfaction — material, emotional, psychological, or intellectual — the message has for the receiver.
2. **People are defensive.** Communicators must recognize that receivers tend to perceive some kinds of communication as threatening. Constructive criticism, for example, may be perceived as a personal attack.
3. **People aren't perfect.** Mistakes are bound to happen, but no one likes to make them. Concentrate on the positive aspects, deemphasize mistakes, and look to the future. We all want to do better in the future than we've done in the past. People respond most favorably to those messages that contain information that can be used to build a better future.
4. **People need specific goals.** Some goals are biological — we all need food, drink, shelter, and a certain amount of sleep to survive. Other goals are psychological — we want to like ourselves and have others like us, too. Through communication we can identify our specific goals and help each other achieve them. When our message will make life a little easier or more pleasant for our receiver, it is sure to succeed.
5. **People do the best they can.** People may do less than we expect of them, but they usually make the best effort they are able to at the time. Although people frequently let emotions get in the way of clear, logical communication, they want to see the world in a rational way and express themselves logically. Even though they don't always succeed, people do their best to value the

positive emotions of joy, enthusiasm, and love, and to disparage the negative emotions of fear, prejudice, and hate.

Logical Expectations

Logical Expectations

Because people value the logical and the positive, communicators must use **patterns of logic, methods of proof,** and **message structures** that will make their logic clear and emphasize the positive elements of their message.

Logical reasoning can follow one of two basic patterns — **deductive order** or **inductive order.** Deductive order begins with a general principle, offers a specific application, and works to a conclusion. To be successful, deductive order requires the following:

Deductive Order

1. A general principle that the receiver already believes. (*People are interested in economy.*)
2. A specific application that the receiver will accept. (*This car is economical.*)
3. A conclusion that is an obvious result of the general principle and the specific application. (*People will buy this car.*)

Inductive order begins with specific data and works to a general principle. To be successful, inductive order requires the following:

Inductive Order

1. Sufficient specifics to warrant a general principle. (*Twenty people buy this car from our dealership every month.*)
2. Specifics that are typical of the general principle. (*The people who buy this car all say that they are interested in its economy.*)
3. No specific that contradicts the general principle. (*No one has bought this car for its luxury.*)
4. A general principle. (*People buy this car for its economy.*)

Both the deductive and inductive patterns can use a variety of methods of proof. The most common of these are as follows:

Methods of Proof

1. Definition: saying what something is or what it is not.
2. Cause and effect: Showing that one thing is the cause of another (indicated by *because, since, then, therefore,* or *thus*).
3. Comparison/contrast: Showing how one thing is similar to or different from something else.
4. Analysis: Showing how all the parts or aspects of something relate to the whole.

Message Structure

To ensure that the positive message receives proper emphasis, each message should be structured so that its positive elements are placed at the beginning and at the end of the message, where the receiver will pay closest attention to them. The structural pattern of a message is based on the objective of that message.

Each objective can best be met with a general structure into which we incorporate an appropriate pattern of logic and methods of proof. The general structure will be either IMMEDIATE or DELAYED, depending on our answer to the receiver's main question, "How will this message benefit me?" When that question has a positive answer, we tell the receiver immediately. When the answer is negative, we delay that part of the message. When we need to overcome resistance to a suggested behavior, we delay specifying the behavior until we have convinced the receiver that he or she will gain.

Immediate Structure
Delayed Structure

An immediate message conveys the most important information — the benefit — in its opening. In a delayed message, the opening prepares the reader for the information that will follow.

COMMUNICATION CHANNELS

Any message a sender may conceive can be transferred to a receiver in a variety of ways. These ways are usually called channels because they are routes through which the message moves from sender to receiver. The three channels which convey messages are **nonverbal, oral,** and **written.**

Our overview here will be brief because we will discuss and illustrate characteristics of each channel at length in later chapters.

Nonverbal

The most important nonverbal components in organizational communication are as follows:

Space

1. Space
   a. Between people (proxemics)
   b. Allocated to people (territory)

Time

2. Time
   a. Amount of time
   b. Kind of time (exclusive or shared)
   c. Who waits for whom

Kinesics

3. Kinesics
   a. "Open" postures and signals, inviting communication
   b. "Closed" postures and signals, discouraging communication

Moral values should not be attached to nonverbal communication components. For example, the "territory" allocated to higher management serves several useful functions.

It provides rewards.
It protects the manager from intrusions that would interfere with accomplishing tasks.
It helps regulate the flow of communication.

Communicators should be aware of the effects of nonverbal indicators. Space, time, and kinesics either increase or decrease the distance (physical and emotional) between people; and every increase in distance brings a corresponding decrease in emotional communication.

Decreases in emotional communication sometimes result in reduced or inaccurate feedback about matters of organizational importance.

Time and kinesics are usually sufficient to maintain high-quality feedback. It is important to keep, and be on time for, appointments. Body movements and eye contact can be controlled to indicate openness, inclusion, and willingness to communicate.

Oral

Even if we exclude extraorganizational oral communication ("Did you see the ball game last night?"), the bulk of the communication activity in organizations is still oral.

Decision Making

Much oral communication is "preliminary" and concerns decision making, and much oral communication takes place between two people or in small groups.

"Open" and "closed" communication stances affect oral communication just as they affect nonverbal communication. For example, an inverse relationship exists between directive leadership and interpersonal distance. Directive — authoritarian — leadership is necessary when the speed of a decision is more important than its accuracy. Nondirective leadership, in which the entire group participates, is preferred when a high-quality decision is required, when accurate feedback is desired, or when morale is low enough to affect performance.

Written

Advantage of Written Communication

Nearly all important business communication is eventually put into writing. The main advantage of written communication is that it provides a fairly permanent record.

As a rule, written messages do not permit effective feedback. For this reason clarity is much more important with a written communication than with an oral message. Also, the psychological impact of a written message deserves close attention, especially when negative information or a persuasive message is involved, because the absence of feedback deprives the sender of the message of the opportunity to modify its content.

SYSTEM SIZE

The operation of communication systems also depends on their size — the number of people the system involves. Systems range in size from two-person exchanges to public information systems.

As a general rule, formality and complexity both increase as the size of a system increases. The larger the system, the greater the need for formal communication, such as written messages and formal oral presentations.

Dyads

The smallest communication system is a dyad — two people. As we explain more fully in later chapters, cultural and psychological factors are important in determining the effectiveness of dyadic exchanges. In organizations, the effectiveness of dyadic exchanges is measured by objective achievement rather than by morale, feedback, or other "human" considerations. Dyadic communications play a significant role in the achievement of specific, task-oriented objectives.

Most modern psychologists disagree with the *mentalist* approach to understanding human behavior advocated by Freud, Berne, and others who discuss "inner" qualities. Behaviorists and other experimental psychologists prefer to explain behavior in terms of external conditioners, which are (or become) rewards or punishments.

Money and power remain the most effective rewards in American culture. Being understood and well liked are also rewarding for most people; achieving personal goals is important too.

Small Groups

Most organizational decision making takes place in small groups. Groups usually solve complicated problems better than individuals working alone, but the speed of problem solving is almost always reduced.

No group can function without leadership. Leadership within a group always involves a certain degree of risk. The lower one is in the organizational hierarchy, the greater degree of risk one assumes in performing the leadership function.

Group objectives can usually be best met by nondirective leadership which encourages the free flow of communication. If communication does not flow freely, managers would be better off making authoritative decisions without wasting the time of the group members.

Public

Public communication is almost always either informational or persuasive. The "public" may consist of the combined membership of the organization or of the extraorganizational public at large.

Whether written or oral, public communication differs from dyadic and small group communication systems primarily by the degree of formality. Public communication, with only a few exceptions (bumper stickers), is more formal than smaller systems. The effectiveness of public communication can be measured in observable, changed behavior.

SYSTEM BEHAVIOR

System Formality

Along with the channel and system size, the degree of formality within a communication system is an important consideration. Some audiences and some channels are by nature more formal than others. For example, written communication for large audiences tends to be formal. Some dyadic exchanges, such as interviews, can be very formal, whereas others are extremely informal. The same is true of small group exchanges.

Whether an exchange will be improved or harmed by formality or lack of it depends on the objective, not on qualities inherent in a particular degree of formality. Informal leadership tends to produce improved morale, higher quality decisions, and slower decision making; formal leadership usually produces quicker decisions. Formal presentations tend to be more persuasive than informal ones.

COMMUNICATION AUDITING

As you can see, effective communication involves several complex components. Each of these communication components operates in every relationship, both in and out of business. Is it any wonder that communication is frequently the least efficient part of an organization's operation? With so many variables, it's difficult for management to clarify communication objectives. Because the task of establishing effective communication systems seems so simple on the surface but is actually so complex, communication systems frequently go unrecognized and unsupervised. For this reason, communication is frequently called the *invisible environment*.

Organizations and individuals can improve communication skills in spite of the number of variables involved. Modern businesses have learned (usually the hard way) that effective communication is a key ingredient in success. It is, in fact, just as important to examine communication systems for effectiveness as it is to have the financial accounts audited for accuracy and reliability.

Communication Auditing

Communication auditing is the process by which organizations identify, evaluate, and improve their communication systems. Each system is evaluated for effectiveness in achieving the organizational goal established for it, and the components of each system are evaluated for effectiveness in achieving immediate, practical goals.

In the following chapters we will show you how these practical goals fit into the larger systems. We will define specific, practical objectives for the various components of communication systems and show you how these goals can best be achieved.

SUMMARY

Communication begins with a perception in the mind of a sender. This perception is the impetus for a message for which the sender selects a channel that will convey the message to a receiver. The goal of this process is the transfer of meaning.

Models are simplified, symbolic representations of the communication process. They help us to understand the process by allowing us to isolate factors for separate study.

Because of the complexity of the communication process, barriers to communication must be overcome if accurate transfer of meaning is to take place. Barriers can be caused by faulty perceptions, semantic misunderstandings, or poor mechanics.

Organizational objectives are not the same as communication objectives. Communication is a tool that management uses to define, clarify, transmit, and achieve other objectives.

Organizational communication systems consist of the communication channel, the system size, and the system behavior. All communication requires at least one element from each of these three areas.

Communication auditing is the process by which organizations identify, evaluate, and improve their communication systems. Each system is evaluated for effectiveness in achieving the organizational goal established for it, and the components of each system are evaluated for effectiveness in achieving immediate, practical goals.

EXERCISES

1. Which one of the communication variables discussed in this chapter is the most important? Why?
2. Ask several smokers and several nonsmokers how they feel about "No Smoking" signs. What causes the differences in feelings?

3. What is the relationship between communicating and thinking?
4. How many is "some?"
5. Does *every* verbal message (written or oral) contain nonverbal components?
6. Does the communication theory presented in this chapter account for any human relations problems you may have had recently?
7. Select an example of an organizational communication and examine it to see how each communication variable is used.
8. Using one of the communication models described in this chapter, analyze the communication situation in your business communication class.
9. How does the saying, "The map is not the territory," relate to communication difficulties?
10. Write a message about 100 words long. Select seven people, and read the message to the first person while the other six can't hear you. Then have the first person *tell* the second person what he or she thinks you said while the others can't hear. Have the second person tell the third person, and so on. Have the seventh person *write* what he or she thinks the sixth person said. Then compare your original message with the seventh person's version.

SUGGESTED READINGS

Berlo, David K. *The Process of Communication.* New York: Holt, Rinehart and Winston, 1960.

Goldhaber, Gerald M. *Organizational Communication.* Dubuque, IA: W. C. Brown, 1974.

Haney, William V. *Communication and Organizational Behavior.* 3d ed. Homewood, IL: Richard D. Irwin, 1973.

Hayakawa, S. I. *Language in Thought and Action.* 2d ed. New York: Harcourt Brace Jovanovich, 1964.

Hayakawa, S. I. *The Use and Misuse of Language.* Greenwich, CT: Fawcett Publications, 1962.

Korzybski, Alfred. *Science and Sanity.* 4th ed. Lakeville, CT: The Institute of General Semantics, 1948.

Schneider, Arnold E., William C. Donaghy, and Pamela Jane Newman. *Organizational Communication.* New York: McGraw-Hill, 1975.

Thayer, Lee. *Communication and Communication Systems.* Homewood, IL: Richard D. Irwin, 1968.

Weeks, Francis W. *Principles of Business Communication.* Champaign, IL: Stipes, 1973.

2

WRITING SKILLS

"The best writing always reflects its oral heritage."

After you have read this chapter, you should be able to

1. **State three reasons why written communication is important.**
2. **Apply the principles of grammar and word usage in your writing.**
3. **Construct logical sentences and paragraphs.**
4. **Identify and use the elements of effective communication.**
5. **Develop a writing style that expresses your personality.**

IMPORTANCE OF WRITTEN COMMUNICATION

Advantages of Written Communication

Because written communication provides a fairly permanent record, it offers certain advantages over other forms of communication. The most important of these advantages are the abilities of writing to transcend time, to transcend distance, and to permit the careful consideration and controlled use of language.

The development of writing permitted primitive people to communicate from generation to generation with an accuracy not possible with oral techniques. Because of writing, legend gave way to history. Writing also enabled people to communicate more accurately over longer distances than had previously been possible. Because of writing, isolated villages gave way to city-states and eventually to empires. And it was only through writing that the complex philosophical, legal, and political concepts important in modern life were developed.

The abilities of writing to trancend time, to transcend distance, and to permit the careful consideration and controlled use of language are the principal reasons that written communication is so important to business. An important rule in business is that if something is significant, it belongs in writing. Important decisions, agreements, and proposals all require written records. And in spite of the increasing use of the telephone and of electronic media to overcome distance, written communication forms convey complex messages better than the communication channels that do not leave a readily accessible record.

Written communication may also provide sender and receiver the opportunity to deal with messages at times convenient for both. Telephone calls can interrupt important conferences, and if the message is important, the sender and the receiver usually will require a written record of the call.

With written communication the sender and the receiver have the opportunity to consider the content of the message carefully over an extended time if necessary. Each word, each phrase can be selected for precise expression and maximum effectiveness. Probably no other channel offers such an opportunity for the full use of intelligence in communication. Oral forms that at first seem to make full use of intelligence — a prepared platform speech, for example — rely on writing to achieve their effects. The paradox of writing, however, is that the best writers are those who never forget that written language is only an extension of oral language. The best writing always reflects its oral heritage in the sense that the message is presented as clearly, naturally, logically, forcefully, and simply as its contents will permit. Written language that cannot comfortably be delivered orally is not good writing. To be right, language must *sound* right to the ear as well as *look* right to the eye.

Paradox of Writing

THE NATURE OF LANGUAGE

Change

Anyone who has ever looked at one of Chaucer's poems is aware that language has changed since the fourteenth century.

> Whan that Aprill with its shoures soote
> The droghte of March hath perced to the roote. . . .

Changing Needs

Language is dynamic. It changes to meet the changing needs of the people who use it. In general, oral forms of the language change more quickly than written forms, and one function of written language is to provide a fairly stable standard against which change can be measured.

Stable Standard

Meaning

Having a fairly specific standard of language usage is important to communication because it helps ensure the accurate transfer of meaning from sender to receiver. The rules governing the way language should be used may sometimes seem arbitrary and unnecessary.

If we write the ungrammatical sentence, "He ain't got no bread," the use of the double negative doesn't interfere with our ability to understand that the person doesn't have any bread. We are much more likely to have trouble understanding how the sender is using the word "bread." Does the sender mean "bread" to indicate food or money? Now look at the message, "Smelling just awful, I drove past the factory." The miscommunication here is a result of the message sender's failure to follow a grammatical rule governing the placement of modifiers.

Rules

The rules of grammar have been established for the same reasons that rules for other human activities have been established. When we all follow the same rules, we can better understand what others are saying. It's also helpful if the rules don't change too quickly. Linguists (language experts) disagree about what constitutes "too quickly." As is the case with any cultural change, some linguists are too eager to change; some refuse to change at all. When language changes too quickly, its abilities to transcend both time and distance are diminished. The balance between the change necessary to keep language alive and interesting and the stability required for maximum usefulness is built into culture. If you are either too far ahead or too far behind what most people accept as "correct," your speech and writing will attract the kind of attention you'd probably rather avoid.

GRAMMAR

Grammar is important — but rather than consider grammatical principles absolute indicators of right and wrong, you should consider them guides to effective communication. We think you'll find that grammar is really quite simple when you concentrate on the few absolute essentials you'll need to communicate effectively. When you think about it, any objection you may have to grammar is probably a result of its arbitrary nature. There is no rational answer to the question "why?" about grammar — it's just the way things are. Keep in mind that the words we use to express grammatical principles are merely symbols for concepts we have about the ways language functions. To be able to discuss the concepts, we need a common terminology.

In discussing language, you'll need to know its components — the parts of speech — and how these parts function in sentences.

Part of Speech	Function
Noun	Names something
Pronoun	Takes the place of a noun
Verb	Expresses action
Adjective	Modifies a noun or pronoun
Adverb	Modifies a verb, adjective, or another adverb
Conjunction	Joins one element to another
Preposition	Shows relationship
Interjection	Expresses strong feeling

Nouns

A noun names a person, place, thing, or idea. In sentences, nouns can function as subjects, direct objects, indirect objects, objects of prepositions, subject complements, and appositives.

Proper nouns name particular persons, places, or things; they are usually capitalized. Examples of proper nouns include *Abraham Lincoln; Washington, D.C.;* and *Blue Ridge Mountains.*

Common nouns name persons, places, or things that are not specific, such as *man, woman, city, state, chair, desk, profits,* and *losses.*

Common nouns may be classified as **abstract** or **concrete.** Abstract nouns refer to intangible things — things that cannot be seen, heard, touched, tasted, or smelled. Abstract nouns refer to qualities or ideas, such as *goodness, freedom, democracy,* and *capitalism.* Concrete nouns refer to tangible things — things that can be seen, heard, touched, tasted, or smelled — such as *chair, noise, skin, fur, apple, smoke* and *fumes.*

Abstract and concrete are, of course, matters of degree rather than absolutes. Most nouns are only abstract or concrete in relation to other nouns. The word *dog,* for example, is less concrete than a specific breed, *English setter,* and less abstract than the word *mammal.*

Pronouns

A pronoun is a word that takes the place of a noun. The noun for which a pronoun stands is its *antecedent*. Pronouns can be personal, relative, interrogative, demonstrative, or indefinite.

Personal pronouns refer to the person speaking, the person spoken to, or the person spoken about.

	Singular	Plural
Person speaking:	I went.	We went.
Person spoken to:	You went.	You (all) went.
Person spoken about:	He went.	They went.

Relative pronouns introduce subordinate clauses by referring to antecedents in the main clause. *Who, whom, which,* and *that* are relative pronouns.

Dolores Powers is an executive who works hard.

Who is a relative pronoun that introduces the subordinate clause; it refers to the antecedent, *executive,* in the main clause.

Interrogative pronouns start direct or indirect questions. Interrogative pronouns include *who, whom, what, which,* and *whose.* (Don't confuse *whose* with the contraction, *who's,* which stands for *who is.*)

Direct question: Whose account is this?
Indirect question: I wonder what stock we should purchase.

Demonstrative pronouns — *this, these, that, those* — point out particular persons or things. This (singular) and these (plural) refer to objects that are near. That (singular) and those (plural) refer to objects that are distant.

Singular:	This is mine.	That is hers.
Plural:	These are mine.	Those are hers.

Indefinite pronouns refer to groups of persons or to things in general. Some indefinite pronouns are:

all	any	anybody	anyone	anything
each	either	every	everyone	everybody
everything	neither	most	much	none
several	some	someone	somebody	something

Verbs

A verb is a word that expresses action or being. A verb is essential to complete the meaning of any sentence. Verbs can be either transitive or intransitive. A **transitive** verb needs an object to complete its meaning; an **intransitive** verb does not need an object to complete its meaning.

Transitive: David completed the project.
Intransitive: Mary Ann sat.

Some verbs are both transitive and intransitive.

Transitive: Fred sells stocks.
Intransitive: Fred sells frequently.

An intransitive verb has no object, but it may have a complement. We discuss complements on page 37. An intransitive verb that joins a subject to its complement is called a **linking** verb. Common linking verbs are *be, seem, appear,* and verbs describing the senses, such as *feel, taste,* and *look.*

Profits seemed high. Profits are good.

Voice

If the subject of the sentence does the action the verb describes, the verb is in the **active voice.** If the subject of the sentence receives the action, the verb is in the **passive voice.**

Active voice: Edward prepared the sales report.
Passive voice: The sales report was prepared by Edward.

Adjectives

Adjectives are words that modify nouns or pronouns.

Short-term profits increased.

Adjectives have three degrees of comparison — **positive, comparative,** and **superlative.** Use the positive degree when the word modified is not being compared with anything else. Use the comparative degree when comparing two things; use the superlative degree when comparing more than two things.

Generally, add the suffix *-er* to form the comparative degree and form the superlative by adding *-est* to one-syllable adjectives. For adjectives of more than two syllables, add the words *more* or *most* (for negatives, *less* or *least*). Two-syllable adjectives may take either form to show the comparative or superlative degree.

Positive	Comparative	Superlative
bright	brighter	brightest
angry	angrier	angriest
	more angry	most angry
appreciative	more appreciative	most appreciative

Some adjectives have irregular forms of comparison.

Positive	Comparative	Superlative
bad	worse	worst
good	better	best

Other adjectives cannot be compared; they are absolutes. *Round, square, perfect,* and *unique* are absolute adjectives.

Adverbs

Adverbs are words that modify verbs, adjectives, or other adverbs. They give information about *when, where, how,* or *how much.* Most adverbs end in *-ly.*

Profits increased *rapidly.*

Often adverbs can be moved from place to place in a sentence without changing the meaning of the sentence. When the sentence contains more than one word that could be modified by the adverb, however, confusion may result.

The profits that had declined sharply rose the next day.

In this example we cannot tell whether the profits "declined sharply" or "sharply rose." **Limiting adverbs** *(only, nearly, almost, just,* and *hardly)* must immediately precede the word they modify.

Only profits declined 18 percent. (Nothing else declined.)
Profits *only* declined 18 percent. (Profits didn't plummet.)
Profits declined *only* 18 percent. (Profits didn't decline 20 percent.)

Conjunctions

A conjunction is a word that connects words, phrases, or clauses. Conjunctions are classified as **coordinate, correlative,** and **subordinate.**

Coordinate conjunctions — *and, but, or, for,* or *nor* — join elements of equal rank.

Both the executives *and* their secretaries planned the program.

Correlative conjunctions connect matched pairs. Some correlative conjunctions are *either . . . or; neither . . . nor; both . . . and;* and *not only . . . but also.*

The bank will have its grand opening on *either* Monday *or* Wednesday.

Subordinate conjunctions connect elements that are not of equal rank. Some subordinate conjunctions are:

after	although	as
because	if	since
so	unless	when

After we save enough money, we will buy a new car.

Prepositions

A preposition is a word that shows a relationship of one word in the sentence — its object — to some other word in the sentence. Common prepositions are the following:

about	between	by
down	during	for
into	over	to

This book is *about* communication.
Evelena is the president *of* Permanent Press Inc.

Interjections

An interjection is a word, generally isolated from the rest of the sentence, that expresses strong emotion.

Wow, did you see that?
Ouch! You hurt me.

SENTENCES

Subject and Predicate

The parts of speech just discussed are used to build sentences, the basic units of communication. A sentence is a group of words that expresses a complete thought and contains a **subject** and a **predicate** (verb).

Profits (subject) increased (predicate).

The subject of a sentence is that part about which something is being said. Subjects can be simple or compound.

Simple: *Jessica* works in marketing.
Compound: *Jessica* and *Jerome* work in marketing.

The predicate of a sentence is that part which says something about the subject. Predicates can be simple or compound.

Simple: Norman *reads.*
Compound: Norman *reads* and *writes.*

In addition to the two essential parts — the subject and the predicate — sentences contain other elements that modify or complete those parts. These elements are complements, phrases, and clauses.

Complements

A complement is a word that completes the meaning of the subject and the verb. Complements are of three kinds: direct objects, indirect objects, and subject complements.

A direct object is a word that receives the action of a transitive verb. Direct objects answer the question *what* or *whom.*

Patricia sold *trucks.* (what?)
Alfonso loved *Olga.* (whom?)

An indirect object always precedes the direct object; it answers the question *to whom, for whom, to what,* or *for what.*

Patricia sold *Joshua* a truck. (to whom?)
Patricia bought *Joshua* a truck. (for whom?)
I gave the *tire* a kick. (to what?)
Reggie bought the *company* a plane. (for what?)

A subject complement is a noun, pronoun, or adjective that renames or describes the subject. Two kinds of subject complements are the predicate nominative (a noun or pronoun) and the predicate adjective.

A predicate nominative is a noun or pronoun that follows a linking verb and renames the subject.

Joshua is the *buyer.* (noun)
It is *he.* (pronoun)

A predicate adjective is an adjective that follows a linking verb and describes the subject.

Margarite is *intelligent.*

Phrases

A phrase is a group of related words that do not express a complete thought. A phrase may contain a subject or a predicate but not both. Phrases may be either prepositional or verbal; both modify other parts of the sentence.

A prepositional phrase is a phrase beginning with a preposition and modifying other words in the sentence.

The cover *of the book* is red.
The book sold *for $5.*

A verbal phrase begins with a verbal — a verb used as a noun, adjective, or adverb. Three kinds of verbal phrases are gerund phrases, infinitive phrases, and participial phrases.

Gerund phrase: *Dictating letters* is not an easy task.
Infinitive phrase: *To become president* was her ambition.
Participial phrase: *Having dictated letters all morning,* the executive was tired.

Don't confuse gerund phrases with participial phrases. Gerund phrases act as nouns; participial phrases act as adjectives.

Gerund phrase: *Making a profit* is necessary to stay in business.
Participial phrase: *Making a profit,* I stayed in business.

Clauses

A clause is a group of words that contains a subject and a verb. Clauses are either main or subordinate. A main clause contains a subject and a verb and expresses a complete thought; it is a simple sentence. A subordinate clause contains a subject and a verb but does not express a complete thought; it needs the main clause to make its meaning complete.

Main clause: *Profits increased rapidly* before the Christmas holidays.
Subordinate clause: *After our profits increased,*we bought additional property.

Uses of Phrases and Clauses

Phrases and clauses are used in sentences as nouns, adjectives, and adverbs. When a phrase or clause modifies a verb, adverb, or adjective, it is an adverb phrase or clause.

Profits increased *in the afternoon.* (adverb phrase)
Because sales increased, profits rose. (adverb clause)

When a phrase or clause modifies a noun or pronoun, it is an adjective phrase or clause.

Profits *on the sales of cars* increased. (adjective phrase)
Profits, *which had been low,* increased. (adjective clause)

When a phrase or clause is used as a noun, it is a noun phrase or clause.

Our company makes *cars.* (noun)
Our company makes *whatever you want.* (noun clause)
After the meeting would be the best time. (noun phrase)
Making profits on cars is easy. (gerund phrase)
To make a profit on a car is easy. (infinitive phrase)

Phrases and clauses may be restrictive or nonrestrictive. A restrictive phrase or clause is one that is essential to the meaning of the sentence. A nonrestrictive phrase or clause is not essential to the meaning of the sentence.

Restrictive: The man *who is director of research* conducted the seminar.
Nonrestrictive: A. W. Wells, *who is director of research,* conducted the seminar.

Kinds of Sentences

Sentences made from the foregoing components may be simple, complex, compound, or compound-complex, depending on what components are present. A **simple sentence** contains one subject and one verb.

Profits increased.

A **complex sentence** contains a main clause and one or more subordinate clauses.

Because profits increased, morale improved.

A **compound sentence** is two simple sentences joined by a coordinating conjunction.

Profits increased and morale improved.

A **compound-complex sentence** contains two simple sentences and one or more subordinate clauses.

Because we raised dividends, profits increased and morale improved.

In constructing sentences, we must consider what kind of influence each component has on the message contained in the sentence. For example, a subordinate clause is "subordinate" because it makes the idea contained in it depend on the idea contained in the main clause.

> Because profits increased, morale improved. (emphasis on morale)
> When morale improves, profits increase. (emphasis on profits)

In the next three sections of this chapter we will briefly discuss three important aspects of writing skills: problems of usage, mechanics, and elements of effective communication.

PROBLEMS OF USAGE

Once you know all the terminology, you're off to a good start. Now all you need to learn is how these components work. "Experts" don't agree about all aspects of language usage, but a few rules are so universally accepted that you should consider them absolutes.

Subject and Verb Agreement

A verb must agree with its subject in person and number. There is usually no difficulty with agreement in person. It's the number — singular or plural — that can cause difficulty.

Singular subjects require singular verbs.

> The *company was* established in 1902.
> *Each* company *has* its own charter.

Plural subjects require plural verbs.

> The companies *were* established in 1902.
> *Most* companies *have* a charter.

When words, phrases, or clauses separate the subject from the verb, they may mislead the writer.

> The *merchandise was* delivered on Thursday.
> The *merchandise* for all the stores *was* delivered on Thursday.

Pronoun and Antecedent Agreement

A pronoun must agree with its antecedent (the word it stands for) in number (singular or plural) and gender (feminine, masculine, common, or neuter).

Singular, feminine:	*Mary* worked on *her* project.
Singular, masculine:	*Bruce* worked on *his* project.
Plural, common:	*They* worked on *their* projects.
Singular, neuter:	The *project* gave satisfaction to *its* author.

Sentence Fragment

Every sentence must contain a subject and a verb and must express a complete thought. If a group of words does not express a complete thought, it is a sentence fragment.

Fragment: When we arrived.
Sentence: When we arrived, they started the session.

Run-On Sentence

Two sentences must be separated by a period, a semicolon, or a comma and conjunction. If they are not, the result is a run-on sentence. The two sentences run into each other.

Run-on sentence: We arrived they started the session.
Sentence: We arrived. They started the session.
or: We arrived; they started the session.
or: We arrived, and they started the session.

Comma Splice

If two sentences are joined by a comma alone, the result is a comma splice. The comma "splices" or joins two sentences that should be separate.

Comma splice: We arrived, they started the session.
Sentence: We arrived. They started the session.

Mismodification

When used properly, modifiers make the meaning of sentences clearer. But nothing can cause more confusion than misplaced or dangling modifiers.

Misplaced or dangling modifiers modify the wrong word, phrase, or clause. Avoid mismodification by placing the modifier as close as possible to the word, phrase, or clause that it modifies.

The client had a large envelope talking to Mr. Polski. (misplaced modifier)
The client talking to Mr. Polski had a large envelope.

While trying to repair the typewriter, the telephone rang. (dangling modifier)
While trying to repair the typewriter, he heard the telephone ring.

Entering the store, her eye spotted the sale sign. (dangling modifier)
Entering the store, she spotted the sale sign.

Progression of Verb Tenses

When you write, be consistent in your use of verb tenses. Avoid shifting from one tense to another unless your meaning requires it. Changing tenses can cause confusion. The verb of the main clause should agree in tense with the subordinate clause in that the time sequence must be logical.

Wrong: After Angela *leaves* the room, Arnold *told* his story.
Right: After Angela *left* the room, Arnold *told* his story.
Right: After Angela *had left* the room, Arnold *told* his story.

Make sure that your verb tense accurately expresses when the action takes place. Table 2-1 summarizes the tenses and their uses.

Table 2-1

Tense	Use	Example
Present	Action occurring now	I go.
Present progressive	Action ongoing at the present	I am going.
Past	Action completed in the past	I went.
Past progressive	Action ongoing in the past	I was going.
Future	Action that will take place in the future	I will go.
Present perfect	Action completed at the present	I have gone.
Past perfect	Action completed before another past time	I had gone.
Future perfect	Action that will be completed before a certain time in the future	I will have gone.

Parallelism

Parallelism is the use of the same grammatical construction for two or more parts of a sentence that have the same function — comparing ideas, contrasting ideas, or coordinating ideas. Match one part of speech with the same part of speech: nouns with nouns, verbs with verbs, phrases with phrases, clauses with clauses, and sentences with sentences.

Her duties included composing, editing, typing, and proofreading.

Faulty parallelism occurs when sentence elements that are alike in function are expressed in different grammatical forms.

Her duties included composing, edited, typing, and to watch for errors.

MECHANICS

As you already know, words aren't the only symbols we use to express ourselves in writing. We use punctuation to help indicate our meaning by showing how we think the words, phrases, and clauses we write should relate to each other. Punctuation marks are the nuts and bolts that hold writing together. We shall now examine the most common uses of punctuation marks and the rules governing capitalization.

The Period

Use the period after:

1. A declarative sentence.
   A distinction exists between brevity and conciseness.
2. An imperative sentence (a sentence that gives a command).
   Make your sentences concise.
3. An indirect question.
   Sue asked if she could write a report on conciseness.
4. A polite request.
   Will you please send me a copy of your bulletin.
5. Abbreviations and initials.
   Mr. J. W. Moltzan Ph.D. Mon. A.M.

The Comma

Use the comma:

1. To separate items in a series.
   They purchased new furniture, appliances, and accessories.
2. To enclose unnecessary expressions.
   Of course, the company will be closed on July 4.
   We will, however, be open on Monday, July 5.
3. To set off appositives (words placed side by side so the second describes the first).
   Mr. Leo Attaway, our purchasing agent, secured the raw materials.
   One-word appositives or those forming parts of proper names do not require commas.
   My sister Betty bought 40 shares of blue-chip stock.
   The manager reminded me of Attila the Hun.
4. To separate two or more adjectives.
   She enclosed a stamped, addressed envelope.
5. To separate the parts of dates and addresses.
   On July 4, 1976, the United States celebrated its bicentennial.
   Dimitri lives at 408 Banburdy Street, Canton, Ohio.
6. To set off nouns of direct address.
   Please, Mr. Holtzen, send us your check for $100.
7. To set off introductory phrases.

Wondering about the sudden increase in profits, the manager flew to Texas.

If the introductory phrase is short (no verb and fewer than five words), omit the comma.

In the report several management techniques were discussed.

8. To separate two main clauses joined by a conjunction.
   The accident occurred in the afternoon, and there were no witnesses.
   If the clauses are short, omit the comma.
   She asked and he answered.
9. To set off introductory subordinate clauses.
   If Jean should call while I'm gone, tell her I'll be back in 20 minutes.
10. To set off nonrestrictive clauses and phrases.
    My mother, needing more information, wrote to the director.
11. To separate two unrelated numbers.
    On June 1, 400 students enrolled.
12. Between contiguous verbs.
    Those who call, call for a reason
13. To indicate the omission of words.
    Last month Allen called two meetings; this month, two.

The Question Mark

Use the question mark after direct questions.

Who has the dictionary?

Exclamation Point

Use the exclamation point after exclamatory words, phrases, clauses, or sentences.

Really! How wonderful! You're kidding!

The Semicolon

Use the semicolon:

1. To join two main clauses that are not joined by a conjunction.
   Darlene is interested in music; Dennis is interested in drama.
2. After each item in a series with an item or items containing commas.
   Agnes visited Ann Arbor, Michigan; Chicago, Illinois; and Gary, Indiana.
3. To separate main clauses joined by a conjunction when both clauses contain a comma or when either clause contains two or more commas.
   Our company president, who winters in Florida, arrived this morning; and as soon as she arrived, she called a meeting of the Board of Directors.

The Colon

Use the colon before a list of items.

The purchasing agent ordered several kinds of typewriter ribbons: silk, nylon, cotton, and carbon.

The Dash

Use the dash for greater emphasis or for abrupt interruptions.

Four of the players — Val VanDyke, Jess Jakowski, Abe Solomon, and Bodo Buelow — were chosen for the national team.

The mistake — if that's what it was — caused a great deal of confusion.

Parentheses

Use parentheses:

1. To separate expressions providing qualifying information not important to the meaning of the sentence.
   Dr. R. Furjanic (Business Education) received his doctorate from Northern Illinois University.
2. To enclose figures or letters preceding enumerated items.
   The following projects are included: (1) Tax Analysis, (2) Time Management, and (3) Human Relations.

Underscore

Use the underscore:

1. For titles of books, periodicals, plays, and newspapers.
   <u>How to Bake Bread</u> (book)
   <u>Journal of Business Communication</u> (periodical)
   Jacques saw <u>Hamlet</u> three years ago. (play)
   Lillian bought today's issue of the <u>Times Gazette</u>. (newspaper)
2. For words that would be italicized in print.
   "Not only <u>what</u> you say but also <u>how</u> you say it, is important."
3. To indicate italics to the printer.
   Do <u>not</u> return to the refusal.

Quotation Marks

Use quotation marks:

1. For direct quotations.
   Vern said, "I'll install your carpeting."
2. For slang expressions.
   "ain't" "goofed"
3. For titles of articles, short poems, songs, subdivisions of books, and unpublished works.
   "Mastery of Typewriting" (article)
   "Ode on a Grecian Urn" (poem)
   "Mack the Knife" (song)
   "Writing Skills" (chapter)
   "A Study to Determine the Significance of Ten-Minute Timed Writings" (dissertation)

Capitalization

1. Capitalize the first word of
   a. A sentence.
      Management is an important executive function.
   b. An elliptical (condensed) expression.
      Congratulations! Really? No. Yes.
   c. A direct quotation.
      Mary Lou said, "The subsidiary should have an independent budget."
   d. A salutation.
      Dear Mr. Bussard
   e. A complimentary close.
      Sincerely yours
   f. A list or an outline.
      1. Period
      2. Comma
      3. Semicolon
2. Capitalize proper nouns and adjectives.
   Berard Building Baltic Colorado River French
3. Capitalize all titles when they precede the name.
   Dr. Reiter Sheriff Saulson Captain Dolez
4. Generally, do not capitalize titles when they follow a name or are used in place of a person's name. Retain the capitalization for a high-ranking official, however.
   Lester Salisbury, production manager
   Our production manager
   Myles Murphy, Senator
   Thomas Goodwin, professor
   His professor
   Charles Powers, Chief Justice
5. Capitalize all titles in addresses and in closing lines of a letter.
   Ms. Kathleen Kennard, Principal
   Adam Blaha
   Director of Research
6. Do not capitalize a title when it is followed by an appositive.
   Our supervisor, Mr. Joseph Anropolis, submitted a report.
7. Capitalize names showing family relationship, but not when preceded by a possessive.
   Uncle Steve and Aunt Louise my mother Dad
8. Capitalize the main words in titles of publications and literary or artistic works. Do not capitalize an article, conjunction, or short preposition unless it is the first word.
   The Silent Majority Speaks up About It. (book)

9. Capitalize the names of specific courses and subjects. Do not capitalize general areas of study unless the word is a proper noun or adjective.

   Business Communication 242
   American History 101
   accounting
   German
   Marketing 303
   Typewriting II
   English writing
   chemistry
   Russian history
   management

10. Capitalize a degree after a name or in abbreviations. Do not capitalize the name of a degree when used as a general term.

    John Arnold, Doctor of Medicine
    B.A. M.A. Ed.D. D.D.S. Ph.D.
    A bachelor of science degree

11. Capitalize the principal words in the names of associations, business firms, clubs, fraternities, governmental groups, religious bodies, and schools.

    American Business Communication Association
    Business Club
    Federal Party
    Alexander High School
    XYZ Corporation
    Delta Pi Epsilon
    First Christian Reformed Church

12. Capitalize days of the week, months of the year, holidays, historical events, and periods of time.

    Monday, January 23
    World War II
    Memorial Day
    Middle Ages

13. Do not capitalize the seasons of the year, decades, or centuries.

    spring summer fall winter
    early thirties twentieth century

14. Capitalize points of the compass when they designate definite regions. Do not capitalize points of the compass when they are used for direction.

    Midwest
    Far East
    South America
    south side of town
    Middle East
    east of Detroit

15. Capitalize nouns followed by a number or a letter. Some nouns, such as page, paragraph, line, or verse are not capitalized.

Building 83	page 23
Lot A	paragraph 3
Chapter X	line 8
Flight 807	verse 46

ELEMENTS OF EFFECTIVE COMMUNICATION

As we said at the beginning of this chapter, grammar and mechanics serve only one purpose: to help you make your communication clear. The prime requisite of communication is the transfer of meaning, but this alone does not make the communication effective. Effective communication requires that your receiver not only understand, but also agree with, approve of, or act on your message.

Transfer of Meaning

In addition to tranferring meaning, effective communication establishes a favorable relationship between the sender and the receiver. In interpersonal situations, sender and receiver can use means other than language to help establish a favorable environment for communication. In written communication, a favorable communication environment must be established through the use of language alone. In many cases, *how* we convey our message is just as important as *what* our message is. In this section we are concerned with how a message should be conveyed.

The elements of effective written communication may be called the **C**s to help us remember that good writing displays the following characteristics:

Clarity
Courtesy
Conciseness
Confidence
Correctness
Conversational tone

Clarity

Clarity is the transfer of thoughts to a receiver without misunderstanding. This is the single most important factor in communication. To achieve clarity, you must put into practice what you learned about barriers to communication in Chapter One. How will your readers perceive your message? Will your readers attach the same meaning as you do to the words you've used?

Words have both denotations — dictionary meanings — and connotations — associated meanings. Connotations may vary greatly from person to person. The words "inexpensive" and "cheap," for example, both denote the same thing, but their connotations are quite different.

Word Choice

Take as much time as necessary to explain things to your readers. Watch your vocabulary: use words your readers will understand. When a technical term is necessary for exactness, use it, but be sure to explain each term your readers may not be familiar with. Keep in mind also that your message will be clearer if you state it explicitly rather than implicitly. The following examples show the greater clarity achieved by being explicit.

Implicit: To complete the purchase of the property, fill in Items 6 and 7 on the enclosed document, noting your relationship to William R. Adams and Susan B. Adams. Also note that, should *the owners* be unable to make a payment, you as cosigner assume that responsibility.

Explicit: To complete the purchase of the property, fill in Items 6 and 7 on the enclosed document, noting your relationship to William R. Adams and Susan B. Adams. Also note that, should *Mr. and Mrs. Adams* be unable to make a payment, you as cosigner assume that responsibility.

A message should be implicit only when:

1. The reader will consider it negative.

   Explicit: You failed to perform the maintenance check on your machine.

   Implicit: A maintenance check on your machine should be performed every 30 days.

2. The reader is sophisticated enough to understand the implication.

   Explicit: With our usual credit terms, you save 2 percent when you pay within 10 days of the invoice date. The net amount is due in 30 days. (audience that may not be familiar with credit terms)

   Implicit: Our usual credit terms are 2/10, n/30. (sophisticated audience)

Structure

To be clear, writing must also have a solid, logical structure. No matter what its objective, any written message — any clear message, for that matter — must have a definite beginning, middle, and end. But as we discussed in Chapter One, the purpose of the message and the receiver's probable reaction to it determine the content of the beginning, middle, and end of the message.

The general structure of a message may be either immediate or delayed, depending on the answer to the receiver's main question, "How will this message benefit me?" When we have something good to tell the reader, we can say it immediately in the first paragraph. When we have a message that the reader will find unpleasant or will resist, we delay that part of the message by putting something positive ahead of it.

When the purpose of the message is to inquire, to provide positive or neutral information, or to grant a request, the structure should be immediate. The most important part of the message — from the reader's point of view — is conveyed immediately.

Immediate Messages

General Structure of Immediate Messages

Beginning (introduction):
- Most important information, question, or answer to a reader's question
- Important conclusions or recommendations
- Good news

Middle (body):
- Supporting details
- Secondary matters
- Answers to secondary questions
- Explanations

End (conclusion):
- Statement of who is to do what next
- Summary (if message is long)
- Anticipation of a positive future

Delayed Messages

General Structure of Delayed Messages

Beginning:
- Something with which the reader can agree
- Clear statement of a problem
- Promise of a benefit

Middle:
- Reasons
- Specific facts and figures

End:
- Positive statement of who does what next
- Suggestions of specific, positive course of action

Specific organizational patterns for specific message purposes will help you to write successful messages. Specific patterns for letters and reports are found in Chapters Three and Four.

Unity
Coherence
Transition

To be clear, a message must also have unity. A unified message has continuity of thought and singleness of purpose. Like structure, unity doesn't just happen; you must plan for it. Group related ideas together, and then arrange the groups into a logical sequence. Eliminate ideas that do not pertain to the topic that is the purpose of your message. Because your readers should always know where they have been and where your message is taking them, each sentence and each paragraph should contain a clear, specific reference to the preceding sentence and paragraph. In this way you can maintain **coherence** of thought and provide clear **transition** from idea to idea. The ways you can achieve coherence and provide transition are the following:

1. **Repetition.** As you move from sentence to sentence, repeat key words or ideas or use pronouns to stand for key words and concepts. Repetition of sentence structure provides coherence and, at the same time, emphasizes the ideas put into parallel structure.

   When checking raw materials, look for quality.
   When checking the final product, look for quality.

2. **Cause and effect.** Use words such as *thus, therefore,* and *because* to indicate that one event is the result of a preceding event. You must be careful, however; this method of achieving transition frequently gets writers into trouble. Make sure that the event you identify as the cause of something else actually is the cause. The following example may or may not be true:

   Because I bought a typewriter, my grades improved.

   If buying the typewriter provided the psychological motivation the writer needed to become a better student, then the cause-effect relationship is stated correctly. It's more likely, however, that the two events were both caused by some other factor — a determination to do well, perhaps — and they simply happened at about the same time. A more accurate statement would be, "After I bought a typewriter, my grades improved."

   Sentences using the words *because, since, therefore, then,* and *thus* should indicate a definite cause-effect relationship between two ideas:

   Because I bought 12 shares of IBM stock, George bought 24 shares. (George bought the shares *only* because I did.)

3. **Comparison/Contrast.** Pointing out the similarities or differences between two concepts or events will also help you keep your reader informed about where your message is going. The verb *compare* can indicate either similarities or differences. When you use it to focus on similarities, it is followed by *with*. When you use it to focus on differences, it is followed by *to*. The verb *contrast* is followed by *with*.

   Brand A has a *better* (or *worse*) flavor than Brand B. Brand B offers some advantages when compared *with* Brand A. Compared *to* Brand B, Brand A comes in a wider variety of colors, sizes, and shapes.

4. **Time and place.** Let your reader know when and where events are taking place. Be sure to relate that *when* and *where* to the *when* and *where* of other events described in your message. Make your references to time and place as specific as you can. When you have several related items to mention, a **numbered list** — as we have used here — is a useful device for showing that they are related parts of a larger whole.

Specificity

Being specific is another important aspect of clarity. By being specific you let your readers know what you're doing and show that you care enough about them and their businesses to provide all the details pertinent to the subject. In any message, specific details make the writing interesting; in a business message, the specific details make the writing not only interesting but also believable.

General: Your car will arrive sometime next month.
Specific: Your Mustang II will arrive on Monday, 27 September.

Be sure to give exact facts, figures, explanations, and examples. Whenever you can, use specific words rather than general ones.

General	Specific
color	red
number	4,000
city	Kalamazoo
contact	call, write, throw a brick

Completeness

To be clear, you also need to be complete. Make sure that you have covered everything you intended to cover and that you have provided sufficient detail for your readers to know exactly what you expect of them. After they have read your message, your readers should know who is going to do what next.

Readability

The final measure of the clarity of a message is its readability. Several authors, of whom Rudolf Flesch and Robert Gunning are the most widely known, have developed mathematical formulas for measuring the educational level a piece of writing is best suited for. Such readability formulas are based on the concept that short sentences and words of few syllables are easier to read than long sentences and polysyllabic words. We suggest that, rather than resorting to a specific mathematical formula, you should check your sentences to see that they *average* about 17 words. Some should be longer, some shorter. Also, make a deliberate effort to use words that will be familiar to your readers.

Courtesy

A courteous message is polite and considerate. The assumption of a courteous message is that writer and reader are both reasonable people with good intentions who can solve problems, make decisions, and understand each other without resorting to any form of psychological or physical force.

Empathy

You-Attitude

A courteous message has empathy: it takes its readers' thoughts, feelings, and point of view into account. Empathy is also known as the you-attitude. Examine everything you write from your readers' point of view. Will your readers welcome your message, or will they resent or resist it? Structure your message to make it as comfortable and nonthreatening for your readers as you can. Always do what you can to help your readers develop positive self-images and maintain their confidence in themselves, even when the situation is unpleasant.

Put your readers and their problems first. That doesn't mean that you should omit all reference to your own interests. Your readers expect you to have legitimate interests and concerns, but they will appreciate your showing them that you understand what their needs are. Emphasize the benefits to the readers. When you can, make the readers the subject or object of your sentences.

Writer viewpoint: We shipped your merchandise this morning.
Reader viewpoint: Your three screwdrivers should arrive by 2 August.

Conciseness

Don't waste words. Make sure that each word and each sentence accomplish something for you, whether it is satisfying the readers' logical expectations or their emotional needs. But don't sacrifice the human aspect in your desire to be brief. Your readers don't want to receive three or four pages when one will do, but neither do they want to feel as though you could hardly wait to get their letter out of the way. **A concise letter takes care of business in the fewest possible words, but it also takes the time required to establish a warm, human relationship.**

Confidence

Confidence in Yourself

Show confidence in yourself. Present your message with confidence that your reader will understand and accept what you have to say. Emphasize the positive aspects of your message, eliminating negative words, phrases, and ideas as much as possible. Always focus on what can be done rather than on what can't be done.

Negative: We cannot ship your merchandise until Friday.
Positive: We can ship your merchandise on Friday.

Confidence in Reader

Show confidence in your readers. Assume that your readers will do what is right until you have absolute proof that they won't. Assume that your readers are capable of overcoming obstacles.

Confidence in Message

Show confidence in your message. Expressions such as *I hope*, *if*, and *why not* may indicate that you don't believe that your message is clear or that your readers will accept it.

I hope that this letter answers your questions.
Why not try a Freeflow pen today?
If you follow my suggestions, you will become rich.

You can avoid the implication that your message may not have done everything it should have by emphasizing the positive or by focusing on the future.

I'm glad to send you this information.
Try a Freeflow pen for 10 days absolutely free.
You will become rich by following my suggestions.

Avoid Overconfidence

While you are working to be confident, remember that overconfidence leads to presumptuousness. When your readers have a choice, make sure that you don't take that choice away from them.

Presumptuous: Send me your dollar today!
Positive and courteous: By sending your dollar today, you can be sure of receiving your Freeflow pen in time for Christmas.

Correctness

Pay Attention to Details

Most readers of business messages expect grammatical correctness. Misspelled words, faulty punctuation, and awkward constructions indicate inattention to details, which many readers would assume was carried over into areas other than writing. Get into the habit of checking spelling, punctuation, and word usage. Your correctness will show that you care about yourself, your reader, and your company's image.

Verify Facts and Figures

In addition to being grammatically correct, correct messages supply the reader with accurate information. Double-check all facts and figures, including serial numbers, dates, and amounts.

Conversational Tone

The final element of effective written communication is conversational tone. Although one great advantage of written communication is its ability to convey complex messages better than the spoken word, good writers never forget that writing should sound comfortable and natural to the ear. Style — the way a writer puts words together in a message, including word usage, sentence construction, and forcefulness — is important. Writers of fiction go to great lengths to develop an identifiable style. Literary writers such as Faulkner, Hemingway, and Mailer have styles so distinctive that readers can identify the writer after reading only a few sentences. Business messages, however, should be written in an inconspicuous style. This doesn't mean that your writing should be dull. Your writing can — and should be — lively, interesting, and indicative of your personality. But remember that you are not writing business messages to impress your reader with your clever command of the language. As a business communicator, you want your readers to focus their attention on what you're saying rather than on how you're saying it. Use the content of your message to hold the readers' attention.

Style

Your style should be natural, conversational, and unpretentious. Use the words that you would use in conversation with your readers. Remember that words are merely symbols for objects and events, so not all people have the same concepts of what words mean. If writer and reader have different concepts of what a word means, confusion is bound to result.

Word Usage

Simple, familiar, and concrete words have fewer related and personal meanings than unfamiliar, abstract words. For greatest clarity, stick to the everyday words your readers are certain to know. Define technical terms, and avoid abbreviations. Watch for combinations of words that result in meanings you don't intend:

Do not break your bread or roll in the soup.

Definition Jargon

Of special danger to business communicators is jargon — words used to impress readers. Such words are frequently used incorrectly. "Parameter" is one example — as in "I have examined the *parameters* of the problem." (A parameter is not an *aspect, limit,* or *perimeter;* it is a constant that varies at a rate determined by another constant — for example, the radii of concentric circles.)

Jargon is popular because it lets people sound knowledgeable without requiring them to be specific. Much jargon is a result of combining perfectly good words into complex phrases: "systematized logistical projection," for example.

Readers are more impressed if they understand exactly what you mean. Use language that shows the clarity, directness, and force of your thinking.

Say this:	Rather than this:
Tell	Beg to advise
Before, after	Prior to, subsequent to
Know	Cognizant of
The enclosed booklet	Please find enclosed
To use	In order to utilize

Good writing consists primarily of the right nouns and the right verbs. Make your nouns specific and concrete; make your verbs vivid. Don't use a clause when a verb will do the same job more economically.

Demosthenes has made the suggestion that. . . .
Demosthenes suggested that. . . .

Variation

Variation will add interest to your writing. Vary sentence structure, paragraph length and construction, and emphasis to create an interesting rhythm and flow in your writing. You can achieve variation in sentence structure in several ways:

1. Combine two main clauses into a compound sentence.

   He read *Newsweek*. His wife read *Time*.
   He read *Newsweek*, and his wife read *Time*.

2. Combine two clauses into a complex sentence by making one clause subordinate to the other.

   Although he read *Newsweek*, his wife read *Time*.

3. Combine several ideas into a compound-complex sentence.

   While reading *Newsweek*, he smoked his pipe and drank a glass of sherry; but his wife, who was reading *Time*, neither smoked nor drank.

4. Embed one sentence in another one.

   He read *Newsweek* out of habit. That made his wife angry.
   His reading *Newsweek* out of habit made his wife angry.

Short, Direct Sentences

Although you must vary sentence pattern and length to keep your message from becoming monotonous, your style will be more readable if you keep most of your sentences short and direct. As we mentioned previously, your sentences should average about 17 words. If your average is much less, your readers will feel that you are "talking down" to them; if your average is much more, even your well-educated readers will be forced to read slowly to be sure that they understand what you are saying.

Variation in paragraph length and construction also helps make your writing interesting and forceful. In general, short paragraphs are easier to read and more forceful than long ones. Paragraph length is more critical when your message is single-spaced. As a general rule, your first and last paragraphs in any message should be no more than four or five lines long, and no paragraph in any typewritten message should be much longer than eight lines.

Emphasis

Proper emphasis of ideas also contributes to the forcefulness of your writing. The means of controlling emphasis are as follows:

1. **Placement.** Where you place an idea influences the amount of attention a reader pays to it. The beginnings and the ends of sentences, paragraphs, and entire messages are the places of natural emphasis. Consider carefully what words you place at the beginning and the end of a sentence. Paragraphs should usually begin or end with the topic sentence. The important, positive concepts belong at the beginning and the end of your written messages.
2. **Proportion.** Allot space to ideas on the basis of their importance to the reader. If item A is three times as important as item B, it merits roughly three times the space.
3. **Language.** Make people, not ideas, the subjects of your sentences. And, except when you wish to de-emphasize something (such as a reader's mistake) use the active voice. A simple declarative sentence has more emphasis than a rambling compound-complex sentence. Concentrate on nouns and verbs: use

specific, concrete nouns and action verbs. Avoid artificial intensifiers, such as *very, terribly, extremely, it is important to note, you can be assured;* they have become meaningless through overuse.

Watch your use of expletives *(it is, there is, there are)*. Too many expletives make for slow, dull reading.

[There are] some business persons [who] always do well.

Sometimes you can use expletives to place the stress on a word you wish to emphasize.

Managing by objectives is a good idea. (emphasis on *managing* and *good idea*)
It is a good idea to manage by objectives. (emphasis on *good idea* and *objectives*)

Put ideas you wish to emphasize in main clauses and ideas you wish to de-emphasize in subordinate clauses.

Since Christmas will be here in two weeks [subordinate clause], the stores are jammed with shoppers [main clause].

4. **Mechanics.** You can also emphasize by underscoring, using color, putting important points in an itemized list, repeating verbal patterns and important words, or surrounding an important statement with extra white space.

SUMMARY

Written communication is important to business because it has the ability to transcend time, to transcend distance, and to permit the careful consideration and controlled use of language.

Essential to all writing is an understanding of the rules of grammar. You'll need to know the parts of speech and their functions to build sentences, which are the basic units of communication. The mechanics of the language — punctuation and capitalization — help you to write clear, concise messages.

In written communication, you must establish a favorable communication environment entirely by the use of language. How you convey your message is just as important as what your message is.

Good writing has a logical structure, a unified message, continuity of thought, and singleness of purpose. Emphasize the positive aspects of your message and, as much as possible, eliminate negative words, phrases, and ideas. Present your thoughts as clearly as possible so your reader will understand what you are trying to say. Examine everything you write from your reader's point of view. Be sure to give exact facts, figures, explanations, and examples. Be specific.

EXERCISES

1. State three reasons why written communication is important.
2. Name the eight parts of speech and state their functions.
3. Explain the differences between active and passive voice and state the uses of each.
4. Supply correct punctuation and capitalization for the following:

   because mr smith empathy is an important concept in written messages you should always consider what the message is going to mean to your reader you should also think about punctuation and capitalization shouldn't you clarity is after all a result of the right words in the right places separated by the right punctuation marks will you write me when you have further questions I'm glad to be of help

5. What is the difference between a fragment and a sentence? Between a sentence and a run-on sentence?
6. Why is parallel construction an important grammatical principle?
7. List and define the six elements of effective written communication.
8. Rewrite the following sentences to make them more positive:

   We cannot ship your table until Friday.
   I hope that you won't be disappointed with the table.
   If you would like to order, use the enclosed order blank.

9. Rewrite the following sentences to make them more empathetic:

   I will ship your merchandise sometime next week.
   I need the Golden Paint as soon as possible.
   I am proud to announce the grand opening of my new store.
10. Rewrite the following to make it clearer, more specific, and more conversational:

    Prior to the receipt of your missive some time last month, in order to utilize the full advantage of the possibilities of having Johan Reich being cognizant of his duty to serve as an interface between your department and ours, I begged to advise him of his obligations in that regard.

A number of managers will be traveling to the city with Johan in the future, so if you would contact me at your earliest convenience, we could make a determination of the possibilities of your being in attendance at said meeting to discuss the parameters of the problem.

Please find enclosed an envelope, which somehow or other managed to become self-addressed, and subsequent to reading the directions on the instruction sheet which I am sending under separate cover, return same to me. I beg to remain your humble and obedient servant.

SUGGESTED READINGS

Brusaw, Charles T., Gerald J. Alred, and Walter E. Oliu. *The Business Writer's Handbook.* New York: St. Martin's Press, 1976.

Crews, Frederick. *The Random House Handbook.* New York: Random House, 1974.

Flesch, Rudolf. *The Art of Plain Talk.* New York: Harper & Brothers, 1946.

Gunning, Robert. *The Technique of Clear Writing.* Rev. ed. New York: McGraw-Hill, 1968.

Himstreet, William C., and Wayne Murlin Baty. *Business Communications.* 5th. ed. Belmont, CA: Wadsworth, 1977.

Kerrigan, William J. *Writing to the Point.* New York: Harcourt Brace Jovanovich, 1974.

Menning, J. H., C. W. Wilkinson, and Peter B. Clarke. *Communicating Through Letters and Reports.* 6th ed. Homewood, IL: Richard D. Irwin, 1976.

Murphy, Herta A., and Charles E. Peck. *Effective Business Communications.* 2d ed. New York: McGraw-Hill, 1976.

Perrin, Porter G. *Writer's Guide and Index to English.* 5th ed. Glenview, IL: Scott, Foresman, 1972.

Reid, James M., Jr., and Robert M. Wendlinger. *Effective Letters.* 2d ed. New York: McGraw-Hill, 1973.

Stewart, Marie M., Frank W. Lanham, and Kenneth Zimmer. *College English and Communication.* 3d ed. New York: McGraw-Hill, 1975.

Wolf, Morris Philip, and Robert R. Aurner. *Effective Communication in Business.* 6th ed. Cincinnati: South-Western, 1974.

3 LETTERS

After you have read this chapter, you should be able to

1. **State four advantages of communicating by mail.**
2. **Name three objectives of letters.**
3. **Use writing skills discussed in Chapter Two to make letters more effective.**
4. **Identify letter-writing problems.**
5. **Use letters effectively in meeting specific organizational objectives.**

ADVANTAGES OF LETTER WRITING

Cost

The cost of doing business by mail, like the cost of everything else, is going up. Although estimates of the cost of an average business letter vary, it's easy to see that postage, supplies, production time, and composition time for a letter add up to a significant sum very quickly.

But in spite of the increasing costs, letters remain the most important single channel an organization has for communicating with the public and with other organizations. Because letters are an important necessity for business, you must learn to handle letter-writing situations quickly and effectively.

As is true for all communication, a letter can only be effective if it makes its purpose clear and, at the same time, establishes empathy between reader and writer. In other words, the writer must make a good impression on the reader. Many customers, clients, and associates form their entire impression of you and your company on the basis of your letters. Important as it is for letters to make a good impression, clarity and empathy are frequently more difficult to achieve in written communication than in oral communication. This is true for two reasons:

1. We tend to be more formal when we write than when we speak.
2. We cannot receive the immediate feedback necessary to alter our message if our receiver doesn't understand what we are saying.

In spite of these difficulties, communicating by letter offers several important advantages.

1. **It provides a permanent record.** Important exchanges of information in business should be retained so each party will have an accurate record of what was said. Letters, like other writing, provide such a record. Phone calls do not, so important calls require follow-up letters.
2. **It provides proof of agreement.** An exchange of letters can constitute a written contract. When two people or organizations agree that certain goods or services should be exchanged for something else, the agreement should generally be put into writing. When the agreement is complex, a formal contract is helpful to specify complicated conditions; but when the agreement is simple, an exchange of letters is enough. For example, when an organization offers you a job, it will probably do so by mail, offering you a specific salary to work at a particular job. When you write back accepting that salary to do that work, you complete a contract.
3. **It puts emphasis on logic.** Because errors in logic are more obvious in writing than in speaking, written communication requires both writer and reader to be more logical than they might otherwise be. Letters enable the writer to rework the message until it says exactly what is meant. Letters also enable the reader to reread the message as often as necessary to comprehend all the implications of everything that is said. For this reason, letters do a better job of conveying complex information than phone calls or other oral channels of communication.
4. **It can be more convenient.** Phone calls are often inconvenient for one party. If an important phone call should arrive in the middle of an important conference, the receiver could not be expected to do justice to either the conference or the call. And you probably know how inconvenient it is to be placed on "hold." Letters, on the other hand, can be written and read at the times most convenient for writer and reader. Because of this, letters usually receive the amount of attention they deserve.

THE LETTER'S PURPOSE

Purpose

As with all written communication, the purpose or function of a letter determines its content and structure. Letters may have the same basic purposes as all other practical messages: to inquire, to inform, or to persuade. Each letter should have a clear, definite objective. Your main purpose might be one of the following:

To inquire . . . about or request a new product or service

To inform . . . the reader that you (or your company) agree to a request

. . . the reader that you do not agree to a request

To persuade . . . the reader to purchase a new product or service

. . . the reader to alter an established behavior

In most cases, the writer should state the main purpose of the letter in one sentence. The rest of the information in the letter can then be organized around the main purpose and be stated concisely, precisely, and logically.

Several Possible Objectives

In many cases writers must select from several possible objectives the one that seems most important. Do you want to *inform* your readers that you are offering a new product or service, or do you wish to *persuade* your readers to purchase your product or service? Do you wish to *inform* your readers that you can't fill their orders for six weeks and suggest that they buy elsewhere, or do you wish to *persuade* them to wait until you can fill their orders?

Reader's Choice

When presented with such choices, you should usually focus on the objective you would most like to achieve and construct your letter around that objective. Although to be honest you must give your reader the facts required to make the right decision, you can certainly emphasize the advantages your objective has to offer.

When your reader has a choice, be sure to indicate what that choice is. Stress the action you would like your reader to take, but don't ignore other possibilities. As we discussed in Chapter One, disappointing material, whether it is a delay in shipment or refusal of a request, belongs in the middle of the letter. The positive aspects — the part of the order you can fill, a statement with which your reader can agree, or positive alternatives — belong at the beginning and the end of the letter.

Apologies

When they're called for, apologies are positive, not negative. If you have made a mistake that can't be corrected, all you can do is apologize and attempt to re-establish a friendly relationship with your reader.

> Your reader discovered a cockroach in a jar of your peanut butter.
>
> One of your salespersons hit your best customer right in the mouth.
>
> You discovered a letter, now six weeks old and requiring an immediate answer, mixed in with a bunch of other papers.

In such cases you *must* apologize, so do that first and get on with the more positive task of re-establishing the relationship. If a letter must include an apology, it should be first and only first. Don't try to subordinate an apology by putting it in the middle of the letter, and above all, *never* apologize at the end of the letter. The end of the letter should always be positive and forward-looking.

Most of the time, however, an apology serves no purpose and should be omitted. When something is your fault but you can fix it, your reader is more concerned with how you're going to fix it than with how sorry you are that it happened in the first place. Fix it, and don't look back.

THE READER'S RESPONSE

The content of your message is only one of three factors that influence the way your reader will respond to your message. Usually, the content is determined by the situation. You probably can't change the nature of *what* you are going to say in any given letter, but you can control *how* you say it, and this will greatly influence the way your reader interprets your message. Because your message tells your readers not only what you are saying but also what you think of them and their problems, the way you state your message is just as important as what you say in determining your reader's response.

Naturally, your previous experience with a particular reader is important. The better you know people, the easier it is to communicate with them. With friends and with business acquaintances of long standing, you have greater assurance that your message will be interpreted correctly.

Most of the following discussion concerns the problems of communicating with people you don't know well — people about whom you must make assumptions because you don't have specific observations to go by. You must rely on inferences and intuition to predict the possible response of such readers to your message.

What You Say

Regardless of the way you phrase and structure it, the content of your message is bound to influence your reader's response.

Is your reader likely to welcome, resent, or resist the content of your message? Will your letter

. . . increase your reader's business?
. . . provide requested information?
. . . grant a special favor?
. . . deny a request that the reader hoped would be granted?

. . . attempt to persuade the reader to take an action he or she may not wish to take?

Although intuition and experience are not absolutely reliable as predictors of the behavior of others, you can use your intuition and your own experiences to make some practical generalizations about the responses of others. What you welcome, resent, or resist, your reader is likely to welcome, resent or resist. Would the message content make you glad, hurt your feelings, or arouse your skepticism? It will probably influence your reader the same way.

How You Say It

Your attitude toward your reader is reflected in your choice of words and phrasing. Do you feel that you are superior to your reader in some way? Do you feel inferior? Do you trust your reader?

Although we are not always conscious of it, our use of language reveals our feelings about our readers and shows the reasons we are writing. Certain negative emotions can detract from the effectiveness of communication:

1. **Indignation.** If we say, "Your letter has been referred to this office for a reply," we are telling the reader that we resent taking the time to write.
2. **Mistrust.** If we say, "You claim that five ceramic figures were broken," we are implying that we don't trust the reader.
3. **Paternalism.** If we say, "We are pleased to grant you permission," we're saying that we are more important than the reader. If we say, "You must order our product now because the only way you can succeed is to offer your customers quality merchandise at bargain prices," we are giving a lecture based on the assumption that the reader is incapable of independent thinking.
4. **Humility.** If we say, "I'm sorry to bother someone as important as you, but . . .", we're placing ourselves in a servile position.
5. **Flattery.** If we say . . . "Only you and you alone can do this job . . .", we are trying to substitute flattery for legitimate praise or honest persuasion.

In addition to avoiding these negative points of view, writers should avoid seeming self-centered; readers respond more favorably to letters that focus on them, their problems, and their benefits.

Reader's Viewpoint

Always attempt to look at the situation from your reader's point of view. When you are writing the same letter to many people — as with direct mail advertising and some insurance correspondence — you

Form Letters

should use a form letter to reduce the expense of writing, printing, and mailing the letters. Readers prefer to be treated as individuals rather than as members of a large group, however. Even when it will be obvious to your reader that your letter is a form letter, personalize your letters by writing to just one reader at a time. Except when your letter is addressed specifically (by name) to more than one person, write as though your one reader is your only concern — even though copies of the same letter may be going to thousands of people.

Keep the Reader in the Picture

When giving explanations, keep your reader in the picture. Refer to the reader — as the subject or object of the sentence when possible — or refer to the reader's company, product, or service.

Empathy — frequently called the "you-attitude" or the "you-viewpoint" — involves putting your reader's interests first. This forces you to concentrate on the *results* of efforts rather than on the actions taken within the company. For example, say "You will receive . . ." rather than "We have shipped . . ."

Readers are naturally more interested in how the action affects them than in what was done, and empathy on the writer's part causes the reader to read more attentively and to believe more readily that the benefits promised are real.

Positive Tone

Our attitude toward customers (and, to a certain extent, our attitude toward business and life in general) is reflected by the language we choose. We should maintain a positive tone.

Negative phrasings and words indicate a negative attitude toward the reader; they also reveal a negative pattern of thinking.

Compare: "We're sorry that we cannot ship until Monday."
to: "We can promise delivery by Wednesday."

By focusing on what we *can't* do, we reduce our reader's confidence in us and our ability to perform. But by emphasizing what we *can* do, we increase our reader's faith in us, even when we are unable to meet certain specific needs. Make an effort to rephrase negative words and expressions whenever you can state the same idea clearly using positive language.

ORGANIZING THE CONTENTS

The organization of your message content is important for two reasons. First, the organization is largely responsible for determining the relative importance of material in the letter. Second, the letter's organization will influence the reader's response.

Because the reader gives special attention to the beginning and the end of a letter, the writer should take advantage of the beginning and the end to stress important, positive points. Because the reader pays the least attention to the middle of the letter, the writer can de-emphasize matters of secondary importance and negative matters by placing them in the middle of the letter.

Emphasizing important, positive points by placing them first and last and de-emphasizing secondary and negative matters by middle placement is common to both immediate and delayed messages. This structure helps in achieving practical communication goals — to inquire, to convey positive information, to convey negative information, and to persuade.

Inquiries

When your main purpose is to request information or the shipment of a product, use an immediate presentation.

1. **Immediate beginning.** Begin the letter with a direct question or a request for what you want.

   What are the differences between Model X and Model Y?
   Please send one dozen copies of *Elmo's Elementary Encyclopedia.*

2. **Explanation.** When an explanation is needed, give it second. But as you explain, refer to your reader, the product, or the company to keep your reader in the picture.
3. **Secondary matters.** Other questions or specifications should follow any necessary explanation. If you use a numbered list for these secondary matters, you will direct your reader's attention to each item separately and greatly increase your chances of getting what you want.
4. **End dating.** It's a good idea to end most inquiries by setting an end date or deadline for the reader. Be polite and give a justification for the deadline.

   I would appreciate receiving your reply by December 1 because I must make my recommendation to the President on the 10th.

   Because my peak season for Halloween masks is in mid-October, I would appreciate receiving my order by the last week in September.

   A word of caution: do *not* thank your reader "in advance." That's presumptuous.

The first of the following examples illustrates common errors in letters of inquiry. The second example shows how inquiries should be written.

Poor

Dear Mr. Dowd:

My name is Allen Acreo, and I have a small manufacturing company here in Winnebega, Montana. We make all sorts of small metallic implements for a variety of farm machinery applications.

About two months ago, Ms. Susan Galligan came to me and applied for a job as my secretary. I really do need a new secretary because my old secretary died. Her funeral, strangely enough, was on the hottest day of the year, July 22.

If I hire Ms. Galligan as my secretary, she will have to take over all of Nancy Johnson's duties. Could she do this? Thank you in advance for your cooperation.

Sincerely yours,

Allen Acreo
President

P.S. Ms. Galligan listed you as a reference on her application.

Notice that the letter:

1. Begins with an explanation rather than with the main question.
2. Contains many irrelevant details.
3. Fails to provide the details the reader will need to supply a complete, accurate answer.
4. Thanks the reader in advance.

Improved

When Ms. Galligan worked
as your secretary, Mr. Dowd...

was she efficient, resourceful, and courteous?

I am considering hiring her as my administrative assistant, and she gave your name as a reference and former employer. The job is an important one, and I would welcome your comments on Ms. Galligan's abilities to handle a variety of complex responsibilities in an efficient, cheerful manner.

In addition to typing, taking dictation, and filing, the job would require Ms. Galligan to assume responsibility for routine correspondence, bookkeeping, and handling of special orders and complaints. In my absence she would be responsible for running the plant, including giving orders to my other 60 employees--all of whom are men.

Do you think that she is qualified for this position?

I'll keep your answers to these questions, and any other information you think will help me decide about Ms. Galligan, strictly confidential.

Because I'm leaving for Europe in mid-February, I must make my decision by 24 January. May I have your answer by then?

I'd appreciate it,

Allen Acreo
President

Notice that the letter:

1. Gets off to a fast start by asking an important question.
2. Gives the explanation second. The explanation keeps the reader in the picture.
3. Provides all the details necessary for the reader to give a complete, accurate answer.
4. Sets an end date and justifies it.

Positive Information

When your main purpose is to convey positive information, use an immediate presentation.

1. **Immediate beginning.** Begin the letter by providing the reader with the information requested.

   Model Y, with 33 horsepower, is available in red, blue, brown, and white. Model X, with 20 horsepower, comes in white.

2. **Secondary matters.** The rest of the information you wish to convey should follow logically, in chronological order, order of importance, or some other natural sequence.

3. **The closing.** When appropriate, add a statement of goodwill or resale — something favorable about a product, service, or idea in which your reader has expressed an interest. But don't be afraid to quit after you've made your last point if that seems most appropriate.

   Call on me again if I can help. Your cause is certainly worthy.

   Your new stereo is fully guaranteed for five years, and it will provide you and your children with many hours of enjoyment.

Compare the following examples:

Poor

Dear Mrs. Motts:

We received your letter regarding your recent experience with one of our garments. A report of this kind is of deep concern to us.

Kiddie Klothes Inc. has been in business for over 50 years and has earned a reputation for making the finest quality children's clothes at affordable prices. We make every effort to have our clothes reach the consumer in as perfect a condition as possible. To do this, our company maintains an on-going program of quality control to check fabrics, pattern making procedures, cutting and sewing of the garments. Furthermore, we have our own laboratory where technicians perform intensive tests on fabrics and garments.

Regarding the item you brought to our attention, our Quality Control department would very much like to examine it. Accordingly, would you be kind enough to return it to me. Upon receipt of the garment, we will send you a replacement of the same style if it is available, or a comparable one.

We are sorry for any inconvenience this may have caused you and appreciate your notifying us. At Kiddie Klothes our objective is not merely to have consumers, but to have satisfied consumers.

Sincerely,

Notice:

1. The first statement is too obvious. If they hadn't received the letter, they couldn't be answering.
2. The language of the second sentence is inappropriate for the situation.
3. How long the company has been in business and how extensively each product is tested has nothing to do with the issue; moreover, by emphasizing how good their products are, Kiddie Klothes is implying that the customer's complaint was unjustified.
4. The apology is unnecessary because the situation can be corrected.
5. The platitude in the last sentence is ineffective.
6. The letter is wordy, pretentious, awkward, and company-oriented. The following phrases are especially offensive:

   deep concern
   garment (instead of the specific kind of garment)
   regarding the item . . .
   accordingly . . .
   we . . . we . . . our company, etc.

Improved

```
Just send it back,

Mrs. Motts, and we'll send you a replacement.  We
try hard to be perfect, but every now and then
we do slip.

When you send your daughter's pants back to us, our
Quality Control Department will examine the fabric to
see if we can find out why the pants wore out so
quickly.  We want your daughter's next pair of Kiddie
Klothes pants to last until she outgrows them.

The enclosed $1 should cover the cost of returning
the pants to us, Mrs. Motts.  Now you know that
we mean it when we say...

They're guaranteed,
```

Notice:

1. The immediate positive answer.
2. The focus on the reader's problem.
3. The demonstration of concern about quality.
4. A positive attitude about the future of the business relationship.

The letter types listed below are all immediate messages; they require the same general structure.

1. Inquiries
2. Positive replies
3. Requested sales
4. Orders
5. Letters of receipt
6. Credit approvals
7. Simple requests
8. Most personal, social, and civic letters

Negative Information

Ego Involvement

If you have negative information to convey, determine whether the information will upset your reader. Will the negative information be something that will cause the reader to lose face? Will it be an "ego blow"?

If your main point is to convey negative information and the reader's ego *is not* involved, a direct beginning is best: "You may purchase a digital watch from Penury's. Zalers no longer manufactures or sells digital watches."

When the reader's ego *is* involved, take advantage of the reduced attention paid to the middle sections of the letter and place the negative information there. Your object is not to hide the fact that the reader has been disappointed in some way. Your purpose is to help the reader save face — and help to preserve positive feelings about you and your company at the same time.

Help your reader maintain a good self-image by beginning with something *related to the problem* that your reader will respond to favorably. Delay giving the negative message, but avoid misleading the reader into thinking that you are giving a positive answer.

Organization of the delayed presentation is as follows:

1. **Delayed beginning.** When you can think of nothing related to the problem that is positive but not misleading, as a last resort you can thank the reader for having brought the matter to your attention.

   Thank you for thinking of us.

   You are certainly right to think that . . .

2. **Reasons for the decision.** After your positive opening has established empathy with the reader, give your reasons for the negative information before actually giving the negative message. Make sure that you get in at least one good reason before the reader can guess that he or she has been turned down.
3. **Subordinated refusal.** The refusal itself should be subordinated as much as possible without sacrificing clarity. If your reasons are good enough, your reader can conclude that the message is a refusal without a direct statement to that effect. You can imply the negative message as long as the message is clear. It's also possible to de-emphasize a refusal by placing the negative aspect in a subordinate clause and by using positive language to make the refusal.

Poor: We don't ship in lots smaller than 12.

Better: To save you and our other customers money, we ship in lots of 12 or more.

Poor: Your test scores are not among the top 500, so you don't qualify for admission.

Better: Your test scores, while not among the top 500, indicate that you have the potential to succeed in college.

4. **Positive close.** After you have made your refusal, get the letter back on a positive footing. Give other reasons you may have, provide positive alternatives for your reader, or do something else for your reader if you can and if it is appropriate. Do *not* return to the refusal, and, most important, do not apologize for your decision.

Compare the following examples.

Poor

Dear Mrs. Motts:

We aren't going to replace the pants which you claim wore out too quickly. It's our policy to replace only those garments worn out from hard play, not those damaged by acid as the pants you sent had been.

All of our products are tested for durability, and the material used in the pants you purchased underwent 32 separate inspections for quality, strength, and colorfastness. You can't possibly expect a product to deliver more than Kiddie Klothes products deliver.

When you buy your next high-quality Kiddie Klothes product, notice the quality stitching, the heavy-duty fabric, and the bright colors. We make the kind of clothes that children find impossible to wear out.

Our name is your guarantee of high quality and satisfaction.

Sincerely,

Notice:

1. The immediate presentation of negative material.
2. The mistrust of the reader indicated by "you claim."
3. The appeal to a vague company policy.
4. The insult implied by the assumption that the reader has been satisfied by either the product or the service.

Better

You're right, Mrs. Motts,

to expect a pair of Kiddie Klothes pants to take the wear and tear of a child's hard play for months and months. That's what they're designed to do.

We work hard to find and use only the most durable materials in all our products, and we appreciate the opportunity you gave us to examine the pants. Our analysis revealed that the holes in the knees of the pants were caused by a corrosive agent, such as acid, rather than by the abrasion of play activity. We guarantee Kiddie Klothes to remain free from defects in materials and workmanship for five years only under normal circumstances.

The next time you are buying clothes for your child, compare the quality of Kiddie Klothes with that of any other brand. You will be able to see for yourself that we double-stitch every seam, use only heavy-duty fabrics, and use the brightest colorfast dyes available.

The enclosed coupon will give you a 10 percent discount on your next purchase of Kiddie Klothes pants. Use it, and...

Enjoy,

Notice:

1. The delayed beginning that "buffers" the negative aspect by focusing on a point of agreement.
2. The natural transition to the reason for the refusal.
3. The absence of "telegraphic" words, such as *however, although,* and *but,* which foreshadow the negative message to come.
4. The subordinated refusal.
5. The future-oriented closing that
   a. Recognizes that Mrs. Motts must continue to purchase clothes for her child.
   b. Suggests that she won't be able to find a product as good as Kiddie Klothes.
   c. Offers an inexpensive inducement to encourage her to buy Kiddie Klothes pants again.

Persuasive Information

When the main purpose of your message is to persuade the reader to take a particular action, you are assuming that the reader is likely to resist your message. The well-tested organizational plan for persuasive messages of all varieties is attention, interest, conviction, and action.

1. **Attention.** First, catch your reader's attention by stating a problem or promising something that will benefit the reader. Successful appeals can be made to people's needs for health, wealth, pleasure, or curiosity. In general, appeals to what readers will gain (positive appeals) are more successful than appeals to what they will lose (negative appeals).

2. **Interest.** You can build reader interest by picturing your reader enjoying the promised benefit or by showing that a solution to the stated problem is possible. Give your main attention to one benefit or one problem. Secondary benefits or related problems should be introduced only if they contribute to the reader's acceptance of your main point.

3. **Conviction.** Base the conviction part of your persuasive message on facts, figures, testimonials, tests, samples, guarantees, or whatever proof your proposal requires. Consider enclosing a descriptive brochure to keep your letter from becoming too cluttered. The factors you choose to establish conviction may vary greatly depending on your proposal. A sales letter, for example, may contain more emotional appeals than would be appropriate in a persuasive request for credit.

4. **Action.** The close of a persuasive message should tell the reader exactly what action to take, give a reason for acting promptly, and provide a return envelope or other aids to make that action easy.

   By returning the enclosed postcard now, you will receive three issues absolutely free.

   By purchasing two Roundex Duplicators before Christmas production begins in October, you will save a minimum of $22,000 by 1 January.

Compare the following letters:

Poor

Dear Teacher:

We have just the product you'll be interested in, and it's only $29.95.

Imagine! Our briefcase is designed to hold a ton of books, papers, and other work. It's a simulated leather executive model and measures 24" x 20" x 6". It has a special compartment for papers, a special compartment for notebooks, and a special section to hold a cassette tape recorder or an electronic calculator. It also has a secret compartment in which a checkbook or important papers could be hidden.

Enclosed you will find a brochure. This brochure describes the briefcase in detail and has some pictures of it.

Teachers all over the country are telling one another about our wonderful, exciting briefcase. Everyone who has received one has written back expressing tremendous satisfaction with the briefcase.

If you want to receive one, you had better act today. The supply is going fast, and it won't last much longer. Order yours now!

Cordially,

Notice:

1. The general opening that betrays the “mailing list” nature of the letter.
2. The “we” orientation of the beginning.
3. The mention of the price (something for the writer) before the benefits (something for the reader).
4. The focus on the product itself rather than on what the product can do for the reader.
5. The early, awkward mention of the brochure, which emphasizes its existence rather than what the reader should look for or get out of it.
6. The unsupported superlatives (exciting, wonderful).
7. The negative closing.
8. The failure to make clear *how* one orders the briefcase.

Improved

```
Every teacher needs
a briefcase that can keep
papers and books nice and neat...

From experience you know how maddening it is to open
your briefcase at the end of a hard day of teach-
ing, only to discover that your students' papers are
so thoroughly shuffled that you need an extra 45
minutes just to get each paper back into its proper
place.

With the Executive Teacher briefcase you won't have
that worry.  We've taken the special design features
of our Executive briefcase and put them in a larger
model that will hold all the books and papers you
need to carry.

We've made sure that you'll have room for...

         ...your cassette tape recorder or
         ...your electronic calculator
         ...your checkbook
         ...important papers you want kept
            separate from your school work

The pictures in the enclosed brochure show you just
how versatile the 24" x 20" x 6" Executive Teacher
briefcase actually is.  To order yours, just complete
the order blank and send it with your check for
$29.95 in the postage-free envelope provided.  In ten
days you can be enjoying the...

neatest papers in town,



As a bonus for ordering in the next seven days, we'll
send you a special edition of the famous Teacher's
Calendar to help you keep your appointments straight.
```

Notice:

1. The first three lines of the letter simulate an inside address, retaining a traditional letter appearance without trying to pretend that the letter isn't a form.
2. The focus on the reader and the reader's benefits.
3. The emphasis on special features by use of an unnumbered list.
4. The late reference to the brochure, which helps to keep atten-

tion focused on the letter until the reader has had a chance to finish reading it.

5. The subordinated reference to the price.
6. The complete instructions for ordering stated in a way that makes ordering sound easy.
7. The return to the main reader benefit at the closing.
8. The inducements to act quickly — telling how soon the reader can expect to enjoy the neatest papers and offering the bonus for ordering right away.

The following messages require a delayed organizational pattern.

1. Negative replies to requests for
   a. Adjustment
   b. Credit
2. Postponements
   a. Reader's fault
   b. Writer's fault
   c. Selling a substitute
3. Persuasive requests
4. Sales letters
5. Collection letters
6. Employment letters

Mixed Messages

Mixed messages are fairly typical in business situations. They usually consist primarily of informing the audience of some kind of change. Because most people resist change unless they see that it is to their advantage, an important secondary objective of a mixed message is to persuade the audience to accept and act on the change without feeling resentful. If, for example, you want to change the way your area representatives submit their weekly reports, you will achieve better results — in terms of both cooperation and attitude toward the company — if you tell your readers not only what you want but also why you want it.

1. **Benefit.** Begin mixed messages with a statement of benefit. You may explain immediately that the reader stands to gain in some way. This opening is much like that of persuasive messages. Or you may define a problem and offer a solution. In either case, describe a specific benefit — an easier or less expensive way of doing things, perhaps.

2. **Information.** As with all explanations, the informative part of mixed messages belongs in the secondary position. Along with your explanation of what you want, explain why you want it. Make sure that your reader understands that the change is not arbitrary but rather serves a specific purpose.
3. **Requested action.** Make sure that your reader knows exactly what you want, when you want it, and how it should be done. Make the action as easy as possible for the reader by providing clear instructions, samples, blank forms, or other aids to action.

Although it's impossible to anticipate every kind of mixed message situation, the following letter illustrates the structure common to mixed messages.

QUALITY INSURANCE COMPANY

5 June 1977

Agency Head
Independent Insurance Sales
2323 North Rose Street
Richmond, VA 23284

QIC AWARDS AND REPORTING PROCEDURES

Special Recognition. Because you and your staff deserve special recognition when you achieve high QIC sales, we are honoring the three salespersons who have the highest volume of QIC sales each week with a $100 cash award.

The weekly winners' pictures with brief biographies will appear in our monthly *Insuring News Bulletin*.

So that you can receive your QIC cash awards as soon as possible when you are eligible, a new, more efficient form of reporting weekly sales is being initiated.

New Report Procedure. In addition to the usual sales report (Form 592), simply complete the attached standard forms for each area of weekly QIC sales:

1. Homeowners and Personal Catastrophe Application

2. Auto Applications

Please complete and mail to me a copy of the new QIC sales forms along with your Form 592 on Friday of each week. Keep the original for your files.

Cash Awards. You and your staff will receive prompt consideration for the QIC cash awards when your sales report forms are submitted correctly and on time. Winners will be announced on Wednesday of each week. Good luck to you and all your staff in your QIC sales efforts.

ALBERT MACHACHECK
Supervisor

Notice:

1. The subject line that mentions both the benefit *and* the necessary filing information.
2. The positive, reader-oriented opening.
3. The embedding of the material that readers are likely to resist.
4. The way the writer makes the new action sound easy.
5. The positive close that returns to the reader benefit.

MESSAGE PRESENTATION

The appearance of a letter is extremely important. Even if you have done everything else correctly, a messy, unattractive appearance may indicate to your reader that you are a careless, unconcerned person. The opposite is also true: a neat, carefully prepared letter suggests that you are well organized and that you have concern for your reader.

Just as you form your first impressions of people by their appearance, so readers form first impressions of writers according to the appearance of their letters. As a writer, you take the risk that your message may not be read if your letter fails to pass the appearance test.

The following elements will help the appearance of your letters:

1. Stationery
2. Letter layout
3. Parts of the letter
4. Punctuation styles
5. Letter format

Stationery

The paper on which you present your message should be selected with care. Select the paper that will best represent you and your company. When selecting your letterhead stationery, you should consider quality, size, weight, and color. The most widely used paper for letterhead stationery in offices today is 25 percent rag-content paper. The standard size for office stationery is 8½″ x 11″; white is the most acceptable color. The generally accepted weight for letterhead stock is 16 or 20 pounds.

Letter Layout

Although the length of a message generally determines the width of margins, a 1½″ margin gives your message ample white space around it and presents a neat appearance. Short paragraphs are more readable than long ones. The first and last paragraphs of letters should be about four lines long. No paragraph in a letter should be much longer than eight lines. The entire letter should appear centered on the page, with the white space of the margins forming a "picture frame" around the message.

Parts of the Letter

The names and positions of the parts of a letter are matters of custom. Figure 3-1 (shown on page 84) shows the standard placement of the parts of the letter.

Punctuation Styles

The two most common styles of punctuating the salutation and the complimentary close of the letter are as follows:

1. **OPEN PUNCTUATION.** No punctuation appears after the salutation or the complimentary close.
2. **MIXED PUNCTUATION.** A colon follows the salutation, and a comma follows the complimentary close.

Letter Formats

The usual formats for business letters include the following:

1. **BLOCK.** In the full block letter format, all parts of the letter and all lines begin at the left margin.
2. **MODIFIED BLOCK.** Modified block format has two ver-

Date	September 23, 19___
4-6 Spaces	
Inside Address	Mr. Andrew Anderson, Manager The Firex Manufacturing Company 408 Henderson Avenue Johnstown, PA 15900
Salutation	Dear Mr. Anderson:
Subject Line	Subject: Policy No. 45903
Body	Your renewal policy is in the mail and should reach your office by September 28. As you requested, Plants A and B are included in the coverage.
Complimentary Close	Sincerely,
Typed Signature Title	John H. Santos Underwriter
Typist's Initial	s
Copy Notation	c E. R. Smith

Figure 3-1. The parts of a letter.

sions. Modified block with blocked paragraphs has all lines beginning at the left margin except the date and the closing lines, which *begin* at the center of the page. Modified block with indented paragraphs is the same as the modified block, except that the paragraphs are indented.

3. **AMS SIMPLIFIED.** In the Administrative Management Society's simplified letter format, all lines begin at the left margin. This format omits the salutation and complimentary close.
4. **PERSONALIZED.** The personalized letter format is a combination of the block and the AMS formats. Like the AMS it omits the salutation and complimentary close, but it retains the traditional block appearance by providing personalized facsimiles of those two standard letter parts.

FORMAT EXAMPLES

Block Format, Mixed Punctuation

Canfield Press
San Francisco

Date	12 July 1977 — *850 Montgomery Street, San Francisco, California 94133*
Inside Address	Mr. Fernando Pushkin Assistant Vice-President for Personnel Margarita Manufacturing Company 1492 Avenue of the Americas San Francisco, CA 92182
Salutation	Dear Mr. Pushkin:
Subject Line	BLOCK FORMAT
Body	You're right, Mr. Pushkin; both block and modified block formats are widely used in all aspects of business. This letter is in block format, a more economical format than modified block. The differences between modified block and block are in the placement of the date and the signature block. In block format they begin at the left margin; in modified block they begin at the center of the page. Many conservative firms still use modified block in spite of the extra cost of producing letters in that format. The other letter format you asked about, the AMS simplified format, is similar to the block format; however, the salutation and the complimentary close are omitted. The format we recommend for all but the most conservative business letters is a combination of block and simplified. It offers some of the economy of the simplified but preserves a more traditional appearance. The enclosed examples illustrate both the simplified format and our adaptation from the two styles. Whichever format you adopt, Mr. Pushkin, the important thing to remember is to be consistent. Use the same format throughout your message for a pleasing appearance.
Complimentary Close	Cordially,
Signature(s)	
Typed Name(s)	Joel P. Bowman Bernadine P. Branchaw
Reference Initial	p
Enclosure Notation	enc 2
Copy Notation	c James E. Freel, Editor

AMS Simplified

Canfield Press
San Francisco
850 Montgomery Street, San Francisco, California 94133

Date March 17, 1977

Inside Address
Mrs. Arlene Dalton, Manager
The All American Paper Company
691 Burdick Street
Austin, TX 78700

Subject Line AMS SIMPLIFIED FORMAT

Body

This letter, Mrs. Dalton, is typed in the simplified format recommended by the Administrative Management Society. To use this modern time-saving format:

1. Use block format.

2. Omit the salutation and the complimentary close, but try to use the reader's name in the first sentence.

3. Use a subject line. Type it in CAPITALS, a triple-space below the inside address; then triple-space from the subject line to the first line of the body.

4. Type the numbers for lists at the left margin; indent unnumbered listed items five spaces.

5. Type the writer's name and title in CAPITALS, at least four line spaces below the body of the letter.

6. Double-space closing notations--reference initials and enclosure and copy notations--after the writer's name.

AMS simplified letter format is not only very efficient, Mrs. Dalton, but it is also quite attractive.

Signature

Typed Name and Title CHARLES CARPENTER, PERSONNEL DIRECTOR

Reference Initial q

Copy Notation c Lou Spataro

Personalized Format

Canfield Press

San Francisco

28 May 1977

850 Montgomery Street, San Francisco, California 94133

Dr. Janet Morell, Dean
College of Business
Kent State University
Kent, OH 44240

You're right, Dr. Morell...

standard letter formats are still correct, but many letter writers are choosing to personalize messages with breezy, "open" beginnings and closings in place of stilted, formal salutations and complimentary closings.

These personalized openings and closings have the advantage of retaining the appearance of traditional formats while substituting something useful for the dull salutation and complimentary close.

Why say	Dear Mr. Griffin: The enclosed check for $2,500 is your refund for overpayment on your medical bill.
When you can say	The $2,500 check, Mr. Griffin... is your refund.
Why say	Dear Ms. Irving: The hand-carved statue of Euripides you recommended for our display arrived this morning. It's everything you said it would be.
When you can say	Euripides arrived, Ms. Irving... and the statue's hand-carved excellence is everything you said it would be.

Why say	Sincerely yours, Sincerely, Cordially, Best regards
When you can say	When you're in town again... Please call, I'm so glad you got the job... Congratulations, Call me at (815) 432-5678... When I can help again,

Dr. Janet Morell 28 May 1977 2

When you use the personalized style, you show your reader that you are a thoughtful letter writer and a person who can think for herself.

Naturally, if you are writing to a very conservative company, you would want to use a more traditional format to make sure that you don't offend your reader. Your format as well as your language should indicate your empathy for your reader.

We'll be glad to help again when you have questions...

Anytime,

Joel P. Bowman Bernadine P. Branchaw

SUMMARY

Letters are the most important single channel an organization has for communicating with the public and with other organizations. Communicating by mail has several advantages: it provides a permanent record and proof of agreement; it puts emphasis on logic; and it is more convenient.

Letters have the same basic purposes as all practical messages: to inquire, to inform, or to persuade. No matter how you phrase and structure your message, its content is bound to influence your reader's response to the message. But how you say it is just as important as what you say.

When your main purpose is to request information or to convey positive information, use an immediate presentation. If you have negative information to convey and the reader's ego is involved, use the delayed presentation. When the main purpose of your message is to persuade the reader to take a particular action, use the delayed organizational plan of *attention, interest, conviction,* and *action.*

Because readers form first impressions of writers by the appearance of their letters, make sure that your letters are attractive. Use short paragraphs and "picture frame" your message. Standard formats for business letters include block, modified block, AMS simplified, and personalized. Whichever format you select for a letter, use it consistently throughout.

EXERCISES

1. What are the advantages of communicating by mail?
2. What are the three categories of objectives for letters?
3. What are the differences between immediate and delayed message structures?
4. How would you begin a letter stating that an applicant to Alabama State University was accepted for admission? How would you close it?
5. How would you begin a letter stating that an applicant to Alabama State University was refused admission? How would you close it?
6. Discuss the attitude toward the reader implied by each of the following sentences:
   a. "Your letter has been referred to this office for reply."
   b. "We are willing to take back the merchandise which you claim was damaged in shipment."
   c. "It gives me great pleasure to give you permission to begin construction of your new home."
   d. "It should be obvious to you that paragraph three of our contract clearly states that no pets are permitted in your apartment."
7. What would you do to improve the attitude in the sentences in Exercise 6?
8. Write a positive answer to the following letter:

Twenty-five months, two weeks, and three days ago I purchased a Westwood Color Television from Werner Von Bucholtz, your dealer here in Williamsburg. Last week, some 40 days after the warranty on the set expired, the television went up in smoke.

```
It was quite a sight.  It gave me quite a thrill.  I
pulled the knob and was greeted by a ball of fire
and a big cloud of black smoke.  My wife called the
fire department; I called Von Bucholtz.  He came
out and looked at the set, but he said that I would
have to foot the bill because the warranty had ex-
pired.  I don't think that's fair.  The set obviously
had a defect which took an extra 40 days to show up.

I think that the only fair thing you can do is extend
the warranty and authorize Von Bucholtz to fix the
set.  My wife and I would both appreciate it.  Once
the living room is repainted, we'll be able to get
back to normal.
```

9. Write a negative answer to the letter in Exercise 8, assuming that you called Von Bucholtz and learned that the reason the set malfunctioned was that an amateur had incorrectly wired a Citizens Band radio into its high-voltage circuitry.
10. During the past six months, certain changes in your company's operations have caused a tremendous increase in your department's responsibilities and workload. Using a little imagination to come up with some specifics, write a letter to persuade your boss to let you hire an administrative assistant to help handle the increase.

SUGGESTED READINGS

Bonner, William H. *Better Business Writing*. Homewood, IL: Richard D. Irwin, 1974.

Brown, Leland. *Communicating Facts and Ideas in Business.* 2d ed. Englewood Cliffs, NJ: Prentice-Hall, 1970.

Himstreet, William C., and Wayne Murlin Baty. *Business Communications*. 5th ed. Belmont, CA: Wadsworth, 1977.

Lesikar, Raymond V. *Business Communication: Theory and Application.* Rev. ed. Homewood, IL: Richard D. Irwin, 1972.

McIntosh, Donal W. *Techniques of Business Communication.* Boston: Holbrook Press, 1972.

Menning, J. H., C. W. Wilkinson, and Peter B. Clarke. *Communicating through Letters and Reports*. 6th ed. Homewood, IL: Richard D. Irwin, 1976.

Murphy, Herta A., and Charles E. Peck. *Effective Business Communications.* 2d ed. New York: McGraw-Hill, 1976.

Sigband, Norman B. *Communicating for Management and Business.* 2d ed. Glenview, IL: Scott, Foresman, 1976.

Wolf, Morris Philip, and Robert R. Aurner. *Effective Communication in Business.* 6th ed. Cincinnati: South-Western, 1974.

REPORTS

After you have read this chapter, you should be able to

1. **State the five advantages of report writing.**
2. **State how reports can be used to satisfy task, maintenance, and human organizational objectives.**
3. **Explain the differences between informational and analytical reports.**
4. **Explain the five common report forms.**
5. **Write a report using headings, itemized lists, visual aids, and timely summarizing statements.**

ADVANTAGES OF REPORT WRITING

Reports Are Used in Decision Making

Report writing is probably as old as writing itself; much of what we know about ancient civilizations comes from their business and governmental reports. Certainly no organization of any size can exist for very long without some kind of formal report-writing system. And the larger and more complex an organization is, the more it tends to rely on written reports to aid in the decision-making process.

Of course, many reports in all organizations are oral. For example, your supervisor stops by your office and asks you how you're doing with a certain account. Your reply is an oral report. Your supervisor's boss in New York calls your supervisor in San Francisco and asks for last month's total sales figures. Your supervisor provides an oral report.

Nearly all important reports, however, are put into writing. This is because (1) written records are fairly permanent; (2)written records help overcome problems caused by time and distance; and (3) written records help managers handle the complex information required to evaluate and make decisions about situations, ideas, and employees.

Reports are assigned and written to provide management with the information needed to make decisions. Most managers in most organizations cannot directly observe the materials, personnel, and other facts involved in running a business. They must rely on the observations of others to make their decisions when:

1. They are too far removed from a particular operation to observe it directly;
2. They don't have the time to supervise an operation directly; or
3. They don't have the technical expertise to make accurate observations.

Reports Require Direct Observation

Reports go from a person who is in a position to make direct, accurate, reliable and objective observations to a person or persons who will make decisions about the observations. This means that reports usually go *up* the chain of command, from lower-ranking personnel to those of higher rank. Some reports, however, are exchanged between people of equal rank. As a rule, reports are distributed *down* the chain of command only as a means of disseminating information.

PURPOSES OF REPORTS

Reports may be written to satisfy the demands of each of the basic kinds of organizational objectives — maintenance, task, and human. Reports written for maintenance and task reasons are assigned jobs. Reports written to satisfy human needs are usually proposals on the part of the writer — the kind of report that is frequently dropped into the company suggestion box.

Maintenance Reports

Maintenance Reports Monitor and Regulate

Maintenance reports are usually a regular part of a job: every week each sales representative submits a report on last week's sales. Reports involving such routine information are also known as *periodic reports.* These reports may be given daily, weekly, monthly, quarterly, annually, or at any set interval — even hourly if circumstances require it. The main function of maintenance reports is to monitor and regulate the sustenance of the organization. Most organizations use printed forms and/or specific guidelines to help writers present the required facts quickly and easily in the desired form. Inventory and manufacturing reports are common examples of maintenance reports.

Task Reports

Task Reports Are Special Assignments

Task needs, however, usually require special reports. Because special reports are "special," — prepared on a one-time basis to deal with a particular problem — report writers must present the information without the aid of printed forms and with only general guidelines. When you are assigned a special report, it will be because you are in a position to make direct observations and to provide management with answers to the following three important questions:

1. **Can we?** The first logical question about any project is whether it is possible. Can a certain thing be done? Many business projects are obviously possible, but some are not. For example, current technology may not permit the accomplishment of a desired goal. Some projects may be possible for one company but not for another because of the new capital, resources, and technology involved.
2. **Should we?** If a project is possible for your company, the next question is whether it should be undertaken. Will the expected benefits outweigh the costs? The benefits, of course, may not always be in terms of profits, though profit cannot be ignored. Will the project contribute to the well-being of the company in the long run?
3. **Which way is best?** Once it has been determined that the project is worthwhile, the means of achieving the goal must be examined to determine the way that will provide the greatest return for the least investment.

Human Reports

Human Reports Motivate

Because management is frequently too far removed from certain observations to know everything about them, intelligent managers are open to suggestions. The people dealing with particular situations on a day-to-day basis can frequently foresee problems before they occur and find better solutions than managers, who are not so well acquainted with the project. Reports of this kind are not assigned, but managers may provide incentives (a percentage of the first year's saving, perhaps) to encourage employee participation in decision making.

Informational Reports

Information Only

Reports may be classified by specific message purpose as well as by organizational objectives. Although all reports provide information, some go beyond the mere presentation of data, analyzing the information presented and offering conclusions and recommendations. Reports without any analysis are known as informational reports. Reports with analyses, conclusions, and recommendations are known as analytical reports.

Most maintenance (periodic) reports are purely informational. Some task (special) reports are also purely informational. For example, an oil company might assign a representative the task of discovering and reporting on the feelings of the residents of a particular town about exploratory drilling in the town's only park, without wanting the representative to draw conclusions or make recommendations.

Analytical Reports

Information and Opinion

Every analytical report begins as an informational report to which the writer adds opinion. Before writing, a writer needs to know whether the report should be informational or analytical. Offering conclusions and recommendations when they are not wanted is presumptuous; not offering them when they are expected is fatuous.

Because most task reports are analytical, and because each report must satisfy the needs of a special task, task reports often give writers difficulty. Each company specifies certain requirements for reports that address common kinds of problems (for example, an engineering firm would have a particular set of guidelines for analyzing and recommending dam sites), but the guidelines for analytical reports are usually general. They must be sufficiently flexible to deal with many special tasks.

DEFINING AND INVESTIGATING THE PROBLEM

Report writers usually receive specific assignments: defining the problem is almost always management's task. Report writing assignments are often given orally, however; so the report writer must clarify the specific problem by restating it in terms of an objective to be met or a question to be answered. For example, you may be called into your boss's office:

Boss: (After the usual exchange of pleasantries) Susan, why have we been having so many accidents on the line in your department?

You: Well, as you know, Malcolm, our presses are old and replacement parts just aren't available anymore. We do the best we can at making our own parts, but the jerrybuilt substitutes don't last. Each time a part breaks, somebody gets hurt. We've been lucky that none of the injuries has been worse.

Boss: You'd better give me a report on the situation right away, Susan, so I can send it in to the home office. We can probably get some new equipment if we can show a definite need.

Susan has just been given a report-writing assignment. But exactly what is she to report? Her first task is to state the problem clearly in writing so that

1. She can be sure she is investigating and analyzing the correct problem;
2. She can have her boss evaluate and approve her line of investigation; and
3. She can refer to the specific statement when she needs to clarify for herself the direction and progress of her investigation.

If Susan chooses to state the problem in terms of an objective to be met, she will use an infinitive phrase:

> To analyze the high accident rate in the Production Department.

She could state the problem as a question:

> What is causing the high accident rate in the Production Department?

Once the report-writing assignment is put into specific, workable form, the report writer needs to determine what areas or items to investigate to solve the problem. The foregoing problem is simple: Susan already knows the cause of the high accident rate, and presumably she will be able to show that each of the recent accidents in her department was caused by a press failure.

Research

Report writers need to research all the information sources available in preparing their reports. Sources of information are either secondary or primary.

1. **Secondary sources.** Secondary sources provide information collected by other investigators. Published materials, such as:

almanacs	brochures	pamphlets
articles	dictionaries	periodicals
books	encyclopedias	newspapers

are examples of secondary sources a writer should check before writing the report. A similar problem may already have been investigated and reported. The best place to search for secondary sources would be a library. In addition to checking the subject entries in the card catalog and the abstracts and indexes, consult the reference librarians. They may save you hours of searching and usually offer invaluable assistance.

2. **Primary sources.** When secondary sources do not provide the answers, the report writer needs to uncover the facts and figures firsthand. Several methods for collecting primary or original data are experimentation, observation, and surveys.

Experimentation. In experimentation, the researcher tests one variable of a problem while holding all other variables constant. The experimenter measures the results and reports these findings, drawing conclusions and making recommendations based on careful analysis of the data collected in the experiment. For example, you might wish to test the effectiveness of a new packaging concept for your firm's product. In conducting your experiment, you would manipulate the packaging (technically known as the independent variable) to see what influence the change would have on sales (the dependent variable).

Observation. In research, observation means recognizing and noting facts. Unlike the experimenter, the observer does not manipulate the environment. Observers merely use their senses to note the physical changes that occur; they report only what they have observed. Observation may also include a thorough search of company records for relevant information. Observation is the only means of recognizing and noting facts about the current and previous environment. Although it is often used alone to record facts — raw data — observation is more often used in conjunction with experimentation and surveys, which help explain what the facts mean.

Surveys. Because observation provides the answers to the *what* questions — what has been observed, what has been found — but not to the *why* questions — why do people react a certain way, why do people perform better under certain conditions — report writers need another research technique to uncover the motives of individuals to solve certain problems. Surveys can be conducted by means of mailed questionnaires, personal interviews, or telephone interviews. Each method has advantages and disadvantages. The report writer must determine which method of research will best provide the answers for the particular problem at hand.

Each report-writing problem presents its own set of circumstances and calls for particular investigative techniques. But, however the facts are gathered, good reports present the facts in similar ways.

THE QUALITIES OF REPORTS

Complex Information

Good writing style for reports is essentially the same as for other kinds of writing. Reports, however, place demands on writers that aren't always present in other communication situations. The information contained in reports is usually much more complex than that in other messages, and that information must be presented both clearly and quickly.

Because reports go up the chain of command and because the person receiving the report has requested it for the purpose of making a decision, reports require greater attention to organization and accuracy than most other kinds of writing.

Need for Organization

Clarity

Organization is the communicator's primary means of achieving clarity. In written communication, organization is the key to success because the writer must anticipate the receiver's questions and answer them without the aid of immediate feedback.

The purpose of a written message governs its basic structure. Letters, for example, have definite organizational patterns based on the writer's specific objectives. Messages to which the reader will react favorably are presented immediately; messages the reader will resist use delayed structure. Similarly, the purpose of a report determines its structure. The basic purpose of all reports is to convey information which may influence decisions; the overall organizational patterns for reports reflect this.

Deductive Order

Reports are arranged to present the most important information either first or last, depending on the reader's expected reaction to it. If the reader will welcome the contents of the report, a deductive order of presentation is better. The writer should put the most important part of the information, including the conclusions and recommendations, first. Deductive order begins with a general principle, offers a specific application, and then works to a conclusion.

The report would begin with:

General Principle: The company needs to reduce operating expenses by at least $10,000.

Specific application: The only possible source of this saving is a reduction in personnel.

Conclusion: Morris L. Burner, the company's least productive employee, should be fired.

The rest of the report would contain the supporting details.

Inductive Order

If, however, the reader is likely to resist the information, the report writer should use an inductive order of presentation, working from specific facts to a general conclusion and saving the recommendation for last. Although the inductive pattern of presentation is similar to the pattern used for persuasive messages, the purpose of the inductive order is *not* to persuade. The purpose of all reports is to communicate accurate, reliable, and objective information; but sometimes report writers will reach conclusions and make recommendations that management will resist. The inductive pattern of presentation may help to ensure an objective evaluation of the information.

Specific fact: Last year the company lost $9,500.

Specific fact: This year the company will lose about $9,750.

Specific fact: Manufacturing costs have risen; production levels cannot be increased because sales have peaked.

Specific fact: The plant will need to be retooled before manufacturing costs can be reduced.

Specific fact: Personnel reduction is the only means of reducing costs until retooling takes place.

General conclusion: The least productive person should be fired.

Recommendation: The president's son-in-law, Morris L. Burner, should be fired.

After selecting the overall structure for the report, the writer needs to organize the data itself. Except for the briefest reports, which usually follow the same organizational patterns as letters, making an outline is essential. An outline forces the writer to divide the topic into approximately equal, logical subdivisions emphasizing the most important points. Full sentence outlines are generally more useful than noun, adjective, or phrase outlines because they force the writer to say something specific about each topic and establish clearly the relationship among topics.

Outlining

The report writer can usually use some version of the initial statement of the problem for the title of the outline and the finished report. The writer should select a title that covers the entire subject and that is suitable for the overall pattern of presentation. For example, the report title "New Presses Will Reduce the Accident Rate in the Production Department" might not receive a fair hearing because management resists the expenditure of money. A better title for such a report might be "Reducing the Accident Rate in the Production Department."

Classifications

Whether the report is deductive or inductive, the title usually implies a certain basis of classification. The writer must use that basis of classification for each of the subdivisions, making all subdivisions mutually exclusive. For example, if you are going to report on the ways religious affiliation influences buying habits, it would not be logical to classify your subjects as *Protestants, Catholics, women,* and *Republicans,* because the categories overlap. A better division would be *Protestants, Catholics, Agnostics,* and *Atheists.*

If your title establishes certain expectations in your reader, your subdivisions should satisfy those expectations. If your title is "Reasons Why . . .," your main subdivisions should form a list of reasons. If your title establishes a comparison leading to a choice, your main subdivisions should form a list of the criteria used to evaluate the choices.

Your outline should clearly indicate the relationship among divisions and subdivisions. Either of the following methods of outlining works fine:

1.0	Main Division	I.
1.1	Subdivision	A.
1.2	Subdivision	B.
1.3	Subdivision	C.
2.0	Main Division	II.
2.1	Subdivision	A.
2.11	Sub-subdivision	1.
2.12	Sub-subdivision	2.
2.2	Subdivision	B.
3.0	Main Division	III.

The following conventions used in outlining are designed to help writers avoid problems with the logical presentation of information:

Relative Balance

1. Divisions should be organized for relative balance. Because equal divisions should indicate equal importance, each division should require about the same amount of space as similar divisions. Each Roman numeral or whole number, for example, should be treated equally. This rule is not absolute, but if one of

your divisions requires three times as much space as another of supposedly equal rank, your organization may not be well balanced.

No Single Subdivisions

2. No single subdivision should occur, since a topic is not divided unless at least two parts result. If you subdivide a part, you must have at least two subdivisions. You can't have I. A. unless you also have I. B.

Parallel Structure

3. Main divisions must be expressed in parallel grammatical form. Subdivisions must be parallel within each division, but they need not be parallel with subdivisions of other divisions. Thus A., B., and C. under main division I. must be parallel with each other, but they need not be parallel with A., B., and C. of main division II.

Parts Must Equal the Whole

4. The total of the subdivisions must equal the main division; the whole of each division must be the sum of its parts. For example, the Roman numerals must cover everything implied by the title.

Three to Seven Divisions

5. Divisions and subdivisions should be selected to help the reader grasp the information quickly and easily. The ideal number of parts in any classification is from three to seven. If you have fewer than three subdivisions, they may be too broad or incomplete; and if you have more than seven, your reader will have a hard time remembering important points. Use a classification that permits a favorable division of parts.

Need for Accuracy and Objectivity

Because the purpose of any report is to furnish management with information necessary to make a decision, management expects the information to be accurate, reliable, and objective. Because, as we discussed in Chapter One, our perceptions are often less than perfectly accurate, we must take special care to ensure accuracy and objectivity in even the simplest informational report. Have you included all pertinent facts, or have you abstracted only those facts that fit certain preconceptions of yours?

Biases

The problem is compounded in analytical reports, where the writer must not only present the facts but also interpret them and provide conclusions and recommendations. All of us have certain biases which interfere with our objectivity. In the problem we introduced earlier, Susan may want new presses badly enough to overlook the possibility that the accidents were caused by careless handling of the "jerrybuilt" replacement parts rather than the fact that the presses were old.

Report writers must be especially careful to determine their pre-

Preconceptions

conceptions and to identify their desired outcomes. Preconceptions (Don't confuse me with the facts; my mind is already made up) can cause writers to ignore some facts and undervalue or overvalue others. And if you desire a particular outcome, you will be tempted — consciously or unconsciously — to slant the facts so they lead to the conclusion you favor.

To achieve accuracy and objectivity in your reports, pay particular attention to the following guidelines:

Fact
Inference
Value Judgment

1. Identify — for your reader and for yourself — statements of fact, inferences based on fact, and value judgments. You can use natural, personalized language and still convey objectivity and believability by telling your reader when you are stating a fact, when you are drawing a conclusion, and when you are stating an opinion. Make sure that you have sufficient evidence to warrant your conclusion, and include this documentation in the report. Avoid hasty generalizations and unsupported opinions.

Accurate Sources

2. Use sources that are accurate, reliable, and objective. Books and articles quickly become dated. Also, their authors may not have been as accurate, reliable, or objective as you must be. People used as sources for questionnaire, survey, or interview data may be uninformed or prejudiced. Check the accuracy of all sources.

Analogies

3. Use analogies to explain and illustrate, but not to prove. Because no two things — however similar — are exactly alike, no analogy can be complete enough to constitute proof. False analogies are a form of stereotyping: Tom and Bill are both white, Anglo-Saxon, Protestant males. Tom is dirty, lazy, and shiftless. Therefore, Bill must also be dirty, lazy, and shiftless.

Cause-Effect Statements

4. Examine all cause-effect statements for completeness and accuracy. Might the effect have more than one cause? Can you identify the specific cause of the effect with certainty? Or might you be dealing with a concurrent effect (one that happens at about the same time and seems related to the main effect) rather than the cause?

Specificity

5. Be specific. Avoid unnecessary modifiers and conditional clauses. Too many adjectives and adverbs make your argument seem emotional rather than logical; too many conditional clauses weaken your argument. Use concrete nouns rather than abstract ones. When possible, use people rather than ideas as the subjects of your sentences.

Documentation

6. Provide adequate documentation. Cite your sources and clarify your methodology so that your reader will be able to estimate

your accuracy and objectivity with some confidence. Document all sources in a way that is acceptable to your audience.

Some common guides of documentation are:

Campbell, William G. *Form and Style in Thesis Writing.* 3d ed. Boston: Houghton Mifflin Company, 1969.

Modern Language Association of America. *The MLA Style Sheet.* 2d ed. New York: Modern Language Association, 1970.

Turabian, Kate L. *A Manual for Writers of Term Papers, Theses, and Dissertations.* 4th ed. Chicago: The University of Chicago Press, 1973.

Special Techniques

The special techniques that make report writing different from other kinds of writing are means to make reports easier to read and understand. Reports are almost always longer than letters, and they usually contain more complex information. Help the reader follow your argument, understand your organizational pattern, and keep track of items of special importance by using the following special techniques.

Headings. Headings are the report writer's main aid to easy readability. A heading is a group of words set off from the text that identifies the content following it. Writers are frequently tempted to use a heading as the antecedent of a pronoun, but because headings are not actually a part of the text, the report must make sense even if all headings were removed. Headings should not be used as pronoun antecedents.

A good heading is both brief and specific, not only showing the topic discussed but also giving an important piece of information. "Advantages of Small Cars" makes a better heading than "Small Cars."

Use headings according to the same basic rules that apply to outlining; make the relative importance of each heading clear by using a uniform system of form and position. In general, headings entirely in capital letters are superior to headings that include lower-case letters, and centered headings are superior to marginal headings in the same form.

Your title should be in a form clearly superior to all other headings in your report. The following system is convenient for use with typewritten material when you need five levels of headings for any one section of your report:

R E P O R T   T I T L E

FIRST-DEGREE HEADING [I. or (1.0)]

Your first-degree headings, which correspond to the Roman numerals in your outline, should be in solid capitals and centered. Headings in solid capitals are not underscored. First-degree headings begin on a new page, two inches from the top. Triple-space after a first-degree heading.

Second-Degree Heading [A. or (1.1)]

Second-degree headings correspond to the major subdivisions of each section in your outline. They should be centered and typed in capital and lower-case letters. Second-degree headings may be underscored. Triple-space before a second-degree heading, and double-space after it.

Third-Degree Heading [1. or (1.11)]

Begin a third-degree heading at the left margin. Use capital and lower-case letters and underscore it. Triple-space before a third-degree heading and double-space after it.

Fourth-degree heading [a. or (1.111)]. The fourth-degree heading is an integral part of a paragraph. It begins the paragraph. Capitalize only the first word and proper nouns in the heading; underscore the entire heading. End the fourth-degree heading with a period or with a period and a dash. Double-space before a fourth-degree heading, and begin typing the paragraph immediately after the separating punctuation.

The fifth-degree heading [(1) or (1.1111)] is an integral part of the paragraph's first sentence. Capitalize only the first word in the heading; underscore the entire heading but not the entire sentence. Double-space before a fifth-degree heading.

Very few reports require five degrees of headings. Though many acceptable formats exist, most short reports require only two or three levels of headings. When four levels are used, the forms shown for first-, second-, third-, and fourth-degree headings are the most common. When only three degrees are needed, the forms shown for second-, third- and fourth-degree headings are the most common. When only two degrees are needed, the forms shown for third- and fourth-degree headings are the most common.

Itemizations. Lists are another technique report writers use to make their writing clear, precise, and concise. When you put important points in a numbered list, you call attention to each fact in two ways: separately and as part of a whole. The entire list must be separated from the text, and each item in the list should be grammatically parallel with every other item.

Numbering the items in a list usually implies a hierarchy — the first point is considered more important than the second, and so forth. Unnumbered lists are useful when all the items in the list are of equal importance, but they require some other means of drawing attention to each item, such as underscoring, an asterisk, or a dash.

Visual Aids. Graphs, charts, photographs, tables, drawings, maps, and pictograms are often necessary to illustrate specific points. Such aids can keep the report from becoming cluttered with statistics and lengthy descriptions. So that your reader will understand your graphic aid, remember to do the following:

1. Introduce the aid *before* your reader encounters it;
2. Emphasize what the reader should get out of the aid rather than focusing on its existence;
3. Label each part of the graphic device clearly, interpreting facts that aren't completely self-explanatory; and
4. Make the graphic aid large enough for easy reading and interpretation.

The three most widely used charts are the line chart (Figure 4-1), the pie chart (Figure 4-2), and the bar graph (Figure 4-3).

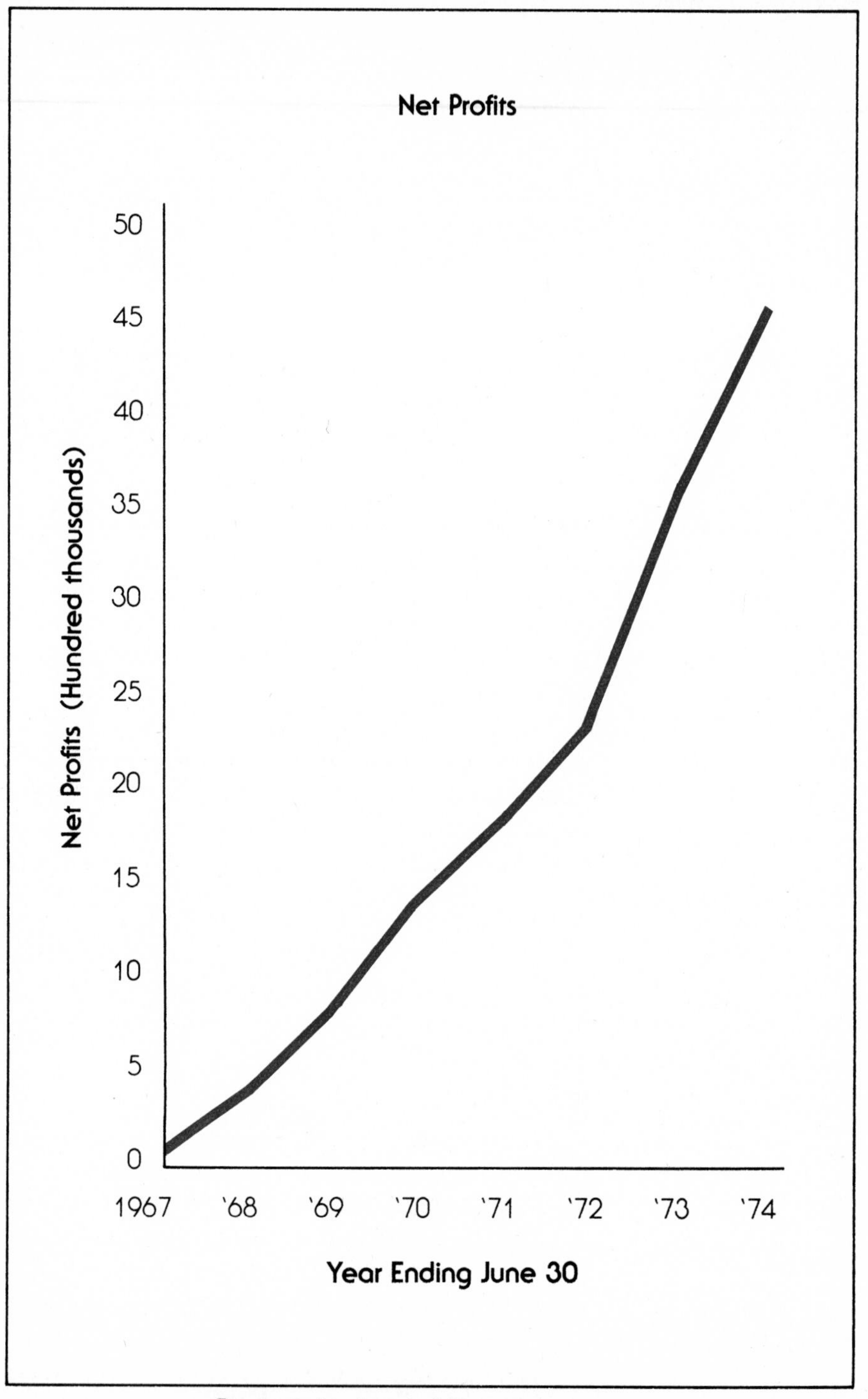

Figure 4-1. A typical line graph.

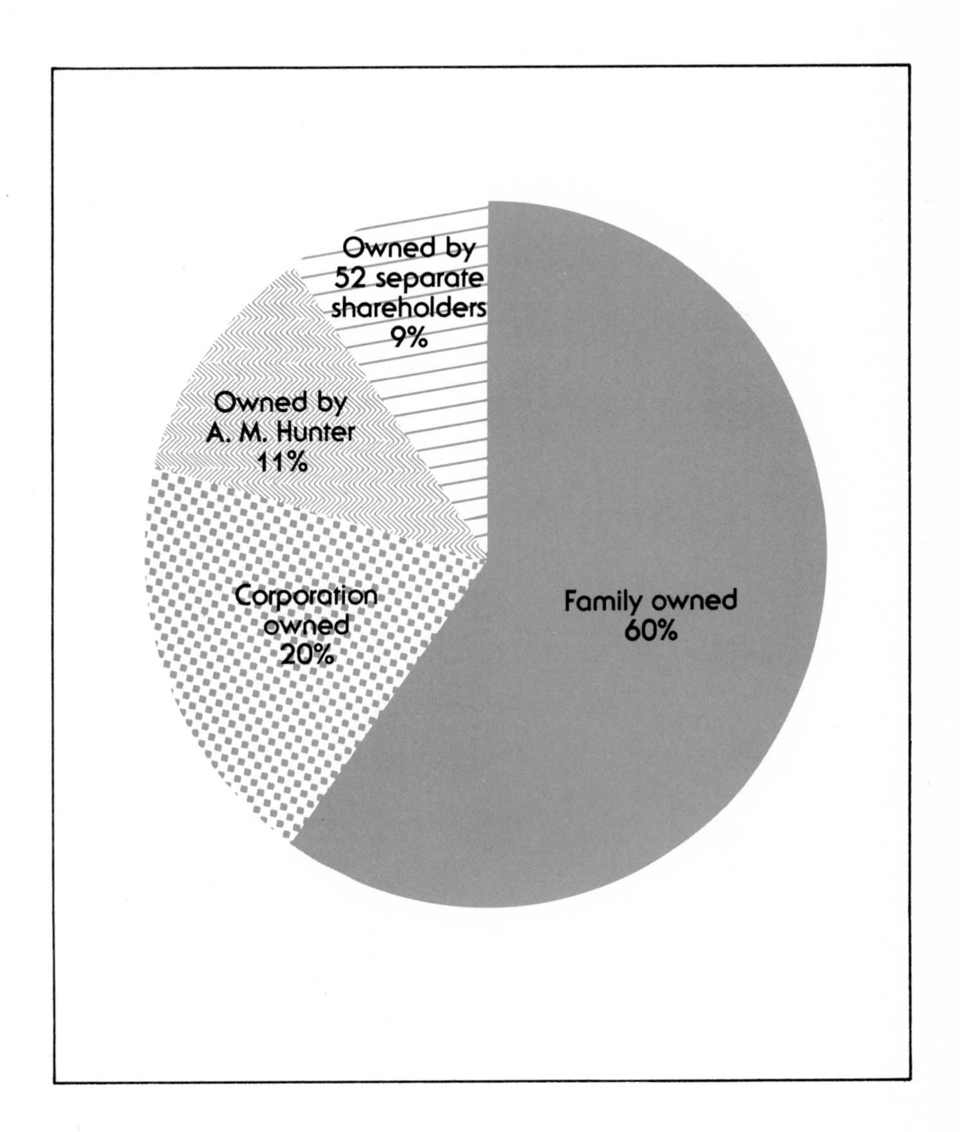

Figure 4-2. A typical pie chart.

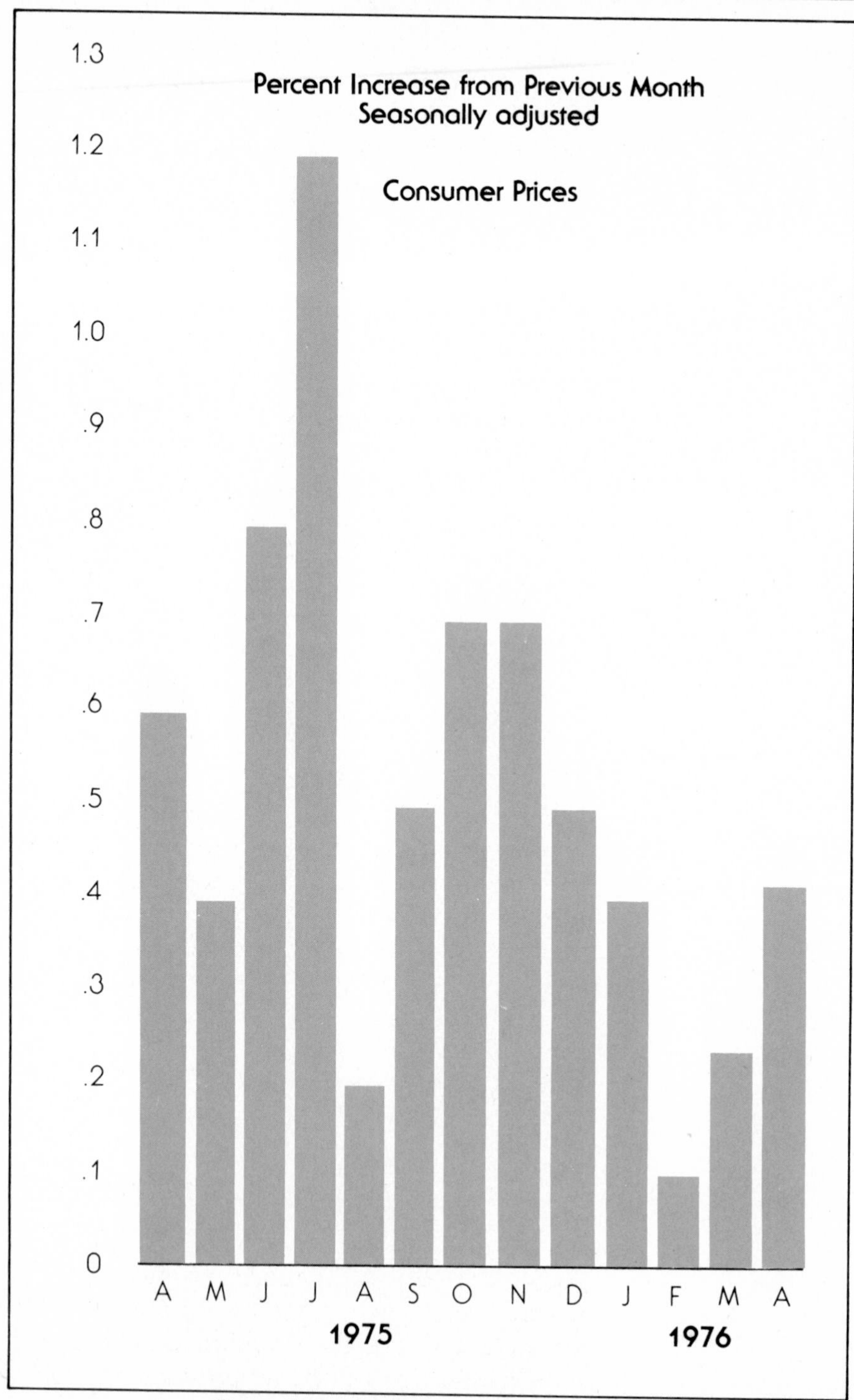

Figure 4-3. A typical bar graph.

Pie charts are so called because they divide a whole (100 percent) into segments in the same way one cuts a pie. Always begin at the 12 o'clock position and move clockwise, starting with the largest segment and proceeding in descending order. Because it is difficult to judge relative sizes, include the value in each "slice." Do not use separate pie charts to compare separate wholes.

Bar graphs are best used to show changes in quantity over time or from place to place. Bars of equal width but varying length represent the various quantities. Multiple bar graphs work well to illustrate comparisons.

Summarizing statements. Summaries also help report readers grasp important concepts quickly and easily. Because of the length and complexity of most reports, it is difficult for readers to keep the important aspects of your argument clearly in mind as they move from section to section. To help your reader, begin each section with a topic sentence that clearly indicates what you intend to do in that section. Conclude each section with a summarizing statement that shows (1) how the material just presented adds up to what was promised in the topic sentence and (2) how it relates to the material that will follow.

Abstracts

When your report is more than three pages long, an abstract or synopsis may save your reader the time required to read the entire report; it will certainly make the rest of your report easier to read. An abstract is a miniature form of the entire report; it is prepared *after* the report is completed. A good abstract should be about 10 percent of the length of the original report, but no longer than one full page. The abstract must be faithful to the original in content and emphasis. Descriptive (topical) abstracts, which, like a table of contents, tell only what the report is about, are less useful than summarizing abstracts, which let the reader know briefly what the report says.

About 10 Percent as Long as the Whole Report

Descriptive and Summarizing Abstracts

COMMON SHORT REPORT FORMS

Each organization has its own requirements for particular report forms. But certain types are very nearly universal, even though their format varies from company to company. The most common short report forms are the memorandum report, the letter report, the justification report, the progress report, and the formal — or short analytical — report.

Memorandum Report

Intracompany Informal Report

The memorandum report is a short informal message that provides a rapid, convenient means of communication between employees within the same organization. Interoffice memorandums — or memos — are the company's principal written medium for internal communication.

Since memos do not leave the organization, you need not be too concerned about public relations: thus you use stationery that differs from letterhead stationery in color, printing, quality, and size. Use inexpensive wood-pulp paper rather than expensive rag-content paper. Sizes of memo stationery range from the full sheet, 8½" x 11", to half sheets, 5½" x 8½". Some businesses prefer half sheets for economy; other companies choose full sheets for ease in filing.

Although most companies prefer white paper for their letters, using colored paper for memos serves to distinguish them from other business papers. Various colors may be used to designate particular departments.

Unlike letters, which use the formal inside address, salutation, complimentary close, and typed signature, memos require only informal headings. Normally, four informal printed headings appear on memo stationery: *To, From, Date,* and *Subject.* Although the arrangement and design may vary among companies, these four headings appear on most forms. Printing of the heading lines may be either vertical or horizontal.

Horizontal

TO:	DATE:
FROM:	SUBJECT:

Vertical

DATE:

TO:

FROM:

SUBJECT:

If your organization does not provide printed forms, you may omit the word *date* and simply type the date.

```
                ARIZONA MANUFACTURING INC.
                   4305 Avenue Palmetto
                   Flagstaff, AZ  86001

    27 September 1976

    TO:        Francis W. Walczak, Production Manager

    FROM:      Henry J. McGraw, Vice-President for
               Personnel

    SUBJECT:   Annual Review of Joshua Sims, Line Foreman


    Please tell Joshua Sims that his appointment for
    annual review is Monday, 4 October, at 10 a.m.

    Please complete the attached form and return it to me
    by Thursday, 30 September.
```

Letter Report

A letter report is a report written in the form of a regular business letter. Unlike the internal memorandum report, the letter report is an external means of communication between organizations.

Letter reports may be used for personnel references, credit evaluations, or auditor recommendations. Many letters requesting or transmitting information are essentially letter reports, but we don't usually call them reports unless they are fairly long and make use of some of the basic report writing techniques.

Letter reports differ from typical business letters in that they are formal and primarily factual. Their objective is to provide the information requested as clearly as possible. Graphs, charts, tables, or drawings may be used to illustrate specific points.

TIME AND MOTION STUDIES INC.
430 Water Street, Flagstaff, AZ 86001

1 October 1976

Mr. Francis W. Walczak
Arizona Manufacturing Company
4305 Avenue Palmetto
Flagstaff, AZ 86001

Dear Mr. Walczak:

As you suspected, you could increase both the efficiency and the capacity of your production line by 30 percent if you installed modern equipment.

We recommend the following substitutions:

IN USE			SUGGESTED REPLACEMENT			
Number	Stock Number	Item	Number	Manufacturer	Item	Cost
15	L-1245-65-11	Power Lathe	1	Smythson	Master Lathe	$15,000
			15	Smythson	Slave Units	1,200 ea
14	DP-9321-59-01	Drill Press	1	Olgivie	Master Press	11,000
			19	Olgivie	Duplicators	900 ea

By reassigning and retraining personnel, you could effect the increase in efficiency and capacity without reducing your work force. We recommend that the personnel who become unnecessary in production be transferred to Quality Control and Packaging. Dorsaneo Management Consultants, 197 Main Street, Flagstaff, is well equipped to help you reassign and retrain your personnel.

Our services and charges are itemized on the enclosed invoice. When we can help further, please call us at 383-1983.

Sincerely,

Linda R. Armbruster
President

Justification Report

A justification report presents a problem and then submits data to justify a recommendation with regard to that problem. Most reports are written at the request of management. Justification reports, however, are initiated by the writer, who has observed a problem and wishes to suggest a solution. Justification reports are always immediate messages and should begin with a clear statement of purpose. Typical headings for a justification report are:

1. Purpose
2. Cost and Savings (or Advantages)
3. Method (or Procedure)
4. Conclusions
5. Discussion

The conclusions should show convincingly that the recommendation is justified by the advantages that will be realized.

HOW SAFETY GOGGLES WOULD SAVE
JACKSON ELECTRONICS $500 A YEAR

Purpose

To save Jackson Electronics $500 a year, I recommend that we purchase 25 pairs of clear glass safety goggles and require the line technicians to wear them during soldering operations.

Cost and Savings

Twenty-five pairs of safety goggles would cost about $750. This investment would save Jackson an estimated $2,000 over the next three years in medical costs and worker's compensation expenses.

Procedure

Each of the 20 line technicians would sign for and receive a pair of safety goggles. The five extra pairs would be available for replacements. Zimmer Glass makes safety glasses appropriate for our needs, and by purchasing 25 we would receive a 10 percent discount. Zimmer's price for 25 would be $748.75. We could have immediate delivery.

Conclusions

Although eye injuries caused by soldering operations do not happen frequently, they are expensive when they do happen. In the last three years two injuries have cost Jackson more than $2,700. The safety goggles would eliminate the eye injuries and associated expenses.

Discussion

In June 1974 a soldering accident cost Robert Johnson the sight in his left eye. Jackson Electronics paid $1,200 for emergency medical treatment, and our insurance costs for the following year increased 15 percent. Though not so serious, our most recent accident, in September, has already cost Jackson $940.

Even though the line technicians are always more careful to follow safety precautions after an accident occurs, it's only a matter of time until someone becomes careless while soldering. Safety goggles should eliminate future eye injuries, and by purchasing goggles now we may be able to avoid costly increase in insurance premiums.

Progress Report

A progress report is a strictly informational report that tells how a project is coming along. Management may have several projects underway at one time, so information about the progress of each of the projects is necessary at various intervals. These progress reports provide management with the following:

1. A brief background of the project;
2. A detailed account of the time period covered; and
3. A projection of the work to be done.

Management needs these reports not only to keep track of what is going on but also to determine whether the project is progressing as planned, whether it is worth continuing, and whether it is encountering any difficulties. When research is involved, progress reports frequently contain preliminary findings and tentative conclusions.

Subject: Progress on Hillcrest Apartments during September

Current Status

1. Construction on the Hillcrest Apartments remains three weeks behind schedule because of the heavy rains during August. During September we lost an additional four days because of rain, but close supervision and some overtime have prevented us from falling further behind.

2. The foundation for the entire complex is complete. Framing on the 14 townhouses is complete, and the framers will begin work on the two-bedroom units on Monday, 4 October. Also on Monday, the electrical and plumbing subcontractors will begin work.

Expected Progress

1. During November, framing, roofing, and siding will be completed. We still expect to be inside of all units by the middle of November, when the early winter rains will probably begin.

2. By 15 November we should be able to reduce our work force by 50 percent.

3. By the first week in December, the electrical and plumbing work should be finished.

Formal Short Report

Special Assignment

In addition to the informal reports just discussed, many organizations require formal short reports on a fairly regular basis. These reports are almost always special assignments, and they are almost always analytical.

Because these reports deal with topics of importance to the organization and because they become an important part of the company's operations and records, the physical presentation of these reports is more formal than those we discussed in the preceding sections.

The formal report includes:

1. A title page, which contains the title of the report, the name and

professional title of the person for whom it was prepared, the name and professional title of the person who prepared the report, and the date the report was completed.
2. A letter of transmittal, including the date and reasons the report was assigned and a brief summary of the important findings and recommendations.
3. Necessary references, tables, and charts inserted within the text itself.

Just because the report is "formal," however, doesn't mean that you should use a stiff, formal writing style. Use the natural, forceful language you use in other writing.

Not: It was concluded that . . . .
But: I concluded . . . .

Remember to use the active voice and, when possible, make people rather than ideas the subjects of your sentences. A sample of formal presentation begins on page 119, after the discussion of the long report.

THE LONG REPORT

A report stops being a short report at about 10 double-spaced pages, but a long report is just like a short formal report in almost every respect but length. Long reports usually deal with more complex problems and involve more data than short reports. Because of the complexity of the problem and the length of the report, long reports include some additional parts to help the reader keep track of the mass of information. These parts are:

Prefatory Parts:
- Cover
- Title Fly
- Title Page
- Letter of Authorization
- Letter of Acceptance
- Letter of Transmittal
- Contents
- Abstract (or Synopsis)

Body of the Report:
- Introduction
- Text
- Summary, Conclusions, and Recommendations

Supplemental Parts:
- Appendix
- Bibliography

Prefatory Parts

1. **Cover.** The cover protects the report itself and introduces the title of the report. Covers may have designs to attract attention, but they should be simple. Keep the cover title short — no more than eight words.
2. **Title Fly.** The title fly, the first sheet of the report, carries only the report title. Your title should be worded to include the *how* of the report and as many of the five *W*s *(who, what, where, when, why)* as possible.
3. **Title Page.** The title page includes the title of the report, the name and professional title of the person (or group, department, or organization) for whom the report was prepared, the name and professional title of the person (or group, department, or organization) who prepared the report, and the completion date.
4. **Letter of authorization.** The letter of authorization authorizes investigation of the problem. It states the problem and the objectives of the investigation clearly. In addition to stating the problem, the letter of authorization specifies the scope and limitations of the problem.
5. **Letter of Acceptance.** Although the letter of acceptance is not usually included in the report, it is the answer to the letter of authorization. It may change or revise the original letter of authorization. The two letters — authorization and acceptance — serve as a contractual agreement between the person (or group, department, or organization) requesting the report and the person (or group, department, or organization) conducting the investigation.
6. **Letter of Transmittal.** The letter of transmittal "transmits" the report from the person conducting the research to the person who authorized it. In addition to saying, in effect, "here is the report," the letter of transmittal may state other relevant issues: (1) the authorization for the study; (2) the statement of the problem, its scope, and its limitations; (3) methods of procedure; (4) a summary of the findings, conclusions, and recommendations; (5) acknowledgments to individuals who helped with the project; and finally, (6) an offer to discuss the project further or to conduct future studies.
7. **Contents.** A contents page should be included if the report is lengthy and has several subdivisions. The purpose of the contents page is to show the reader at a glance on what page a

particular division or subdivision begins. The contents page must be prepared last, because it gives the page numbers for the various divisions. If the report contains several charts, tables, and illustrations, a separate list may be made for each of them. These pages would be called "Figures," "Tables," and so forth.

8. **Abstract.** The abstract (or synopsis) is a brief overview of the entire report. Because it is a summary, it must be prepared after the report has been completed; it should be no longer than one page. The purpose of the abstract is to give the busy reader a quick, comprehensive survey of the report.

Body of the Report

The body of a report generally consists of the introduction, the text, and the summary, conclusions, and recommendations.

1. **Introduction.** In addition to giving the reader the background of the report and detailing its authorization and subject, the introduction orients the reader to the problem, purpose, scope, limitations, and procedure and defines key terms.
2. **Text.** The text of the report presents the data gathered and the analysis. This is the central and largest part of the report.
3. **Summary, conclusions, and recommendations.** The summary of the report summarizes its main points; the conclusions are objective statements based on the findings of the report; and the recommendations are somewhat subjective statements based on the conclusions.

Supplemental Parts

1. **Appendix.** Appendices contain copies of the letters, questionnaires, forms, or blueprints used in obtaining information for the report. They also contain other supplementary material that is not actually used in the report itself. The report may direct the reader to an appendix for further reference or clarification. Because readers do not usually read appendices, nothing important should be put in an appendix.
2. **Bibliography.** The bibliography lists all the references — books, periodicals, journals, speeches, interviews, and newspapers — used in the report.

SAMPLE FORMAL REPORT

The following sample illustrates a few of the elements covered in the preceding discussion. We have omitted some parts (such as the cover and the title fly) because they are too simple to require illustration. Others we illustrate only in part because of space limitations. But in general, your report should look like this:

Title Page

HOW MACDOUGAL'S RESTAURANTS COULD INCREASE PROFITS

TWENTY PERCENT BY SERVING BREAKFASTS

Prepared for

William J. MacDougal

President, MacDougal's Restaurants

Prepared by

Sally K. DeRyke, Associate Director

Field Studies Division

Omaha Management Consultants Inc.

691 Westlake Road

Omaha, Nebraska

68100

16 February 1977

Letter of Authorization

MACDOUGAL'S RESTAURANT

1120 Short Road, Omaha, NE 68100

William J. MacDougal, President
(402) 798-3318

December 4, 1976

Dr. Kathleen M. Saxby, Director
Omaha Management Consultants Inc.
691 Westlake Road
Omaha, NE 68100

Dear Dr. Saxby:

This letter confirms our phone conversation of December 3. For a fee of $8,500 Omaha Management Consultants will investigate the operations of the 14 MacDougal restaurants in Nebraska and recommend ways for MacDougal's to increase efficiency and achieve higher profits.

The subjects for in-depth study should include:

1. Opening for breakfast;
2. Restaurant operation; and
3. Training program.

I understand that you will complete the first report on the feasibility of opening for breakfast no later than February 20 and that the other reports will follow at 30-day intervals. I agree to pay Omaha Management Consultant $2,833.34 upon receipt of each report.

Sincerely,

William J. MacDougal
President

Letter of Transmittal

Omaha Management Consultants Inc.
691 Westlake Road
Omaha, Nebraska 68100

8 February 1977

Mr. William J. MacDougal, President
MacDougal's Restaurants
1120 Short Road
Omaha, NE 68100

Dear Mr. MacDougal:

Here is the report you requested on 4 December studying the feasibility of opening MacDougal's Restaurants for breakfast. Other members of Omaha Management Consultants are now preparing the reports about your operation and training program.

This report shows that with only a small investment in new equipment and a slight increase in personnel, MacDougal's could increase its profits by about 20 percent. As a fast-food chain, MacDougal's is in a good position to compete for breakfast business.

At present, the large motel chains capture most of the breakfast market. This is true primarily because those restaurants must open to accommodate their guests, whereas most other restaurants in Nebraska do not open until 11 a.m. Many commuters who now eat at home or in motel restaurants would prefer the prompt, courteous service offered by MacDougal's.

I have enjoyed preparing this report for you, Mr. MacDougal, and I have learned some interesting things about the restaurant business and MacDougal's while preparing it. Please call me directly at 798-7761 when I can be of further help.

Sincerely,

Sally K. DeRyke

Table of Contents

Contents

Extracts from the Text

Synopsis

With a total investment of only $38,000, MacDougal's Restaurants could begin providing breakfast service at its 14 locations in Nebraska and increase its annual profits by approximately 20 percent.

According to surveys of potential customers in Omaha, Lincoln, Kearney, and David City, the demand for a fast-food breakfast restaurant is high and currently unsatisfied. As an established chain, MacDougal's could easily meet this need....

MacDougal's should convert its five restaurants in Omaha first. Because the Omaha restaurants already open at 9:00 a.m., two hours earlier than the restaurants in other cities, and because they now offer some breakfast foods, the conversion to an earlier, full-time breakfast operation would be easier in Omaha. Also, many Omaha residents already view MacDougal's as the best place to have a quick late breakfast.

* * * * * * *

The Breakfast Business

Purpose

The purpose of this report is to discuss the feasibility of opening MacDougal's Restaurants for breakfast. During my investigation, I discovered that in the four cities in which MacDougal's are located, the demand for a fast-food breakfast establishment is high.

Methodology and Limitations

To determine whether MacDougal's should compete for the breakfast business, I studied the competition, the clientele, the required investments and changes, and the potential for increased profits. For three weeks I surveyed customers eating breakfast at restaurants in each of the four cities, and in each city Omaha Management Consultants conducted a random-sample telephone survey to determine the breakfast market.

* * * * * * *

The Competition

At present no fast-food restaurant in Nebraska offers breakfast. Restaurants that offer breakfast fall into three general categories: hotel/motel coffee shops, hotel/motel restaurants, and family-owned downtown coffee shops. Each of these establishments caters to a particular clientele. . . .

In Omaha

Omaha presents a unique opportunity for MacDougal's because only three coffee shops offer. . . .

SUMMARY

Reports are assigned and written to provide management with the information needed to make decisions. Reports go from a person who is in a position to make direct, accurate, reliable, objective observations to a person or persons who will make a decision based on the observations.

Reports are written to satisfy the demands of each of the basic kinds of organizational objectives — maintenance, task, and human. Maintenance reports are usually a regular part of a job and are generally known as periodic reports. Task reports are special reports, assigned on a one-time basis to deal with a particular problem. Human reports are invited but unassigned reports submitted by individuals who are dealing with particular situations on a day-to-day basis.

Reports may be informational or analytical. Informational reports contain no analysis; analytical reports provide information, analysis, conclusions, and recommendations.

Report writers must research all available sources of information, both secondary and primary. Secondary sources — books, dictionaries, encyclopedias, periodicals, and newspapers — provide information collected by other investigators. Primary sources of information originate with the writer; they include experimentation, observation, and surveys.

Common types of short reports are the memorandum, letter, justification, progress, and short formal reports. The long report is a longer version of the short formal report.

EXERCISES

1. What are the advantages of report writing?
2. What are the differences between informational and analytical

reports?

3. How are reports used to meet maintenance, task, and human organizational objectives?
4. What three questions do task reports answer?
5. What are two means of clarifying a problem for investigation?
6. Explain primary and secondary sources and give examples of each.
7. When should report writers use deductive order? When should they use inductive order?
8. What is the relationship between outlining and headings?
9. Name five common short report forms and state their functions.
10. On a topic of your choice, write a formal report of whatever length your instructor requests, making use of secondary sources and *at least one kind* of primary source, and using the special techniques of report writing.

SUGGESTED READINGS

Campbell, William G. *Form and Style in Thesis Writing*. 3d ed. Boston: Houghton Mifflin, 1969.

Damerst, William A. *Clear Technical Reports*. New York: Harcourt Brace Jovanovich, 1972.

Himstreet, William C., and Wayne Murlin Baty. *Business Communications*. 5th ed. Belmont, CA: Wadsworth, 1977.

Lesikar, Raymond V. *Business Communication: Theory and Application*. Rev. ed. Homewood, IL: Richard D. Irwin, 1972.

Lesikar, Raymond V. *Report Writing for Business*. 4th ed. Homewood, IL: Richard D. Irwin, 1973.

Menning, J. H., C. W. Wilkinson, and Peter B. Clarke. *Communicating through Letters and Reports*. 6th ed. Homewood, IL: Richard D. Irwin, 1976.

Modern Language Association of America. *The MLA Style Sheet*. 2d ed. New York: Modern Language Association, 1970.

Murphy, Herta A., and Charles E. Peck. *Effective Business Communications*. 2d ed. New York: McGraw-Hill, 1976.

Sigband, Norman B. *Communication for Management and Business*. 2d ed. Glenview, IL: Scott, Foresman, 1976.

Shurter, Robert L. *Written Communication in Business*. 3d ed. New York: McGraw-Hill, 1971.

Turabian, Kate L. *A Manual for Writers of Term Papers, Theses, and Dissertations*. 4th ed. Chicago: University of Chicago Press, 1973.

5

READING AND LISTENING

After you have read this chapter, you should be able to

1. **Identify and explain the three phases of receiving information.**
2. **Explain the differences among scanning, skimming, and reading.**
3. **State how to improve your own reading skills.**
4. **Identify and explain the techniques of effective listening.**
5. **Explain how to apply the eight steps of effective listening.**

INFORMATION SOURCES

Receiving Messages

So far in this book we have been concerned primarily with showing you how to improve your communication by concentrating on your responsibilities as a sender of messages. As we indicated in Chapter One, however, your responsibilities as a receiver of messages are also important. In this chapter we focus on two of the primary means you have for receiving messages: reading and listening. You speak and write to inform, to inquire, and to persuade; but you read and listen to *learn*.

You cannot possibly communicate effectively unless you can read and listen effectively. The quality of your communication output depends completely on the quality of your communication input. What you read and hear — and the conclusions you draw because of what you've read and heard — controls what you write and say.

Even more than with speaking and writing, most of us tend to think of our reading and listening skills as well developed; in fact, reading and listening are so fundamental that we frequently take these skills for granted. Most of us read and listen very inefficiently, however, missing much that we should learn from the messages we receive.

The act of receiving messages can be broken into three phases, all necessary for full understanding. First, we must observe the message in its entirety; second, we must analyze the message; and third, we must draw certain specific conclusions on the basis of our observations and analysis.

Observation

Most of us are in the habit of ignoring much of our environment. How often, for example, have you caught yourself "reading" a book — looking at and turning each page — without understanding a word you've seen? How often have you been "listening" to a lecture, only to catch yourself lost in thought about some completely unrelated topic?

Observation begins with attention, and as we discussed in Chapter One, attention is a selective process. We can pay attention only to a limited part of our environment. By a process called abstracting, we select and focus on certain stimuli and ignore others. For us either to read or to listen effectively, we must make a conscious effort to focus our attention on the subject matter and ignore distracting stimuli, such as background noise, the uncomfortable chair we're sitting in, or our increasing hunger pangs.

Focus Attention on Subject Matter

We must also be aware of the following special barriers to observation:

1. We pay closer attention to aspects of the environment that we consider directly relevant to our goals and objectives than to those for which we can see no immediate use.
2. We pay closer attention to stimuli that confirm our world-view than to stimuli that contradict our beliefs.
3. We pay closer attention to unexpected or unfamiliar stimuli (such as a loud bang) than to expected stimuli (such as the ticking of a clock).
4. We pay closer attention to stimuli from sources we consider especially credible than to stimuli from unknown or routine sources.

The selective process of observation has its advantages. We don't need to read or listen to everything with full attention. But we must have the ability to give full attention to a book, lecture, or conversation when the situation requires it.

Analysis

By itself, observation is not sufficient for us to grasp the meaning of written and spoken messages. We must also analyze the message, examine each of its parts, and find and separate facts, inferences, and value judgments. In the process of analysis, we ask ourselves questions about the message:

What are the facts?
How do we know what is fact and what is opinion?

Do we agree with the message?
What is our attitude toward the source? Toward the content? Is our attitude toward the source or content influencing our reception of the message?

Conclusions

The final phase in receiving messages is the formulation of conclusions. The answers we reach in our analysis will largely determine our conclusions. We may, for example, conclude that the message has no meaning for us and promptly forget it. Or as we perform our analysis, we may conclude that some parts have no meaning, other parts are meaningful and true, and still other parts are meaningful but not true.

In reaching conclusions and summarizing the content of the message, we organize the material in the way that will best enable us to remember it. The act of receiving the message is not complete until we have come to some conclusion about it.

READING

Receiving and Understanding Messages

Both reading and listening involve problems with the reception and understanding of messages, but the problems involved in observing, analyzing, and drawing conclusions differ because of the different characteristics of the communication channels involved. With written messages, for example, receivers have no opportunity to request clarification as they usually can when listening; but readers have the opportunity to re-examine the message as many times as necessary to reach a full understanding of it.

In some ways reading is a less complicated activity than listening. In listening we must observe two channels of communication, oral and nonverbal, and weigh them both in our analysis. In reading we can usually focus fairly directly on the message itself. And most of us have had much more formal training in reading than in listening, so we're more attuned to careful reading than to careful listening.

Because reading is our primary means of learning complex material, we can benefit greatly from improving the efficiency with which we read. We spend more time listening than reading, but the time spent reading is usually more "concentrated," because the written message was sufficiently important or complex to be put in writing in the first place, and because all extraneous matter has been eliminated from the central aspect of the message.

Techniques of Effective Reading

Speed

Accuracy

Comprehension

Effective reading calls for mastery of three related but essentially separate skills: speed, accuracy, and comprehension. Speed is determined by the number of words we can read a minute. This aspect of reading is the easiest to measure. Reading accuracy is determined by how correctly we perceive the contents of the message, and comprehension is measured by how well we understand the message. Accuracy and comprehension are easily confused, but they are actually separate skills.

Accurate reading consists of seeing each word for what it is. Reading with comprehension consists of grasping the meaning of the message as a whole, whether or not each word is seen specifically. Suppose that you read the sentence, "Communication is essential for all human relations; it makes civilized, cooperative life possible, and it gives us our ability to build and shape our environment." You can read somewhat inaccurately, omitting a few words entirely (human, civilized *or* cooperative, build *or* shape) and still comprehend the idea the sentence conveys.

The better you read, the faster you will be able to read with complete accuracy and full comprehension. But all readers have a point beyond which every increase in speed results in a loss of accuracy and comprehension. Because the brain processes about 400 words a minute, even the best reader cannot read every word and still read faster than about 400 words a minute. Whether they recognize it or not, people who read faster than 400 words a minute are *skimming* rather than reading. Comprehension may remain high, but accuracy always drops at reading speeds faster than about 400 words a minute. Such readers take the risk of missing something important.

To be a good reader, you need the ability to read everything at the fastest speed that will permit the degree of accuracy and comprehension required. If you must understand something fully, and if each word is crucial for that understanding, you will have to sacrifice speed for greater accuracy and comprehension. But when all you need is the gist of something, you can increase speed by skimming for the central ideas without worrying about accuracy or complete comprehension.

Improving Speed

Readers accustomed to placing a premium on accuracy and comprehension are often uncomfortable when they try to read more quickly than the rate which lets them read each word and consider its meaning carefully. Overcoming this discomfort is usually their biggest obstacle to reading faster. You don't need to read everything with the same kind of care, however. You may, for example, learn all you need to know about current events by skimming a daily newspaper and one or two news weeklies; on the other hand, you may need to read a subordinate's market analysis report for your company's new product with extreme care.

Improving speed requires practice and determination. You can't read faster without forcing yourself to do so, and you can't read faster without suffering at least a temporary reduction in accuracy and comprehension. If you are already reading 400 words a minute, you can't read any faster with absolute accuracy.

To read at the highest possible speed, 400 words a minute, the act of reading must be a direct relationship between your eye and your brain. Using other muscles (except for using your hands to turn the pages) can only slow you down. If, for example, you tend to use your finger to follow the text, you are limiting yourself to the speed with which you can point to individual words.

Avoid Vocalization

If you vocalize by moving your lips or by reading almost aloud, you're limiting yourself to reading at a speaking rate, about 125 words a minute. You can test yourself for vocalizing by placing the fingers of one hand lightly over your lips as you read. If you detect any tendency toward lip movement, make a conscious effort to read without vocalizing, keeping your fingers over your lips as a constant reminder.

Avoid Subvocalization

If you aren't vocalizing, you may still be slowing your reading speed by subvocalization, the forming of words with the vocal cords without moving the lips. You can test for any tendency toward subvocalization by placing your fingers lightly on your larynx (Adam's apple) and checking for movement.

When you've practiced until reading is a direct act involving only the eye and the brain, you should be able to achieve a maximum reading rate of about 400 words a minute. At speeds faster than 400 words a minute, you are either *scanning* or *skimming* the material rather than reading it. Scanning is looking quickly through material to find specific points or answer specific questions. Skimming is looking quickly at the whole message to see what's there.

Scanning
Skimming

Once you realize that at speeds greater than 400 words a minute you are skimming rather than reading, overlooking a word or two, or missing a fact or two, doesn't seem quite so serious a matter. You can improve your speed by selecting material that you don't need to know thoroughly and forcing yourself to read it faster than you find comfortable.

But it doesn't do any good to skim something so rapidly that you

Testing for Accuracy and Comprehension

understand and remember *nothing* about it. So you should test yourself for accuracy and comprehension. A news weekly that you're going to read anyway is probably the most convenient material to use for self-help in improving speed. Pick an article. Read it as quickly as you can, timing yourself (use a stopwatch if you have one, but absolute exactness isn't essential).

1. Pay close attention to headings, the first paragraph, and the last paragraph.
2. Look for main ideas. The topic sentence of a paragraph is often the first sentence in the paragraph.
3. Look for names of people, places, events, and things.
4. Ask yourself the five W questions — *who, what, when, why,* and *where.*
5. If you miss something, don't worry about it. Forge ahead.

Determining: Speed

When you've finished skimming and noted the time it took to skim the article, write down everything you can remember about the article. When you've written down all you can, estimate the number of words in the article by counting the words in five lines, dividing that total by five, and multiplying that answer by the number of lines in the whole article. When you've calculated the number of words in the article, divide that figure by the number of minutes it took you to read the article.

Accuracy Comprehension

Next go back and reread the article carefully. List the specific facts in the article. Comparing your original list with the list you've prepared from the article will reveal your accuracy. To determine your comprehension, add the number of correct facts in your original list (the central ideas must be substantially correct, but it's okay to count two "half-right" facts as one correct one). Then divide by the total number of facts in the article. Your answer will be a percentage that indicates your level of comprehension.

If, for example, you skim an article containing 4,275 words in 3.75 minutes, you would compute your speed and comprehension as follows:

Speed: 4,275 words divided by 3.75 minutes equals 1140 words a minute.

Comprehension: 12 remembered facts essentially correct divided by 18 facts actually in the article equals 67 percent.

You should strive for a skimming rate of about 2,000 words a minute, with a comprehension level of about 80 percent. It's impossible to achieve or maintain such a level without regular practice, but the time spent mastering this technique will save you many hours that you would otherwise spend reading some material much more closely than is useful to you.

Improving Accuracy

Although you should always strive to read everything as quickly as the material and its importance will permit, accuracy and comprehension must sometimes take precedence. Some messages are so important that you can't afford to skim them; you must observe and comprehend the entire message correctly. The key to accurate reading is a well-developed vocabulary. A good vocabulary will enable you to read even the most complex material at close to the maximum reading rate of 400 words a minute because you'll recognize all the words instantly and understand how they are being used in the sentence.

Vocabulary

Unfortunately, there's no short cut to building vocabulary. If you already have a fairly well-developed vocabulary, you can probably expand it by writing down words you aren't absolutely sure of when you encounter them, looking them up, and memorizing them — including spelling, pronunciation, definition, and use. If your vocabulary needs a lot of work, several good paperback books are available which can help you start to build your working vocabulary in just a few weeks. As with improving reading speed, you must invest some time, but the return you'll receive in ability to read accurately will make it a worthwhile investment.

Improving Comprehension

Comprehension and accuracy are closely related. You must observe the message accurately before you can achieve total comprehension, so vocabulary is a key to comprehension as well as accuracy. Sometimes, however, you may know quite well what's being said from sentence to sentence without being able to comprehend the message in its entirety. You can improve your comprehension if you pay special attention to the following:

1. **Getting ready.** "Preread" the material by surveying the title, table of contents, chapter headings, main headings, and introductory comments. Write down questions you anticipate finding answers for in the message.
2. **Searching for main ideas and details.** Make sure that you understand the vocabulary being used. Look for topic sentences and

key paragraphs, and try to discover the organizational pattern of the material.

3. **Analyzing and interpreting.** Pay special attention to the author's principal statements. Are they facts, inferences, or value judgments? Do you agree or disagree with the author? Is the author a recognized, unbiased authority? Is the research sound, including sufficient facts to support generalizations?
4. **Organizing and remembering.** After you've read the entire message, can you recall the major points in their proper order? If the message is important enough, you should probably take notes, either in brief outline form or as a quick summary.

LISTENING

Reading and listening have a lot in common, but effective listening is probably more difficult to achieve. In reading you can proceed at a pace that permits you to understand the message, and you can always go back and reread sections that you don't fully comprehend.

In listening you must adapt to the speaker's pace; although you can sometimes ask the speaker to repeat something, the repetition will probably be a paraphrase rather than an exact statement of what was said earlier, and it may not convey exactly the same idea. In addition, most of us have been taught a greater respect for written messages than for speech. We tend to pay closer attention to material that's been put into writing, and we certainly give it greater credibility.

Importance of Listening

The importance of listening is frequently underemphasized. Throughout school you learn more about reading every year; but you are generally expected to know how to listen when you begin school. Yet studies of listening activity have shown that of the 70 percent of the waking day that most of us spend in communication activity, we spend more time listening — about 45 percent — than reading, writing, or speaking. Studies have also shown that **most of us listen with about 25 percent efficiency;** that is, we remember about 25 percent of what we hear, forgetting 75 percent almost immediately after hearing it.

Listening and Hearing

Listening is much more than hearing. Hearing is a physical, passive communication process; **listening is a mental, active communication**

process. We hear words but we listen for meaning. Hearing is easy; listening is work.

We hear with our ears; we listen not only with our ears, but with our eyes and mind as well. As we listen we also search for nonverbal signs of communication. We study the speaker's facial expressions, body movements, gestures, tone of voice, and voice inflections. We're born with hearing abilities, but we must develop our listening skills through practice. Hearing is a gift; listening is an art.

One of the reasons listening is a more complex activity than reading is that it occurs in a wide variety of situations. Reading is essentially a private affair. If distractions interfere with your reading, you can always reread the material at a more opportune time. Listeners, however, must deal with distractions as they occur.

Public and Interpersonal Listening

Although listening situations range from extremely informal to very formal, listening tasks fall into two broad categories, public and interpersonal. Public listening situations are those in which listeners are attempting to learn everything they can from a formal presentation, lecture, or media (TV or radio) speech. Interpersonal listening situations are those that encourage exchange — questions, answers, or conversation — between speakers and listeners. In public listening situations, the listener has little chance for *personal* interchange with the speaker.

Listening in public situations requires many of the same skills as reading. In public situations, the listener's main tasks are to observe, to analyze, to draw conclusions, and to remember what has been said. In interpersonal situations, listening involves an additional set of tasks: nonverbal messages must be observed, analyzed and weighed against the spoken message.

The techniques we'll suggest here for improving your listening effectiveness apply primarily to receiving the spoken message accurately, whether the situation is public or interpersonal. We'll save our discussion of nonverbal factors and other complications of interpersonal situations for later chapters.

Listening Barriers

Barriers to effective listening may be caused by either external or internal distractions of one sort or another. These are self-explanatory, but they are worth stating:

External	Internal
Hearing problems	Emotions
Physical condition	Attitudes
Fatigue	Biases
Hunger	Opinions
Distractions	Prejudices
Noise	Semantics
Voice inflections	Assumptions
Accents	Cultural differences
Volume changes	Social differences
Interruptions	Inferences

Techniques of Effective Listening

Effective listening is usually an eight-step process. In some situations you won't need all eight steps, but if you master them all, you'll be able to handle any listening situation.

1. **Prepare.** Before you enter a listening situation, make sure that you know enough about the subject to understand what will be said. You can't always control this, of course, but when you know that you will be listening to a message about a difficult subject, "prelisten" by reading enough about the subject that the vocabulary and concepts will be somewhat familiar to you. Relate the subject matter to your goals and objectives and explore your attitude toward the subject. Prepare to deal with your internal barriers to perceiving the message accurately.
2. **Pay attention.** Stop talking and concentrate. Listen to the speaker's full message without interrupting; save your own ideas for later. Whether you are listening to a formal speech or an informal discussion, identify the central subject matter and the organizational pattern. Formal speeches are usually arranged either inductively (specifics followed by conclusions) or deductively (generalizations supported by specifics). The pattern in informal discussions is associational and often chronological.

   Be alert for main points, topic sentences, and transitions. Focus on the message rather than the speaker, the delivery, or your own feelings. As an aid to focusing your attention and remembering the message, identify each point as evidence (specific facts) or conclusions (generalizations or inferences) and assign one or two key words to each point to serve as memory aids.
3. **Summarize.** Keep track of what the speaker has been saying. Use your key words to help you summarize what the speaker has

already covered. As each new point is added, review the points that have led up to it. Each time you review your lengthening list, you are reinforcing the key points.

4. **Anticipate.** Guessing the speaker's next remarks will help you pay attention to the message whether or not you anticipate correctly. If you guess correctly, the confirmation of your expectation will help you to focus on the message; if you guess incorrectly, the contrast between your expectation and the actual message will help you to observe and remember the message delivered.
5. **Listen between the lines.** Listen not only to what is said, but also to how it is said. Watch for emotionally charged words that form a "smoke screen." Is the speaker attempting to convince you by using language that arouses strong emotional responses and thus interferes with your objectivity? While you're listening between the lines, question yourself about the message. Do you agree or disagree with what is being said? Can you think of additional supporting evidence? Do you know of any facts that contradict the speaker's evidence? (Your *feelings* about the subject and speaker don't count.) A speaker who uses emotional language may still have a valid point. See if you can discover the real message underneath the bombast.
6. **Ask questions.** When you have the opportunity to ask for clarification and amplification, do so. Discover what the speaker *means* to say. Make sure that you understand the speaker's use of language to eliminate as many semantic barriers to communication as possible. You should also provide other kinds of feedback to help the speaker. In both formal and informal situations, smile at the speaker. When appropriate, you can also indicate your interest in the speaker by providing other verbal and nonverbal cues. Eye contact, nodding your head, and saying "Uh huh," "Yes," "I see," and other short "I'm listening" comments will encourage the speaker to make a complete statement.
7. **Take notes.** When you need to remember the message for any length of time, you should take notes. The key to good note taking is to listen more and write less. You cannot possibly take down every word a speaker utters, and attempting it will only cause you to fall behind, become confused, and miss most of what is said. Restrict yourself to recording the most important principles. Use the key words you've selected (see point 2 in this list) to stand for the principles. Usually listing one or two supporting facts for each principle will be enough to help you recall the other supporting evidence. As soon after the speech as possi-

ble, review your notes and type a more complete summary of the message for your records.

8. **Evaluate.** After you've heard the entire speech or discussion; after you've had a chance to question the speaker, examine the evidence, and consider the usefulness of the material; and after you've made sure that barriers have not distorted your perception of the message, you're ready to make an accurate judgment or a fair, sensible reply.

REMEMBERING WHAT YOU READ AND HEAR

Observe

Accurate observation of what you read and hear is the most important single factor influencing your memory of the message. Because you must *remember* the significant facts from a message to have learned anything from it, you should strive to commit the most important details to memory. Your notes should be an aid to accurate learning rather than a substitute for learning.

Associate

In addition to observing accurately, you must be able to associate the information you are reading or listening to with something you already know. Our associations are usually subconscious; we form them without being aware of the process. When these associations are good ones, we remember the material; when they are not, we forget. Our interest in the material usually governs the quality of the associations. When we're intensely interested in the subject, we tend to remember everything about it. When we aren't so interested — or when our interest is governed by an outside motivator (such as a grade in a course or a promotion) — we tend to remember the material only as long as we need it to achieve the goal.

Although you can't always control your interest in material that you need to learn, you can improve your ability to remember essential facts by consciously associating those facts to something you already know. When you attend a lecture or read to learn, you have a reason for doing so. Thus the material should already have some meaning for you. State that meaning in a simple sentence or phrase — one that says something permanent about the subject rather than about your feelings toward it or its contribution to a short-term goal. Using the key terms from that sentence or phrase, form a conscious association with the first point. Then proceed from that association to form a conscious association with the second point, and so on.

Visualize

In forming associations, use words or concepts that you can visualize easily. Select concrete, specific nouns and vivid verbs for your key words. Avoid generalities and abstractions. For some reason, ridiculous associations work better than natural, commonplace associations.

You can make ridiculous associations most easily by exaggerating the size or numbers of items involved or by having inanimate objects perform unusual actions.

Make a vivid mental picture of each association. For example, to remember the eight steps required for effective listening, you need to form associations among concepts that are difficult to visualize: prepare, pay attention, summarize, anticipate, listen between the lines, ask questions, take notes, and evaluate. But by using your imagination, you can form mental pictures that will help you recall the eight steps.

For *prepare,* picture yourself in a lecture hall reading a book. The speaker steps to the podium and throws a gavel which hits you on the head. He yells, "*Pay attention.*" He is beginning to speak about his summer *(summarize)* vacation when millions of ants *(anticipate)* begin to march down the aisles and onto the stage, forming lines *(listen between the lines).* When the ants start *asking questions,* you start *taking notes.* The speaker marches out with the ants, and you are left to *evaluate* what you have seen and heard.

Although the same images will not work for everyone, you will find that by making your own conscious associations — ridiculous, active, and in proper sequence — you'll be able to remember the major points of almost any speech or article.

Summarize

In addition to forming conscious associations among the main points in the message as you read or listen, you are also summarizing the material as you go along, thus reviewing and reinforcing each of the associations. The notes you're taking will also reinforce your memory.

SUMMARY

We speak and write to inform, to inquire, and to persuade; but we read and listen to learn. We cannot communicate effectively unless we can read and listen effectively. The act of receiving messages has three phases: first, we must observe the message in its entirety; second, we must analyze the message; and third, we must draw certain specific conclusions on the basis of our observations and analysis.

Because reading is our primary means of learning complex material, we can benefit from improving the efficiency with which we read. Effective reading calls for the mastery of three related skills: speed, accuracy, and comprehension.

Listening is much more than hearing. Hearing is a physical, passive communication process; listening is a mental, active communication process. We hear with our ears; we listen not only with our ears, but with our eyes and mind as well.

Effective listening usually involves eight steps: prepare, pay attention, summarize, anticipate, listen between the lines, ask questions, take notes, and evaluate.

EXERCISES

1. Explain the three steps involved in receiving messages.
2. What three factors determine the effectiveness of reading?
3. What are the differences among reading, scanning, and skimming?
4. What is prereading?
5. Use the techniques described in the chapter to determine your current reading speed. Practice the techniques we suggest and test yourself again after one week.
6. Why is listening important?
7. What are the differences between listening and hearing?
8. List the barriers to effective listening.
9. List and explain seven techniques for improving listening skills.
10. Have a friend or your instructor list 25 key terms taken from an article or speech. Practice making associations to link each term to the following term until you can recall all 25 terms in proper sequence.

SUGGESTED READINGS

Anastasi, Thomas E., Jr. *Communicating for Results.* Menlo Park, CA: Cummings, 1972.

Barker, Larry L. *Listening Behavior.* Englewood Cliffs, NJ: Prentice-Hall, 1971.

Borden, George A., and John D. Stone. *Human Communication: The Process of Relating.* Menlo Park, CA: Cummings, 1976.

Furst, Bruno. *Stop Forgetting.* Rev. and expanded by Lotte Furst and Gerrit Storm. Garden City, NY: Doubleday, 1972.

Huseman, Richard C., James M. Lahiff, and John D. Hatfield. *Interpersonal Communication in Organizations.* Boston: Holbrook, 1976.

Lorayne, Harry. *The Harry Lorayne Mental Magnetism Course.* New York: Information, 1969.

Lorayne, Harry, and Jerry Lucas. *The Memory Book.* New York: Stein and Day, 1974.

Werner, Victor. *Short-Cut Memory.* New York: Paperback Library, 1971.

Young, Morris N., and Walter B. Gibson. *How to Develop an Exceptional Memory.* Hollywood, CA: Wilshire, 1966.

6

NONVERBAL COMMUNICATION

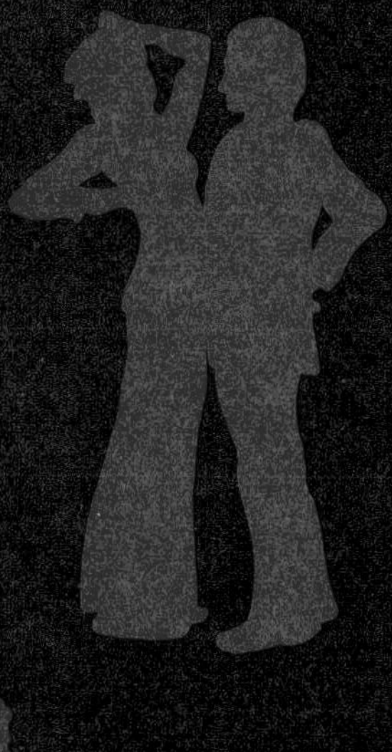

After you have read this chapter, you should be able to

1. **Define nonverbal communication.**
2. **Explain the importance of nonverbal communication.**
3. **Define proxemics and explain its functions.**
4. **Define territory and explain the relationship between status and territory.**
5. **Identify and explain the three factors involved in time as a form of nonverbal communication.**
6. **List the main functions of gestures.**

IMPORTANCE OF NONVERBAL COMMUNICATION

Definition: Nonverbal Communication

Nonverbal communication includes a wide variety of communication activity, most of which occurs below our conscious level of awareness. In other words, we don't usually transmit or receive nonverbal messages deliberately. Rather, we send and "read" these messages without being fully aware that we are communicating. Nonverbal communication is the transfer of meaning without the use of language. A wave of the hand to say goodbye, a smile to indicate happiness, and a hug to show friendship are a few straightforward examples.

Nonverbal Messages Transmit Attitutes, Feelings, and Emotions.

Nonverbal communication may emphasize, contradict, repeat, regulate, or replace verbal communication, either written or oral; it is an extremely important facet of interpersonal and organizational relationships. Nonverbal messages transmit attitudes, feelings, and emotions; and because they are more difficult to control than verbal messages, nonverbal messages usually carry more "truth" than verbal ones. When a verbal message and a nonverbal one conflict, most receivers will believe the nonverbal message.

"It's not *what* you said; it's *how* you said it."

Although the term *nonverbal communication* includes almost everything from which meaning can be derived except verbal (written and oral) communication, the most important aspects of nonverbal communication behavior are use of space, time, kinesics, symbols, and paralanguage.

The meaning attached to specific nonverbal messages varies widely from culture to culture. South American concepts of time and space are not the same as North American concepts. In fact, many of the problems involved in international communication result from differences in the cultural norms that establish codes for nonverbal communication.

Problems of this sort occur among subcultures in the United States as well. Blacks and whites, for example, tend to have different patterns of eye contact: this can result in misunderstandings. Although whites maintain and expect eye contact during verbal exchanges, blacks have a tendency to avoid eye contact at those times. They prefer instead to maintain eye contact when verbal information is not being exchanged — the times when whites tend to avoid eye contact. Even though these tendencies are disappearing in American culture, some whites still conclude incorrectly that blacks "never look me in the eye." Because of space limitations, this chapter will concentrate on patterns of nonverbal communication readily observable in American business organizations. You should be aware, however, that different cultures and subcultures interpret the same nonverbal behavior differently. To be understood by members of other cultures, you need to learn both their verbal and their nonverbal languages.

SPACE

People use space to indicate two categories of feelings toward others. *Proxemics,* or the distance between people, indicates the people's attitudes toward each other. *Territory,* the amount of space a person controls, indicates status.

Proxemics

We can't always control the distance between us and others, but when we can, distance is an excellent indicator of the closeness of the relationship. It's a literal fact that the closer we are physically, the closer we are emotionally. In this culture, proxemic distance is divided into four zones: intimate, personal, business and social, and public.

1. **Intimate zone.** The intimate zone covers the distance from touching to about 18 inches. This is the distance of lovemaking, nurturing, and protecting. Paradoxically, the intimate zone is also the distance of fighting. We must get close to hurt or to give pleasure effectively. In the intimate zone, the senses of smell,

touch, and even taste are all likely to be involved. When you and someone else choose to share this zone, you communicate: (1) your acceptance and appreciation of that person for what he or she is and (2) your trust that the other person accepts and appreciates you for what you are.

Verbal communication in the intimate zone is usually abbreviated and almost entirely emotional. This is because intimate distance out of choice encourages us to concentrate on the other person rather than on ideas or concepts. When forced to share intimate distance with strangers or with people we don't like, we compensate by pretending that we have more space than we actually do and by protecting the space we have left.

The next time you are on a crowded elevator or bus, observe the way people avoid eye contact. They stare at the floor, the ceiling, or a newspaper; they tense their muscles and assume a rigid posture. In such situations we usually remain silent to help ourselves and those around us maintain the illusion of more space.

2. **Personal zone.** The personal zone extends from about 18 inches to 4 feet. This is the zone we share with our friends; the distance between two people who are sharing this zone reflects their feelings for each other. The closer they sit or stand, the better they like each other. At this distance the senses of smell and touch are still important. In the personal zone people speak quietly and supplement their verbal communication with touching and increased eye contact.

   When circumstances force us to share our personal zone with strangers or people we don't like, we protect our space much as we do when a stranger enters our intimate zone. We avoid eye contact, turn away, and become silent.
3. **Business and social zone.** The business and social zone includes distances from 4 feet to about 10 feet. People in this zone usually have a specific reason for being together. This is the distance of most business discussions and social events. Within this zone, the lesser distances are typical of informal meetings, and the greater distances are usual for formal meetings. At this distance we tend to ignore strangers unless the situation makes a brief greeting mandatory.
4. **Public zone.** The public zone begins at about 10 feet. At this distance we may safely ignore other people without feeling defensive or guilty, as we would at closer distances. Communication at this distance tends to be formal; verbal communication

becomes more important than nonverbal behavior because with increasing distance nonverbal cues are not so discernible.

Territory

The second principal way we use space to communicate is through territory. Just as each of us has fairly definite concepts of personal space, we also know what constitutes our territory. **Our status determines:**

> **the amount of territory we control;**
> **how well protected our territory is; and**
> **the degree of access we have to the territory of others.**

A look at any organization illustrates the relationship between status and territory.

1. As your status in the organization increases, you receive more and better space. You've undoubtedly noticed that those just beginning their careers work at small desks in large rooms shared with many other people. With advancement in the organization, the person moves into offices that provide increased space, privacy, and comfort. Permanent offices with doors, for example, indicate higher status than offices made with half-wall partitions. Offices with windows and those on higher floors indicate higher status than offices without windows and those on lower floors. Carpeting, size of desk, number of nonfunctional furnishings (paintings, sofas, coffee and end tables, and so on), and a nameplate on the door are also clear indicators of a person's status.
2. As your status in the organization increases, your territory becomes better protected. You can illustrate this principle for yourself by trying to see the president of any large organization. Before you can make an appointment to see the president, you will have to talk to several secretaries, an administrative assistant or two, and the president's private secretary. In most organizations, executives with high status have offices located so that those with lower status must go through several doors and explain their purpose to several aides before they can gain access to top management.
3. As your status in the organization increases, it is easier for you to enter the territory of others. Although your office is primarily your territory, it also falls within your boss's territory. Subordinates expect their bosses to have ready access to their offices,

but subordinates don't have ready access to their bosses' offices.

The principles of territory extend outside the organizational sphere as well. People with higher status tend to have better space and to keep it better protected than those with lower status. Also, higher status makes it easier to enter the territory of others. Your boss, for example, would generally feel more comfortable visiting your home than you would visiting your boss's home.

TIME

As a rule, time can be spent in one of three ways: working, sleeping, or relaxing. Most of us are geared to working an 8-hour "day" and a 40-hour "week," beginning at about 8:00 on Monday morning and ending at about 5:00 Friday afternoon. The way we spend time is determined in part by culture, in part by our values and attitudes, and in part by nature, which gives us periods of light and dark, seasonal changes, and a fairly predictable aging process.

Time Is Important

In American culture time is especially important. "Time is money" is an axiom of business. Being "on time" is an important indicator of efficiency and responsibility. Even in American culture, however, the use of time varies enough that it can be used only as a rough indication of attitudes and feelings. Compare military personnel who are considered "on time" for an 8:00 meeting only if they arrive 5 or 10 minutes early to college professors, who are considered "on time" for the same meeting if they arrive no more than 10 or 15 minutes past the hour. Although the use of time does vary from context to context, it can be extremely effective in communicating attitudes and feelings.

Imagine the following scene:

You make an appointment with the mayor of Anytown to discuss the possibility of building a new $10,000,000 shopping mall. The mayor's secretary calls and cancels that appointment, gives you a new one for a week or so later, cancels the second appointment, and schedules a third one another week later for 3:00 Friday afternoon. You arrive a few minutes early. The secretary tells you that the mayor is still "out to lunch" but that he will return "soon." Ten minutes pass. Fifteen. Finally, at 3:30, the mayor arrives and leads you to his office. Without closing the door, he asks you to be seated and to tell him about your plans. As you talk, he reads and signs several letters, his secretary brings him coffee, he takes several phone calls, and three men enter the office carrying golf clubs. He insists that he is listening and asks you to continue while he gets his golf clubs out of his closet . . . .

At what point did you get up and walk out?

Time can indeed convey a specific message — one that those who share a common culture can read quite well. Most American businesses operate on some aspect of "commercial time"; that is, time is equated with both status and money. In "reading" the nonverbal language of time in business, we need to pay special attention to three factors:

1. How much time is alloted.
2. What kind of time is alloted.
3. Who waits for whom and for how long.

How Much Time

Generally speaking, we allot more time to people and things we consider more important. Certain aspects of time allotment are firmly established for us by nature and custom. We have 365 days in a year marked by certain seasonal changes. We have 12 months, each with a specified number of days. We have weeks consisting of 7 days each. And each of our days has 24 hours and includes periods of day and night.

Time Is Limited

Because time is limited, the way we spend our time reflects our values, attitudes, and priorities. What would you think of a person, for example, who spent 18 hours a day eating? watching television? bathing? By allocating large blocks of time to any particular activity, we emphasize its importance to us. Saying to a student, "You were watching the football game on television when you should have been studying," is really saying that the student should value knowledge more than televised football.

What Kind of Time

In American culture, high-quality time is exclusive time. When something or someone is important to us, we tend to focus on that thing or person exclusively. We shut out all distractions. Shared time is low-quality time. When we have an interview with someone, we don't want to share that time with other people, with phone calls, or with other business matters. Even if the interview is short, we want it to be all ours.

Who Waits?

Who waits for whom (or what) and for how long is another indicator of values, attitudes, and status. Universities, for example, once had rules specifying how long students had to wait for teachers. The times specified were 5 minutes for graduate assistants, 10 minutes for instructors, 15 and 20 minutes for assistant and associate professors, respectively, and 30 minutes for full professors. Teachers weren't required to wait for their students. To the best of our knowledge, no school still has formal rules about waiting, but the same basic rules still operate on an informal basis. The person with lower status waits for the person with higher status; and the greater the difference in status, the longer the person with lower status will wait without feeling insulted and without an apology being required.

KINESICS

Definition of Kenesics

Our uses of time and space are essentially cultural and are fairly straightforward. We are conscious that the way a person uses time and space says something about that person. Kinesics, the study of body movements and postures as a communication system, is much more complex because of the great number of variables. Consider how much can be communicated by facial expressions alone: joy, surprise, interest, disappointment, sadness, anger, disgust, or nearly any mixture of these emotions.

Most of us unconsciously "read" the body movements of others and interpret them correctly. We all know an "icy stare" when we see one, and we all suspect that a person with "shifty eyes" is less than completely honest. When communicators are conscious that their bodies and those of their receivers are communicating something specific, they can better understand the full message. Rather than attempting to detail the full range of body expressions, we will concentrate on indicators of openness and closedness and certain types of gestures.

Open and Closed Expressions

Facial and body movements that indicate willingness to communicate, interest in the other person or persons, and empathy with the other person are called "open" expressions. "Closed" expressions indicate an unwillingness to communicate.

1. **Eye contact.** Although skilled communicators, including many con artists, can use it to deceive, eye contact is probably the best indicator of a person's openness or closedness. When we like somebody, when we wish to communicate — either to send or to receive — or when we are in accord with somebody, we establish eye contact. And when we wish to emphasize the accord, we wink.

On the other hand, when we wish to hide our feelings or avoid communication, we usually avoid eye contact. Generally, when we wish to deceive someone or wish to show a lack of interest in what that person is communicating, we avoid eye contact. Paradoxically, eye contact can be combined with facial expressions to show either respect or dominance. Managers perceived as having high status receive more eye contact from their subordinates than managers perceived as having low status. Eye contact can also be used to produce fear in others; those who wish to convey superiority "look right through" the other person.

2. **Body rhythms.** People who like each other and agree tend to be "synchronized" with each other. We use rhythms to communicate agreement and understanding: when we agree, we nod our heads. Larger body movements also indicate the same thing. People who are in accord lean forward and backward at the same time and use similar motions of hands, arms, and legs. People in accord who are sitting next to each other even tend to cross and uncross their legs at about the same time.

   When we dislike people, our body rhythms indicate our opposition. When the other person turns toward us to make a point, we turn away just enough to indicate that we don't want to listen.

3. **Posture.** Sitting up straight indicates both interest and respect; slouching indicates the opposite. Other aspects of posture also indicate openness and closedness. By leaning back in our chair and folding our arms across our chest, we are saying that we are closed to the communication we are receiving. We may be closed to it because we dislike the sender, because we are tired, or because we disagree with the message. By leaning forward and relaxing our arms, we indicate our openness and willingness to listen.

   In group situations, the way we sit or stand also indicates our attitude toward the others present. Do we position ourselves so that all persons are included, or do we sit or stand with our backs to those we disagree with?

Gestures

Another important aspect of kinesics is the use of gestures, specific body expressions that contradict, complement, or substitute for words. People who like each other, for example, greet each other with "reaching" gestures. The hitchhiker's thumb is another gesture. Pointing, rhythmic nodding of the head and sticking one's tongue out at someone all have fairly specific meanings. If your supervisor keeps looking at the clock while you describe the movie you saw last night, that gesture has a clear and specific meaning. Public speakers reach out to the audience to elicit sympathy; clench their fists and pound the podium to show strength of conviction; and use their fingers to illustrate points one, two, and three.

People also use gestures unconsciously to communicate their feelings about situations; this happens especially when they need to compensate for feelings of inadequacy. If members of your audience scratch their chins, run their fingers through their hair, wipe their foreheads, or smoke, they are using compensatory gestures to reduce their level of anxiety.

SIGNS AND SYMBOLS

Symbols

All nonverbal communication is symbolic in the sense that the nonverbal language stands for concepts and ideas in the same way the verbal language does. But certain aspects of nonverbal communication are deliberately symbolic in that we use those aspects to establish a particular identity or to communicate a specific idea consistently. In this culture the best-known examples include the obscene gesture of the upraised middle finger, the "V" for victory (or peace, depending on your generation), and the clenched fist representing power and solidarity. When the symbol mimics the appearance of the thing or concept it signifies, it is called a sign.

Nonverbal communication is symbolic whenever we use nonverbal means to convey a fairly specific message. Our means of symbolic communication include our appearance, space, time, posture, gestures, and aspects of our environment.

Appearance

Physical Appearance

Our physical appearance is probably the most symbolic of the nonverbal messages we send about ourselves. With our style of dress, cut of hair, and degree of neatness and cleanliness, we show our political, social, and occupational affiliations. We adopt the "uniform" of the group with which we wish to identify, be it the obvious uniform of the military or the nursing profession, the formal attire of the business community, or the jeans and T-shirt fashionable on many college campuses. Occupational differences have long been indicated by the terms "white collar" and "blue collar," and despite an increased tendency for people to dress as they choose, people still evaluate others on the basis of dress. In addition to clothing and hair, people use jewelry and emblems in a symbolic fashion. A wedding ring is an obvious example, as are the various pins, badges, and patches that make specific political, religious, and personal statements.

Space

Symbolic Use of Space

In addition to the specific nonverbal messages discussed earlier, space also has generalized, symbolic functions. A room can be arranged to encourage or discourage particular types of interaction. A circular table, for example, encourages each person to communicate with all the others; it indicates that all those seated at the table have equal status. Rectangular tables encourage leaders to take the "head" of the table; they also indicate status by nearness to the head and encourage those present to choose sides.

Time

Time also has symbolic functions. For example, most people in this culture eat three meals a day according to a fairly regular schedule: *noon* means *lunch*. We also make symbolic statements about ourselves through our use of time. Is your daily schedule extremely rigid, indicating that you are inflexible — or is it merely "regular," indicating that you are well organized?

Symbolic Use of Time

If you have *deliberately* chosen to avoid any semblance of a regular schedule, that is also symbolic. Other symbolic uses of time include choosing to arrive at a party late (if you *always* arrive late "by accident," you've undoubtedly made the choice unconsciously); deliberately making someone wait for you (again, the choice may be an unconscious one); or deliberately rearranging your daily schedule to make time for someone.

Gestures and Posture

Symbolic Use of Posture

Most of the gestures discussed earlier are obviously symbolic; they are made deliberately to express specific ideas. The hitchhiker's thumb and the military salute are examples. The traffic cop's hand signals are also symbolic gestures. When posture is used in a symbolic way, it is also a gesture. For example, deliberately turning your back on someone to avoid communication is sufficiently specific to be considered symbolic. When men consciously pull in their stomachs and stick out their chests to impress someone with their masculinity, they are assuming a symbolic pose.

Environment

Men and women have always altered their environments to make their surroundings an extension of themselves. Paintings and other art objects, color schemes and furniture give an environment a "mood" that says something about the person who structured it. Detailed analysis of the symbolic meanings of specific environmental components is beyond our scope here, but you should be aware of the effects environments can have on communication.

Warm, Soft, Intimate Environments

In general, warm, soft, intimate environments facilitate communication, whereas cold, hard, public environments discourage communication. *Warm* and *cold* refer to qualities other than the temperature (which influences behavior but is more closely related to metabolism than to communication). Carpets, drapes, upholstered furniture, wood (as opposed to metal or plastic), and art objects or other nonfunctional furnishings all contribute to a room's warmth and softness and thus aid communication. Small rooms also facilitate communication. If you want to lecture, a large room is fine; if you want a discussion, a small room is a necessity.

Small Rooms

Other extensions of human beings also convey nonverbal messages. Just as the physical appearance of a written message says something about the writer, the quality of workmanship on any given product is a nonverbal message about the person or company responsible for it.

PARALANGUAGE

Paralanguage Defined

The last aspect of nonverbal communication we will mention is paralanguage. Paralanguage consists of *nonverbal* vocal elements such as laughing, crying, throat clearing, inflection, volume, tone, rate, pitch, and enunciation. In short, any sound or variation in sound patterns is paralanguage because it communicates a nonverbal message.

Like other means of nonverbal communication, paralanguage communicates attitudes and emotions rather than concepts. Laughing and crying are the obvious examples, but most of us are fully aware of the influence of vocal elements and voice qualities on communication. Depending on tone and inflection, for example, "Would you go to the movies with me" could be a question, a polite request, or even a command.

USING NONVERBAL COMMUNICATION EFFECTIVELY

Many people feel a little guilty about learning to read and control nonverbal behavior. They think that consciously reading someone's nonverbal cues constitutes an invasion of privacy, and that controlling their own nonverbal signals is a misrepresentation of their true selves. But understanding and using nonverbal communication more effectively has a valid goal: to improve interpersonal relationships by understanding the attitudes and feelings that accompany verbal communication.

Most of us "read" nonverbal cues quite accurately on an unconscious level, but we can make ourselves more effective communicators by becoming conscious of the nonverbal signals we are sending and receiving. Obviously, we all use a great deal of nonverbal communication every day, and we couldn't avoid using it if we tried. Because we use so much of it, we can't possibly be aware of each and every signal. Yet to base a judgment on too small a sampling of nonverbal cues is the same kind of hasty generalization that one makes in any kind of stereotyping.

You will be most successful in using nonverbal communication effectively if you concentrate on the generalities of openness and closedness rather than looking for specific meaning in every posture, gesture, or room arrangement. Whether the totality of a person's nonverbal communication indicates openness and willingness to communicate is more important than any single gesture — the one time the person keeps watching the clock while you're talking, for example.

SUMMARY

Nonverbal communication includes a wide variety of communication activity, most of which occurs below our conscious level of awareness. Nonverbal messages transmit attitudes, feelings, and emotions; and because they are more difficult to control than verbal messages, nonverbal messages usually carry more "truth" than verbal ones.

People use space to indicate two categories of feelings toward others. Proxemics, or the distance between people, indicates the people's relationships with each other: intimate, personal, business and social, or public. Territory, the amount of space a person commands, indicates status. Status determines the amount of territory a person controls, how well protected that territory is, and the degree of access that person has to the territory of others.

In reading the nonverbal language of time, we must pay special attention to three factors: how much time is allotted, what kind of time is allotted, and who waits for whom and for how long.

Kinesics, the study of body movements and postures as a communication system, is a complicated subject. The main body expressions may indicate either an open or a closed attitude toward communication.

Nonverbal communication is symbolic when we use nonverbal means to convey a fairly specific message. Our means of symbolic communication include our appearance, space, time, posture, gestures, and aspects of our environment.

Paralanguage consists of nonverbal vocal elements such as laughing, crying, throat clearing, inflection, volume, tone, rate, pitch, and enunciation.

EXERCISES

1. What is nonverbal communication?
2. Explain the differences between verbal and nonverbal communication.
3. Explain what happens when a conflict occurs between a verbal message and a nonverbal message.
4. Discuss organizational uses of territory.
5. How are the clothes you are currently wearing a nonverbal indicator of who you are?
6. Under what conditions do you use eye contact with someone else? When do you avoid it?
7. How does culture transmit information about nonverbal communication from generation to generation?
8. Why can nonverbal messages cause problems in communicating with someone from a different culture?
9. What kinds of complex messages can nonverbal communication transmit?
10. Why is one picture worth a thousand words?

SUGGESTED READINGS

Birdwhistell, Ray L. *Kinesics and Context.* University Park, PA: University of Pennsylvania Press, 1970.

Borden, George A., and John D. Stone. *Human Communication: The Process of Relating.* Menlo Park, CA: Cummings, 1976.

Cronkhite, Gary. *Communication and Awareness.* Menlo Park, CA: Cummings, 1976.

Goldhaber, Gerald M. *Organizational Communication.* Dubuque, IA: W. C. Brown, 1974.

Hall, Edward T. *The Silent Language.* Greenwich, CT: Fawcett Publications, 1959.

Hopper, Robert. *Human Message Systems.* New York: Harper & Row, 1976.

Huseman, Richard C., James M. Lahiff, and John D. Hatfield. *Interpersonal Communication in Organizations.* Boston: Holbrook, 1976.

Knapp, Mark L. *Nonverbal Communication in Human Interaction.* New York: Holt, Rinehart and Winston, 1972.

Stewart, John, ed. *Bridges Not Walls: A Book about Interpersonal Communication.* Menlo Park, CA: Addison-Wesley, 1973.

Stewart, John, and Gary D'Angelo. *Together: Communicating Interpersonally.* Menlo Park, CA: Addison-Wesley, 1975.

7

ORAL COMMUNICATION

After you have read this chapter, you should be able to

1. **Explain the importance of oral communication.**
2. **Identify and explain the five factors that influence the effectiveness of oral communication.**
3. **Identify and explain oral communication techniques.**
4. **Plan, deliver, and evaluate short oral messages.**
5. **Dictate messages for transcription.**

IMPORTANCE OF ORAL COMMUNICATION

Oral communication is both much older and much more common than written communication. Long before writing was developed, primitive civilizations had highly-refined oral communication skills. In fact, the widespread use of writing is a fairly recent occurrence in the history of civilization. Before use of the printing press became common in the sixteenth century, written communication was confined to handwritten manuscripts, laboriously transcribed with quill pens on parchment. For the few who could read and write, letters took a lot of time. Although churches, courts, and a few businesses had scribes whose duty was to record important transactions, almost all business was conducted orally.

Oral Communication before the Twentieth Century

As long as oral communication was the primary means of sending and receiving information, people were very careful to develop their speaking and listening skills. At the turn of the twentieth century, for example, the oral communication skills of the educated were excellent. Because people still relied primarily on oral communication to convey complex messages, conversation was a well-developed art. Reading aloud, dinnertime discussions, and conversations about current events, politics, and religion occupied people's attention in the same way television and radio do today. Oral communication, however, has one important difference. It is an active, two-way process, but "listening" to radio and "watching" television are essentially passive. We let ourselves be entertained without thinking about the messages we're receiving.

Today we're not likely to be so careful about our oral communication as our turn-of-the-century relatives were, even though most communication is still oral. In fact, most of us spend much more time speaking and listening than we do writing and reading. It's true that in modern businesses, writing and reading are generally preferred to speaking and listening for more important, more complex messages. But this, too, is a recent phenomenon.

Business Needs Written Records

The invention of the typewriter is primarily responsible for the reliance of modern business on written communication. At the turn of the century, oral agreements constituted the only contracts in a wide variety of business situations because written contracts were too much trouble to bother with unless the situation was very complex and the sums of money involved were large. But relying on oral communication presented problems.

As we pointed out in Chapter One, people tend to hear what they want to hear, regardless of their intentions. And with the passage of time, people tend to change and interpret oral messages in light of their own desires. The necessity for better written records was the mother of the invention of the typewriter.

Before the typewriter, people probably paid closer attention to what others said and took more care with what they said themselves. Literal veracity was expected, assumed, and relied on. We still value that kind of oral honesty — we all admire someone "whose word is his or her bond." But the need for records in modern business, the increasing ease with which records can be made and stored, and the fact that no two people ever remember the same conversation the same way have combined to decrease the importance of oral communication. In a reaction against the way things had been done, twentieth-century business became overprotective. Until the past few years, business has tended to emphasize the legal aspect of any relationship, especially as embodied in written agreements. Recently, however, business has discovered that the human aspect of relationships may ultimately prove more important than the legal aspect.

Oral Communication Is Human

Does it matter what two people *said* about something once the contract has been written and signed?

You bet it does.

Is it important to be able to articulate ideas about complex subjects orally, even though we know that most people will better grasp our message when we put it in writing?

You bet it is.

The written contract may be the legal "instrument" that finally determines who performs what action for what compensation, but the *quality* — and meaning — of the relationship between the people will be determined by what they say to each other and how they say it. Written communication, in spite of its abilities to provide a permanent record and to convey complex information, remains essentially a substitute for oral communication; and as we pointed out in Chapter One, the best written communication shows its oral heritage.

The Meaning of a Message

Skillfully handled, oral communication can provide a clearer insight into the meaning of a message because message transmission and feedback are immediate. In most oral situations we need not quit until we understand and have been understood. The give and take of a discussion, for example, can achieve consensus much more readily — and quickly — than a written exchange of the same information. Another advantage of oral communication is that as we speak and listen to one another, we have the opportunity to explore each other and the message more fully than we do when writing.

The term *oral communication* covers a broad spectrum of communication activity. The greeting given in passing and the formal platform speech are both oral communication activities, but they have as many differences as similarities. In this chapter we will concentrate on the similarities of oral communication situations. In later chapters we will discuss certain common and specific applications: face-to-face communication and interviews in Chapter Eight; small-group communication and leadership in Chapter Nine; and formal presentations in Chapter Ten.

You will recall from Chapter One that oral communication is influenced by several factors:

1. The setting and circumstances;
2. The purpose of the communication;
3. The size and attitudes of the audience;
4. The techniques used in delivering the message; and
5. The observation and analysis of feedback.

SETTING AND CIRCUMSTANCES

The setting and circumstances that make up the physical and psychological environment — excluding the audience's attitudes toward the speaker and the subject, which we shall discuss separately — are nonverbal aspects of the communication situation to which the oral communicator should pay particular attention. Setting and circumstances cannot usually be changed; they are "givens" to which the communicator must adjust.

Setting

Conducive Environments Are Warm, Soft, and Relatively Small

In Chapter Six we discussed some of the ways the physical environment can constitute nonverbal communication. The nonverbal message of the setting influences both the sender and the audience, even though they may be doing their best to concentrate on the oral message. When you can select a warm, soft, conducive environment for an oral communication situation — whether it is an informal interview or a formal presentation — you should feel lucky. Most of the time the environment will be selected for you, and the setting frequently will work against you rather than for you.

If the room is not conducive to effective communication because it is cold, hard, noisy, or excessively large for the number of people present, a skilled communicator attempts to compensate for the setting's shortcomings by

1. Keeping the message as short as possible.
2. Deliberately drawing attention to the sources of difficulty and asking the audience to help overcome the barriers.
3. Emphasizing the most important points of the message by using repetition, nonverbal cues, and strict organization.
4. Watching carefully for nonverbal feedback.
5. Soliciting and listening very carefully to verbal feedback.

Circumstances

Some people and events are "a hard act to follow," and sometimes even the best of communicators must yield to circumstances.

. . . You're supposed to address the convention at the same time that the social hour is scheduled to begin.

. . . Just as you're about to ask your boss for a raise, her husband calls and tells her that he's driven their new Lincoln Continental through the garage and greenhouse and into the swimming pool.

Circumstances Influence But Do Not Determine Attitudes

For effective communication, you need to know something about the circumstances that establish the psychological atmosphere of your setting. It's important to recognize that circumstances influence but do not determine your audience's attitude toward you or your subject. You may have something funny to say, but a funeral wouldn't be the best place to say it. You may have a well-planned speech to give on the importance of life insurance, but who would listen during a tornado?

Circumstances can vary so greatly that it's impossible to catalog them completely. You probably know an impossible circumstance when you see one. In general, however, circumstances are either formal or informal; and your message as you've planned it will be appropriate, with modifications, or inappropriate for the circumstances. Only after you've considered the circumstances should you decide to forge ahead as planned, modify your message to suit the current mood, or postpone your message until the circumstances are more favorable.

THE MESSAGE: PURPOSE AND STRUCTURE

In situations calling for written communication, it's easy to overlook the fact that if we fail to answer a letter we are sending a very definite message. In face-to-face communication situations, however, we have no choice but to communicate. Failure to respond to an oral greeting is an immediate, direct insult — a message that hits with much more impact than a letter not answered.

Identify the Purpose

Because most oral messages contain many more emotional components than written messages, oral communicators must be just as careful to identify the main purpose of any oral communication as they would be in identifying the purpose of a written message. Obviously, many oral situations leave you very little time to think about the purpose and presentation of your message: you'll be asked a question and you'll have to answer, or you'll be asked to "say a few words" when you hadn't expected to be called on.

Formal and Informal Situations

Fortunately, the less formal the situation is, the less critical your audience will be of your message presentation. In informal situations you'll receive more and better feedback, and you'll have greater opportunity to clarify your message. And, as a rule, the more formal a situation is, the more opportunity you will have to prepare. You make appointments for important interviews, for example, and you know in advance if you're to deliver a platform speech.

Regardless of the formality of the situation, the logical organization of thoughts is just as important to effective oral communication as it is to written communication. And effective organization of oral messages depends on the purpose of the message: to inquire, to inform, to persuade, or to entertain.

When Your Purpose Is to Inquire

Inquiries range from extremely informal ("How's the wife, Joe?") to extremely formal (employment interviews). We've learned how to handle most informal inquiries during the process of growing up. In general, however, remember that when the main purpose of your oral communication is to obtain information, the quality of the answers you receive will depend directly on what you ask and how well you ask it.

You will obtain better results if you do the following:

Ask questions rather than make statements. It seems obvious that the way to obtain information is to ask for it. But because we are all self-centered, we tend to think that our own observations and opinions are more interesting than those of others; and unless we're careful, we end up giving more information than we receive.

Ask only those questions necessary to obtain the information. Most people don't like to answer a long string of questions. Although one of the main advantages of oral communication is that you can ask for clarification when you don't understand something, even your best friends won't appreciate "the third degree." When you must ask several questions, break them up by explaining why you need the information and what you will do with it and by giving positive feedback for useful answers and cooperation.

Avoid questions that trap your audience. Remember that you want to obtain information rather than make your audience defensive. Stick to questions the audience can answer without self-incrimination. Don't force your audience to justify a particular behavior. For example, rather than asking, "Why didn't you tell me you received a 'D' in your business communication course?" you should ask, "How do you feel about your communication skills?" or, "What have you done to improve your communication skills since you took business communication?"

Ask easy questions first. When you have several questions to ask, ask the easy ones first. You would also be wise to keep related questions together and to save personal questions until you've established rapport with your audience. Simple questions — those that are clear without any explanation and that elicit short answers — should precede difficult questions (frequently involving *how* or *why*) which require extended answers. Give your audience a chance to warm up.

When an inquiry is lengthy, it is usually impossible to plan or suggest a specific structure in advance. Answers may suggest questions not included in the original structure. Therefore, in addition to the foregoing suggestions, the two main keys to successful inquiries are as follows:

Remain flexible.
Practice the techniques of effective listening.

When Your Purpose Is to Inform

Most of us know how to convey simple information in most informal situations. We run into trouble only when the information is fairly complex or when the situation is quite formal. It's easy to see why this is so.

Narration

Most informal messages use the technique of narration — storytelling — and use chronological and descriptive patterns of organization. These patterns are easy for us because they represent the way we observe and remember things. Most of the time we use these patterns naturally and correctly, but each presents particular problems.

We can improve our use of the chronological pattern by remembering that

Include the Audience

1. The story is based on our own observations and interests rather than on the audience's. Make a special effort to include the audience's interests and to emphasize those points of greatest interest to the audience.

Make Transitions Clear

2. Unless we make transitions and time references absolutely clear, the chronology won't be clear to our audience. Use transitional words and phrases (*next, while, two weeks later*) so your audience will be able to follow your story.

Make a Point

3. The story needs an identifiable point or message if it is to have meaning for the audience.

We can improve our use of the descriptive pattern by

Be Specific

1. Being specific. Whether you are conveying technical information, attitudes, feelings, or sensory experiences, select words that will convey your meaning precisely. You can describe a daffodil, for example, either technically — "a narcissus that has long, narrow leaves and yellow flowers with a trumpetlike corona" — or, as Wordsworth did, experientially:

   A host, of golden daffodils;
   Beside the lake, beneath the trees,
   Fluttering and dancing in the breeze.

   Both descriptions are good; both are useful, but they have different uses. The thing that makes each one good and useful in its context is its specificity for a particular audience.

Use Analogies

2. Using analogies. When you're describing something that's unfamiliar to your audience, begin by relating it to something your audience already knows. An analogy is especially useful when you need to explain a technical subject to a nontechnical person. Remember, though, that analogies illustrate but do *not* prove (see page 102).

As the formality of the communication situation increases, the organizational structure of the message must also become more formal; and as it does so, its organizational pattern increasingly resembles those used for written messages.

When your audience is likely to accept your information, you should use some form of *immediate* presentation, stating your main point (which may be a conclusion or recommendation) first and putting the supporting details second.

When your audience is likely to object to your information, use some form of *delayed* presentation, saving your conclusions and recommendations until after you've presented supporting material. You may wish to review the immediate and delayed organizational patterns presented in Chapters One, Three, and Four.

When Your Purpose Is to Persuade

When the main purpose of your oral message is to persuade, use the same basic pattern you would use in writing a persuasive message. The main difference between delivering a persuasive speech and writing a persuasive letter is that when you deliver your message orally, your degree of personal involvement and conviction are more obvious to your audience. It's easier to fake conviction when you write than when you speak.

Group Influences

You must keep in mind that persuading a group is *not* the same as persuading one person because in any group the members are under internal and external pressures to conform. Evangelists sometimes "plant" people in their audiences who will act when the appropriate time comes to help overcome people's reluctance to act. Keeping in mind that setting and circumstances are also important variables, the general group influences you need to remember are that the larger the group:

1. The more formal you will have to be.
2. The more important it is that you assume a leadership role before attempting to persuade.
3. The greater your chances of encountering resistance to your message.

In any situation, you should end your persuasive message by asking for the most decisive action you can expect. If you can't achieve full commitment in one message, strive for partial commitment, which frequently leads to full commitment with additional messages.

When Your Purpose Is to Entertain

Our main purpose is to show you how to use communication to achieve business objectives, and speaking for the sole purpose of entertaining is not usually appropriate in business. But whether your purpose is to inquire, inform, or persuade, humor — and entertainment in general — is more appropriate in oral situations than in written business communication.

Comic Relief

A little "comic relief" almost always makes oral communication more enjoyable and therefore more effective. Stories and jokes can help make the listener's job easier. Humor is tricky, however. Not everyone can tell the same joke with the same success. And some people feel foolish telling stories. You'll have to discover for yourself what works best for you, but we can give you a few hints to get you started.

Stories and Jokes

1. Stories and jokes can be effective icebreakers. When you begin your presentation with a story or joke, both you and your audience have a chance to relax and become comfortable with each other before the more difficult message begins.

Current Material

2. Make sure that your material is current. An old joke is worse than no joke at all. It doesn't help to ask your audience to stop you if they've heard it before. Even if they have heard it, they won't stop you — they'll let you make a fool of yourself.

Entertainment as Filler

3. Make sure that your entertainment material is kept separate from your main message. Emphasize the points of your message; use the entertainment material only as filler.

Good Taste

4. Keep the material in good taste. What your audience will appreciate will vary greatly from group to group. If there is any doubt in your mind about whether the audience is "ready" for a particular joke or story, don't use it.

THE AUDIENCE

Common Interests

The audience is an important variable in any communication situation; but as a rule, analyzing an audience in an oral situation is easier than analyzing an audience for the purposes of written communication. You and your audience are in the same place at the same time, frequently for a specific purpose. You have at least that one interest in common.

You should also have some information about your audience's other interests as well as ages, sex, educational level, and perhaps occupations. Based on analysis of this information, you should be able to make some predictions about how the audience will receive you and your message.

The attributes of your audience that will have the greatest influence on the presentation of your oral message are size, attitude toward you and your subject, and previous knowledge about the subject.

Audience Size

The size of the audience is an important influence on any oral communication situation. People behave differently in group situations than in one-to-one relationships. In general, the larger the group, the more difficult it will be for you to get your message across. In fact, just gaining the attention of a large group can prove difficult.

Variations in audience size will force you to make certain specific adaptations in presenting your message. In the next three chapters we will discuss some of these adaptations at length. In general, however, the larger the audience:

The Larger the Group, the More Difficult the Communication

1. The less cohesive it is.
2. The less its members have in common.
3. The greater the variation in attitudes, knowledge about the subject, and educational level.

For the communicator, these rules mean that with every increase in the size of the audience, there is an increased possibility of failure to communicate with some of the audience. You can't please all the people all the time. You should, however, try to maximize your effectiveness by

1. Making sure that your entire audience can hear you.
2. Adapting your message so it will have meaning for everyone in your audience. Explain technical terms for nontechnical audience members.
3. Avoiding jokes and references that only a few in your audience will appreciate.

Audience Attitude

The attitude of the audience toward you and your subject can vary in several ways. The audience can

Like you and like your subject;
Like you but dislike your subject;
Dislike you but like your subject;
Dislike both you and your subject;
Like or dislike you and be neutral about your subject;
Be neutral about you and like or dislike your subject; or
Be neutral about you and your subject.

Analyze the Audience

A previous experience of one sort or another is the only possible explanation for audience attitudes other than neutrality. If the audience has a positive attitude toward either you or your subject, you're off to a good start. If your audience dislikes either you or your subject, try to discover the source of the negative attitude. Have you made an unpopular decision? Is your audience known to oppose the subject you're advocating?

When you know beforehand that your audience has a negative attitude, you must make a special effort to be positive at the beginning of the message. If you've discovered the reason for the negative attitude, can you deal with it directly and eliminate it as an influence? Can you overcome the negative attitude by focusing on the future rather than the past?

Keep Smiling — Someone Is Listening

When you can't discover the reason for the negative attitude, or when you don't discover it until you've already begun delivering your message . . . keep smiling anyway. Someone in your audience may like your smile, and that's a start.

Audience Knowledge

What does your audience know about your subject? What is the educational level of your audience? Adapting an oral message to your audience requires all the techniques for adapting written messages and more. When a written message is complex and introduces new ideas, the audience has the opportunity to read slowly, reread, underline, and use the dictionary. A speaker's audience, on the other hand, must struggle to grasp the message as it is delivered. Make it easy for your audience.

Communicate at Their Level

1. Use a vocabulary that all will understand.
2. Explain technical terms.
3. Use an organizational pattern appropriate for your purpose.
4. Make your organizational plan obvious.
5. Emphasize key points by repeating them and drawing attention to them.

ORAL COMMUNICATION TECHNIQUES

In the foregoing sections of this chapter, we've presented the chief variables you'll encounter in oral communication situations and discussed some of the ways you can respond to those variables. But whatever situation you find yourself in, the techniques you need to be an effective oral communicator remain the same. Regardless of the situation, you must **plan, establish credibility, deliver the message,** and **obtain feedback**.

Plan

Think First; Speak Second

At its simplest level, planning means thinking before you speak. And at one time or another, we've all suffered the consequences of speaking first and thinking later. In face-to-face communication, that's a good way to lose a friend or make an enemy. At the business-group level, it's a good way to get fired. Not being careful enough about what we say earns us the nickname "blabbermouth." On the other hand, being too careful robs us of spontaneity and earns us a reputation for "never saying what we think." The question is, how do we keep the mouth hinged to the brain? Unfortunately, there's no easy answer.

At the very least, you should ask yourself whether what you're about to say is positive. If what you're about to say has *any* negative element — whether that element concerns a person, place, idea, or thing — give it a second thought. Ask yourself what purpose you will serve by making your negative statement. Weigh the advantages against the disadvantages before you speak.

Plan for the Subject and Situation

How much planning you must do before you speak depends on the complexity of the subject and the formality of the situation. Complex subjects require more planning than simple ones, and formal situations give you less margin for error than informal situations. Some situations may require months of research, preparation, and rehearsing. Rehearsing is tricky business. You should rehearse enough to be familiar and comfortable with your message, but not so much that your delivery is stiff and tired.

As you plan, don't expect to make your message perfect. You can't prepare for every contingency; you can't know everything about your subject, the circumstances, or the audience. But you owe it to your audience to present what you do know about your subject in a clear, truthful, and interesting way.

Planning also includes preparing whatever notes you'll need. Effective oral communication precludes the reading of a manuscript or the memorization of a speech. Well-prepared notes let you bring the results of your preparation with you but do not interfere with your natural relationship with the audience.

We suggest that you type your notes on regular 8½″ x 11″ typing paper and triple-space to ensure readability. Emphasize your main headings, topics, and transitions by underlining them (with a red felt-tip marker, perhaps). Fill in the details from memory. Your notes should give structure to your talk but leave you flexible enough to change the details of your presentation to suit your particular audience.

Establish Credibility

Credibility Through Expertise

Your credibility as a message source has an important influence on the reception an audience gives your message. You can establish *long-term credibility* only by becoming a recognized expert in a given area. Once you have established yourself as an authority, you carry this credibility with you into new situations calling for your expertise. Long-term credibility in one area also has a "halo effect," increasing credibility in other areas as well. An audience assumes that if you've always been truthful and "right" about one thing, you'll probably be truthful and "right" about something else too. For example, movie stars who have established credibility with audiences sometimes find it easy to become politicians because of this halo effect.

Credibility Through Honesty

Even if you possess long-term credibility, you will need to establish *short-term credibility* with your audience each time you speak. You do this by making clear distinctions among facts, inferences, and value judgments, and by telling your audience how you know what the facts are.

Deliver the Message

In addition to the structure and content of your message, the way you deliver it will also have an influence on its reception. Whatever the size of your audience, the skills you need to make an effective delivery are the same. They are essentially the same as the conversational skills you've been using all your life. Unfortunately, the larger the audience becomes, the easier it is to forget those skills. For some reason, most of us find large audiences at least a little intimidating. But even though we're using them in a different context, the basic skills that make our communication effective on a one-to-one basis also make it effective with larger groups. Regardless of group size, once you have planned and determined your means of establishing credibility, you're ready to communicate. So:

1. **Relax.** You know that you have something worth saying. Even if your audience has a negative attitude toward you or your subject, it's worth your while to deliver your message. It's also worthwhile for your audience to hear your message, so forge ahead. Use natural gestures and movements, but avoid pacing, fiddling with your hair, snapping your fingers, and other nervous mannerisms that might detract from the content of your message.
2. **Involve everyone.** Whatever the size of the group, maintain

contact with the individual members of your audience. Talk to individuals, not to the group as a whole. Look around the room; take the time to establish eye contact with each person present. Smile.

3. **Be positive.** If you are interested in your message, your audience will perceive this interest and will find you interesting. Your voice should indicate your interest. Project. No one likes to listen to a mumbler. You should be heard clearly and distinctly by everyone in your audience, but don't shout. If your natural voice, well projected, can't be heard by the entire audience, use a sound system. Your appearance should also show your interest in your message and the audience. Dress that is inappropriate for the occasion will detract from the content of your message. Let your audience know that you like and respect them and appreciate the opportunity to speak to them. Always begin with something positive. Save any limitations or negative material until *after* you're off to a good start.
4. **Stick to your subject.** Jokes, stories, and other material inserted for "entertainment" purposes must be related to your message closely enough that the audience can see the connection. After all, your message is the reason you are speaking. The entertainment material is useful only if it helps you convey your message. Don't let it compete with your message.

Obtain Feedback

You need to be concerned with obtaining feedback for two distinct reasons. First, you need feedback to make sure that your audience heard and understood your message. Second, you need feedback so that the next time you deliver an oral message, you will do a better job.

To make sure that your audience is hearing and understanding your message:

1. **Use eye contact.** If the entire back row has fallen asleep, you're probably not speaking loud enough. If people can hear you, their attention should be focused on you.
2. **Invite questions.** Let your audience know in advance when you want to receive questions: at the end of the entire message, at the end of each logical division in the message, or as you go along. Some speakers think that in formal situations questions should wait until the end of the message or at least until the end of logical units. We think, however, that an audience should be able to ask questions whenever they arise, because the clarity of the

Audience's Understanding the Message Is the Most Important Factor message is more important than the formality of the situation.

To do better next time, keep in mind that:

1. In informal situations, your audience probably won't be too critical. If your audience understood your message and responded favorably to it, you did all right. If your audience didn't understand, analyzing their questions will let you know where you failed.
2. In formal situations, you should arrange in advance for some kind of evaluation. Ask your boss to keep track of how you're doing, or prepare an evaluation sheet for your audience to complete.

Act on Feedback

Remember that the feedback does you no good unless you act on what you've learned. Paying attention to feedback — listening — is part of your responsibility as a communicator.

DICTATION

Dictation Combines Oral and Writing Skills

Another kind of oral communication common in business is dictation of messages for transcription into written form. Dictation calls for a combination of written and oral communication skills. The composition of the letter follows the procedures outlined in Chapter Three, but the presentation of the message goes through a preliminary oral channel before it is put in writing. Because the final message will be written, dictators must transmit the oral message with the ultimate written channel in mind.

Whether you are dictating to a secretary or to a machine, the following pointers will help you to dictate quickly and easily:

1. **Plan what you are going to say.** If your message is to inform, to inquire, or to persuade, use the basic organizational patterns discussed in Chapter Three. If you're dictating a report, use the organizational format discussed in Chapter Four.
2. **Be organized.** Set aside a time of day when you're apt to have the fewest interruptions — perhaps in the morning after the mail has been distributed. If you're answering a letter, have that letter available for easy reference, for correct spelling of names, for the correct address, and so forth.
3. **Give complete information.** Before you begin dictating the message, give complete information about it. Is the message a memo? a letter? a formal report? a speech? Do you want a copy to be sent to someone? Is the message to be sent special delivery? certified mail? Do you want to enclose material with the message?

4. **Speak slowly and clearly.** Don't chew gum or smoke.
5. **Visualize your reader.** Talk as though your reader were sitting across from you.
6. **Spell all names.** Repeat dates and figures.
7. **Keep a log.** When using machine dictation equipment, be sure to prepare required index slips of materials dictated.

SUMMARY

The quality of the relationship between people is determined by what they say to each other and how they say it. Written communication, despite its ability to provide a permanent record and to convey complex information, remains essentially a substitute for oral communication.

Oral communication is influenced by the setting and circumstances, the purpose of the communication, the size and attitudes of the audience, the techniques used in delivering the message, and the gathering and analysis of feedback.

The logical organization of thoughts is just as important to effective oral communication as it is to written communication. Effective organization of oral messages depends on the purpose of the message: to inquire, to inform, to persuade, or to entertain.

The audience is an important variable in any oral communication situation. You should know something about the interests, ages, sex, education, and perhaps occupations of your audience; and based on that analysis, you should be able to make some prediction about how they will receive you and your message. Regardless of the situation, the techniques for oral communication are planning, establishing credibility, delivering the message, and obtaining feedback.

Dictation calls for a combination of oral and written communication skills: plan and organize what you are going to say, give complete information, speak slowly and clearly, visualize your reader, spell all names, and keep a record of materials dictated.

EXERCISES

1. What are the main advantages of oral communication? What are the disadvantages?
2. How does the setting influence oral communication?
3. What factors must you keep in mind when using oral communication to obtain information?

4. In what way is entertainment useful to the business communicator?
5. In what ways does the audience influence an oral message?
6. Identify and explain the four steps of oral communication technique.
7. Would you prefer to dictate to a secretary or to a machine? Why?
8. Use a tape recorder to record a lecture or a class discussion. Analyze the speaker's presentation or the oral communication skills of the class members. Listen for evidence of planning. What parts of the lecture or discussion went especially well? Why?
9. Plan and deliver a short oral message (less than five minutes). Have your audience evaluate your presentation, both orally and in writing, immediately after your presentation.
10. Have your instructor select a letter- or memo-writing problem. Dictate your solution to a tape recorder or to someone who takes shorthand. Then have your solution transcribed. Does the transcribed message meet the objectives for written messages?

SUGGESTED READINGS

Anastasi, Thomas E., Jr. *Communicating for Results.* Menlo Park, CA: Cummings, 1972.

Anderson, Ruth I., Dorothy E. Lee, Allien R. Russon, and Jacquelyn Wentzell Crane. *The Administrative Secretary.* 2d ed. New York: McGraw-Hill, 1976.

Borden, George A., and John D. Stone. *Human Communication: The Process of Relating.* Menlo Park, CA: Cummings, 1976.

Carnegie, Dale. *Public Speaking.* New York: Pocket Books, 1970.

Cronkhite, Gary. *Communication and Awareness.* Menlo Park, CA: Cummings, 1976.

Himstreet, William C., and Wayne Murlin Baty. *Business Communications.* 5th ed. Belmont, CA: Wadsworth, 1977.

Hopper, Robert. *Human Message Systems.* New York: Harper & Row, 1976.

Stewart, John, and Gary D'Angelo. *Together: Communicating Interpersonally.* Menlo Park, CA: Addison-Wesley, 1975.

INTERPERSONAL COMMUNICATION

After you have read this chapter, you should be able to

1. **Define interpersonal communication.**
2. **Explain the importance of interpersonal communication.**
3. **Explain the assumptions that the three principal schools of psychology make about human motivation and behavior.**
4. **Name and explain three ways of dealing with interpersonal conflict.**
5. **Name and explain the four stages in the life cycle of a dyad.**
6. **Identify and explain common interview questions and types.**

WHAT IS INTERPERSONAL COMMUNICATION?

All communication is interpersonal in the sense that it takes place between people, but the term *interpersonal communication* has a generally accepted, more limited meaning. Interpersonal communication places as much emphasis on the *personal* as on the *inter;* and the communication requires that the communicators go beyond understanding each other's messages to understand their common humanity.

Most interpersonal communication is face-to-face and takes place in dyadic — two-person — situations. However, interpersonal communication also includes other situations in which the communication behavior is similar to that in dyads. Three or four good friends talking together are probably communicating interpersonally rather than as a small group. Telephone conversations are interpersonal communication, though they are not face-to-face.

Definition

Interpersonal communication is communication that involves an exploration of human psychology and motivation. Using what is already known about psychology is not interpersonal communication. When we use psychological insights to motivate or to reduce the impact of a negative message, we are applying information learned in an interpersonal context to another, more structured communication situation. Interpersonal communication requires exploration and discovery —

the learning of something new.

Although exploration of psychology and motivation may also take place in other situations, the interchange between two people is the best context for sharing inner qualities. For this reason, most interpersonal communication takes place in dyads, and we'll center our discussion on the one-to-one situation.

IMPORTANCE OF INTERPERSONAL COMMUNICATION

Oral and Nonverbal Skills

Interpersonal communication is the foundation of all human relationships. Our relationships with others are determined by the sum of our communication with them. Because most interpersonal communication takes place on a face-to-face basis, listening, speaking, and sending and interpreting nonverbal messages are the skills that determine how well we handle interpersonal communication situations.

In addition to the particular techniques we use when listening, speaking, and handling nonverbal messages, our interpersonal communication is influenced by the assumptions we make about ourselves and other people.

THE PSYCHOLOGY OF HUMAN RELATIONS

Our behavior toward others results primarily from certain assumptions we make about the reasons they behave the way they do. Throughout history motivation has been a principal subject of philosophical speculation, and the speculation continues in the modern discipline of psychology. Motivation and behavior — both normal and abnormal — are complex subjects about which many books have been written. For our purposes, however, we can reduce theories of motivation to a choice among three simple assumptions. Though the language has changed, modern psychologists offer essentially the same three answers offered by the ancient Greeks. People behave the way they do because they are (1) inherently bad, (2) made good or bad by the influence of environment, or (3) inherently good. These categories are oversimplified, of course, but they clearly differentiate the possibilities. Communicators must be aware that all motivation theories have been influenced primarily by one or another of these modes of thinking.

Three Schools of Thought

Psychoanalytic Psychology

Psychoanalytic psychology is a modern version of the "people are inherently bad" school of thought. According to psychoanalytic theory, each individual is motivated by aggressive inner drives which must be sublimated to enable the person to behave in a socially constructive way. The natural tendency is to kill, cheat, and steal to achieve immediate gratification of one's needs; this tendency is (just barely) held in abeyance because the competing needs of others make immediate gratification dangerous. We delay receiving the pleasures we seek only to avoid the painful consequences of being too eager.

Behavioristic Psychology

Behavioristic psychology holds that people begin life with no predispositions. People are *conditioned* to become what they are as a result of external stimuli, some of which are pleasurable (reinforcers) and some of which are painful (punishers).

Humanistic Psychology

Humanistic psychology argues that people are inherently good — capable of self-awareness, self-actualization, self-fulfillment, and self-transcendence when society permits opportunities for psychological growth. According to humanistic psychology, people find events and situations pleasurable or painful, depending on whether these externals contribute to or hamper the psychological growth that will lead to self-transcendence.

Motivation, Behavior, and Assumptions

Differences Prompt Communication

Each of the three schools of thought has accurate insights; none gives a full account of human behavior. Fortunately, however, we don't have to understand fully our own behavior or that of others to achieve successful interpersonal communication. In fact, were we to understand others — or ourselves — fully, we would have no need to communicate. Our differences and our lack of knowledge about one another make communication necessary.

This lack of knowledge also makes the behavior of others often appear irrational and mysterious. Not only may we fail to understand why someone has acted in a particular way, we may also fail to understand what the person says about that action. For effective interpersonal communication we must make five assumptions.

Actions Are Always Meaningful

1. The actions and communication of others have meaning to them, even if we don't know what that meaning is.

   In some cases the psychoanalysts are right — the "meaning" of a behavior or statement is an unconscious, inarticulate feeling that is *displaced* from one time and place to another. A frequently cited example of this is the man who has had a hard time at the office and who vents his anger and frustration on his wife and children after going home. The man's anger is meaningful although misdirected.

A person's behavior is always meaningful in the sense that the person expects to receive some kind of pleasure (or relief from pain) as a result of that behavior. The gratification may not be fully conscious. In the foregoing example, the man knows that he is angry, and he probably knows that his hard day at the office made him angry. What he almost certainly doesn't realize is that he is attempting to bolster his own self-image by hurting the self-images of his wife and children.

We Communicate to Understand and Control What Will Happen Next

2. We communicate to increase the control we have over our own behavior and the behavior of others. We communicate to find out why someone — either ourselves or someone else — does something, so that in the future we can control, influence, predict, cause, or avoid that behavior. We are all more comfortable in an environment we can understand and make predictions about. We feel better when we know what is likely to happen next.

Communication Is Always Meaningful

3. Regardless of the content of a message, all acts of communication are meaningful in that they have either a positive or a negative influence on the self-images of the sender and the receiver. Whenever we communicate, we make our receivers feel either better or worse about themselves. No communication is neutral. A simple "Good morning" may make your receiver feel better or worse, depending on whether you say it as though the person is important or unimportant to you. The sender's self-image also changes for better or worse with each act of communication — in the same direction, and to about the same degree, as the self-image of the receiver.

People Are Both the Same and Different

4. All people have the same basic biological and psychological needs, but their perceptions of what constitutes satisfaction of those needs varies for cultural and personal reasons.

We Need to Communicate to Be Happy

5. For any of us to satisfy many of our needs for any length of time, we must cooperate — and communicate — with others. Because most people aren't mind readers, we must begin by
   a. Asking questions to discover what the needs of others are and doing what we can to help them fulfill their needs and improve their self-images.
   b. Letting others know what our needs are and specifying ways they can help us achieve our goals.

Conflict Resolution

Interpersonal communication skills are put to the test only in situations involving some kind of conflict. When we're getting along well, we're building each other's self-images and making ourselves feel good at the same time. When everybody agrees, communication comes easily. When conflict arises, however, what happens between people is all too often not communication. People tend to engage in simultaneous monologues rather than in dialogue.

Perceived Threat

Conflict is the result of our inability to alter a behavior we *perceive* as a threat to our well-being or to our self-image. Because we are all defensive to some extent, we frequently perceive a threat where none actually exists; and because we are all self-centered, we tend to wish to control the behavior of others without first trying to understand them. If, for example, a supervisor asks a subordinate, "Have you finished the report yet?" the subordinate may view the question as a threat — a comment on his or her efficiency — and conflict might result. In this case both the supervisor and the subordinate might be trying to control the behavior of the other — the supervisor to get the report written more quickly and the subordinate to convince the supervisor to reduce the work load. The unexpressed messages cause conflict.

The Importance of Self-Image

Rational differences of opinion do not result in conflict. For conflict to result from differences of opinion, the emotional self-images of the persons must be involved. We are not defensive about our ideas in themselves. We are defensive about our self-images. When someone criticizes an idea or attribute of ours, we can respond in one of three ways:

1. Defend or deny the idea or attribute.
2. Attack the criticism.
3. Delay the conflict by trying to discover whether a threat actually exists.

In general, our response to a perceived threat depends on the way our self-image compares with our image of the other person. When we perceive the other person as our superior, we tend to defend. When we perceive the other person as our inferior, we tend to attack. When we perceive the other person as an equal, we tend to delay. In some instances, of course, people may respond to a perceived threat by attacking a superior or defending against an inferior. Context is an important influencing factor. Either attacking or defending, however, cuts off the exploration required for effective interpersonal communication.

Because the constructive resolution of conflict requires that all par-

Intelligent Questions Rather Than Self-Expression

ties achieve an enhanced self-image, the third response — delay — always produces better results than either of the others. Effective interpersonal communication requires more intelligent questions and attentive listening than self-expression. If we delay our response by exploring what the other person means, we may discover that what we heard was not what the other person meant. Of course, we might discover that some defense or attack is necessary because the threat is real; but because we delayed our response, we should be in a position to respond more intelligently.

THE NATURE OF DYADS

Dyad Means Two People

Two people in a face-to-face communication situation form a dyad. The major variables in dyadic communication are how well the people know each other and whether they perceive one another as equals.

Dyadic Life Cycle

Any dyad, inside or outside an organization, has a life cycle that begins when two people first meet and ends when the two no longer engage in interpersonal communication. The life cycle is composed of four general stages: initial, formative, mature, and severance.

First Impressions Count

1. **The initial stage** is very short, lasting at most about 10 minutes. But the character of the dyad is usually fully established by the end of this stage. First impressions do count. The initial stage of interpersonal communication generally includes exchanges of demographic information such as where and when the people were born, grew up, and went to school. At this phase each participant has the power to terminate the dyad; the exchange of demographic information helps the participants make inferences about differences of opinion, other matters of potential conflict, and common interests and beliefs. Some self-disclosure at this stage helps to insure the continuation of the relationship, but excessive self-disclosure discourages a lasting relationship.

Discussion and Conflict

2. **The formative stage** may last for an indefinite period, beginning after the initial stage is over and continuing until the equilibrium of the mature stage is achieved. In the formative period, the participants discuss attitudes and opinions and establish the emotional tone of the relationship. Several types of conflict may arise at this stage. For example, one person may wish to be more intimate than the other; one may wish to control the other more than the other wishes to be controlled; or one may respond to sit-

uations in ways that the other finds inappropriate.

3. **The mature stage** also lasts an indefinite period. At this point the participants have "defined" each other and their relationship. They have reached a perceived equilibrium: they think they agree about how intimate they will be, about who will control whom, about how decisions affecting both of them will be reached, and about what jokes are funny.

Participants Think They Agree

Some relationships never reach true equilibrium. The participants behave as though they agree about matters of importance to the relationship, but in actuality they disagree. This happens when one participant does not engage in honest self-disclosure. *A dyad based on inaccurate information cannot last.* The *amount* of self-disclosure can vary greatly in ongoing relationships, but the information must be accurate if the dyad is to continue. This is true of any dyad, from a purely professional relationship in which a bare minimum of personal information is disclosed to the fully intimate relationship of lovers.

Honesty Is Important

In mature dyadic relationships, each participant can judge with fair accuracy how the other will respond in any exchange between them. It is possible, however, for one participant to upset the equilibrium by altering an established conception of the relationship. Suppose, for example, that after 15 years of marriage and raising three children, a wife tells her husband that she wants to go back to school and become a microbiologist. The husband liked things the way they were. When this sort of conflict arises, the dyad returns to the formative stage and the participants must work to reestablish equilibrium if the relationship is to continue.

If the dyad is important or valued, it's generally worthwhile to change the equilibrium slowly rather than dramatically. (It's easier to climb stairs than to leap tall buildings in a single bound.) In the foregoing example, the wife could achieve her objective by letting her husband adjust first to her taking a few courses, then to her working toward a degree, and then to her completion of a graduate program.

4. **The severance stage** is the final stage. Ours is a mobile society: people not only change their residences fairly often, but they also change their values, beliefs, and expectations quite rapidly. This rate of change greatly increases the complexity of interpersonal communication. Some people respond to the uncertainty in the future of relationships by avoiding intimacy; others respond by trying to effect intimacy in all relationships. Any

Relationships Change

interpersonal relationship involves some risk, of course, and the more intimate the relationship, the greater the risk that severance will be painful.

THE MATURE ORGANIZATIONAL DYAD

Dyads in the organizational setting follow the same life cycle as other dyads. Interpersonal relationships greatly influence the success of an organization because the total of the interpersonal relationships in the organization determines both the efficiency and the morale of the company. A company's success is determined by who communicates with whom and how well those people get along with each other. Three factors control dyadic communication in organizations:

Interpersonal Relationships Determine Morale

1. The communication climate,
2. The formality of the dyad, and
3. The dyad's ratio of surface to hidden meanings.

Communication Climate

Dyads have a tendency to be either open or closed to communication. Some variation occurs from day to day, but most dyads are fairly consistent with respect to the amount and kind of communication that takes place. The people in a dyad usually reach an agreement about the way they will treat each other, though the agreement may not be fully acceptable to both people.

Closed Climates

Closed communication climates — those which discourage communication — give people the feeling that they are being judged, evaluated, and criticized. In a communication climate that is essentially closed, even the most innocuous piece of constructive criticism will probably be perceived as a threat. In open communication climates, people perceive communication more accurately and are more willing to communicate honestly themselves.

Open Climates

Although it takes two people to form a dyad, the person in the superior position usually has a greater influence on the communication climate. Management and first-line supervisors have the organizational authority to establish the communication climate because their occupational superiority can readily be perceived. High social status functions the same way. Compare these approaches:

Boss No. 1: You've only been back from vacation three days, and you've already fallen behind in your work. I want the report on the Johnson account on my desk by 9:00

A.M. tomorrow, and I won't take any excuses. Is that clear?

Boss No. 2: I know you've only been back from vacation three days, but I have an important meeting with Johnson tomorrow morning at 10:00. I'll need the report you're working on by 9:00 to make an effective presentation. Can you do it?

Boss No. 1, at the time of this statement at least, is closed to communication. The tone of the statement is accusatory, judgmental, and absolute, emphasizing the superior-subordinate relationship and manipulating the receiver. The closing question does not solicit honest feedback but simply emphasizes the superior position of the boss.

Boss No. 2, at the time of this statement at least, is open to communication. The information contained in this statement is essentially the same as in the first one, but boss No. 2 gives a reason in support of the request. This puts the emphasis on problem solving rather than on the superior-subordinate relationship. The judgmental tone is absent, and the statement solicits honest feedback.

Communication Climates Have a History

Neither of these statements would occur in isolation, of course. Each would have a communication history. Boss No. 1 may have learned the hard way that the person addressed won't do the work unless challenged by ultimatums. In general, however, open communication climates produce higher morale and higher-quality work than closed climates. The following lists of climate characteristics show why this is true.

Open Climate	**Closed Climate**
Observational	Judgmental
Problem Solving	Manipulative
You-Oriented	We-Oriented
Equal	Condescending
Flexible	Dogmatic

Open communication climates lead participants to feel that they are part of a problem-solving team, making valuable contributions. Closed communication climates lead participants to feel that they are on trial, defending themselves against attack.

Formality

A mature dyad has a fairly consistent degree of formality, established almost entirely by the participant who is higher in the organizational

Informal Dyads Encourage Self-Disclosure

hierarchy or who has the higher social status. The main difference between formal and informal dyads is that the former discourages self-disclosure, whereas the latter encourages it. Other aspects of communication are not necessarily influenced by the degree of formality. Generally speaking, however, long-lasting, valued relationships are less formal than relationships the participants feel will be temporary and unimportant.

Conventions Count

Dress and outward appearance do not indicate degrees of formality. Two businessmen in blue suits, white shirts, and conservative ties may be much less formal with each other than two college students wearing cutoffs and T-shirts. The conventions of the business dyad differ from those of the college-student dyad, but formality is measured not by the conventions of behavior themselves but rather by which — or how many — conventions the participants ignore in their dealings with one another.

Context Determines Degree of Formality

Although inappropriate informality in the initial or formative stages of a dyad might lead to an imbalanced relationship, informality in a mature relationship is a sign of trust. The participants in such a relationship have agreed that the absence of certain conventional forms of behavior does not endanger the relationship. Excessive formality, on the other hand, is an element of distance that may indicate a closed communication climate. For example, if one participant in the dyad tends to use a written channel rather than an oral channel for routine communication, the message "keep your distance" is clear.

The appropriate degree of formality can be established only by the two people in the dyad, but for the dyad to be successful, the participants must agree about how much formality is required.

Surface and Hidden Meanings

How comfortable we are in interpersonal relationships depends on our concept of what communication is taking place on the surface and what meanings are being hidden from us. Surface meanings include all those communication components — both verbal *and* nonverbal messages — which one participant in the dyad offers to the other as a means of conveying meaning. Surface meanings may be either explicit or implicit, as long as they are clear to the intended receiver. A private joke, for example, is still a surface meaning.

Hidden meanings are meanings that we know are there, but we can only speculate about their nature. Suppose, for example, that a "friend" comes to you and says, "I've heard that if the new company president has his way, your department won't need its typewriters any more." When pressed for details, your friend says, "I don't know any more; besides, I've said too much already." Because the surface meaning does not make complete sense to you, you're left to speculate about possible hidden meanings.

> Did your friend make up the story?
> Is there any truth to the story?
> Where did your friend hear the story?
> Does the new president want to eliminate your department?
> Will your secretaries be moved to a typing pool?
> And so on.

Because the meaning is unclear, you must speculate about your friend's veracity, motives, and statements. Prevarication and hypocrisy are both difficult to deal with; when they occur, both make interpersonal relationships unpleasant.

Messages with Multiple Meanings

More typical in organizational situations than outright prevarication or malicious hypocrisy are dyads in which one or both participants use statements with multiple meanings to conceal, reveal, or test for the truth. This behavior is typical of the formative stage of the dyad's life cycle, but in the mature stage it indicates a manipulative personality and creates an atmosphere of mistrust. The communicators are acknowledging that they do not fully trust one another, at least with some category of information.

Your "friend" with the story about your department's typewriters may want to let you know that your job is insecure without telling you directly. On the other hand, he may want to convince you that your job is insecure to cause trouble between you and higher management. All you can be sure of is that, for one purpose or another, you are being manipulated.

People who habitually manipulate others in this way tend to assume that messages contain hidden meanings even when none are actually present. They become like the two psychiatrists who were walking down the street when a third psychiatrist passed them saying, "Good morning." When the third psychiatrist was out of earshot, the first said to the second, "I wonder what she meant by that?"

Manipulation Fosters Counter Manipulation

Speculation about what people mean can only be that — speculation. Accurate communication, good interpersonal relationships, and organizational efficiency cannot be based on speculation and mistrust. No one likes to be manipulated, and manipulation fosters countermanipulation. When this goes on, everyone in the organization suffers.

THE INTERVIEW

Most of what we've said about dyads applies to the interviewing process; but interviews differ from other dyads in that they usually have a serious, specific purpose and a more definite, formal structure than other kinds of interpersonal relationships. Of course, other dyads may be purposeful, maintained so that the participants can achieve particular goals; but an interview is almost always deliberately established by one participant to give, obtain, or exchange information.

Although interviews are conducted for various purposes, their similarities are more important here than their differences. For this reason, we will concentrate on interview structure and procedure.

Interview Purposes

In arranging for an interview, one of the participants always has a specific purpose in mind. The specific purposes usually fall into one of the following six categories:

1. **Employment.** The employment interview is probably the best-known of all interview types. It's difficult to get a job without some kind of interview, so most of us have had at least limited experience with an employment interview. Employment interviews have three specific purposes. First, the interview should determine whether the applicant is the right person for the job. Second, the interviewer should give the applicant enough information about the job and the company so the applicant can make a decision about the job on the basis of personal goals and the prospects for advancement with that company. And third, the employment interview should create good will for the company.

Obtain Information

Give Information

Create Goodwill

2. **Orientation.** The orientation interview functions to supply or obtain facts, policy information, or other job-related data. Orientation interviews are routinely used to introduce new employees to the work situation. Orientation interviews also serve to acquaint employees with pertinent, new information.

Provide Job-Related Data

3. **Performance appraisal.** Performance appraisal interviews help evaluate job performance. They are also used to discuss job, personal, and performance goals and to define job problems and expectations. Most companies conduct formal performance appraisal interviews on a regular basis. At the end of the interview, both employer and employee should have a clear understanding of the other's abilities and expectations.

Evaluate Job Performance

4. **Problem-solving.** In problem-solving interviews, the inter-

Search for Solutions

viewer and the interviewee discuss a job-related problem and explore possible solutions. This type of interview is also used when either the employer or the employee needs to familiarize the other with a particular problem.

Discuss Job and Personal Problems

5. **Counseling-grievance.** When the employer or the employee has a particular problem that the other can solve, a counseling-grievance interview is helpful. Counseling includes not only advice about personal problems, but also advice about correcting identifiable job performance deficiencies. Grievance interviews reflect the employee's "right to petition" the employer to change a particular behavior.

Understand Employee Turn-over

6. **Exit.** The main purpose of an exit interview is to help the employer understand the reasons for employee turnover. Exit interviews also serve to express appreciation for the employee's work and to ensure that the employee leaves with a positive attitude toward the company.

INTERVIEW STRUCTURE

A successful interview follows a particular pattern planned by the interviewer, although the actual content of the interview may vary. The interview plan and structure must be flexible enough to allow for some unscheduled discussion. Planning, then, is the first essential part of the interview. The others are the opening, the body, the closing, and the follow-up.

Planning

Planning entails selection of a specific purpose for the interview, collection of pertinent information, preparation of important questions, and determination of a time allotment.

Opening

The opening of the interview should make the purpose of the interview clear and establish an open climate for communication. The interviewer should clarify the objectives of the interview and help the interviewee to feel that the interview setting is comfortable rather than threatening.

Body

Questions and Answers

The body of the interview is an opportunity for the participants to exchange the pertinent information. This portion of the interview consists of questions and answers; the main requirements for success are careful statements and effective listening. Participants must resist the temptation to argue or lecture. Both interviewer and interviewee should remember that each can gain from the other, whatever the circumstances or the nature of the interview. Each must remember that the other may not be capable of expressing observations or inferences adequately, and each should seek clarification on matters of disagreement or misunderstanding before reaching an evaluation.

Closing

The closing provides the interviewer the opportunity to review and summarize the key points of the discussion, emphasizing points of agreement and follow-up actions that the participants are to undertake. Both participants should express appreciation for the interview.

Follow-up

The follow-up consists of recording important decisions and agreements, and planning the follow-up action. In performance appraisal and counseling-grievance interviews, both participants should receive copies of the written summary and evaluation.

Types of Questions

All interviews consist of a series of questions and answers; the success of an interview depends primarily on the kinds of questions asked. The serious nature of an interview makes it a potentially threatening situation for many people, so participants must be especially aware of the communication climate they are establishing with their questions and answers. Creating and maintaining an open climate is essential to the success of the interview in eliciting clear, accurate information. Certain kinds of questions help to establish an open climate; other kinds of questions cut communication off.

Open Climate Questions

Open climate questions include leading questions, direct questions, open questions, probes, mirror questions, and hypothetical questions.

1. **Leading questions** guide the interviewee to a specific response. The interviewer should avoid leading questions unless certain that the socially approved response will result. When used to confirm known information, leading questions help the interviewer and interviewee relax with one another. "You went to Iowa State University, didn't you?" "You majored in marketing, didn't you?" "Isn't it true that you received a football scholarship?"
2. **Direct questions** call for a limited response, often yes or no. "Where were you born?" "Did that influence your decision to apply for a job with us?" Certain direct questions, such as "Did you go to college?" are open climate questions only in certain contexts. If a direct question poses a possible threat, it should be asked only after an open climate has been established.
3. **Open questions** require the interviewee to develop an extended answer. They are, therefore, the interviewer's main tool for discovering what the interviewee is like. "Tell me a bit about yourself." "What do you expect to be doing 10 years from now?" "What do you do for relaxation?" "What would you consider

your major accomplishments during the past year?"

4. **Probes** are direct or open questions that pursue some aspect of a previous response. "Why would you like to be a district manager?" "Which do you prefer, fishing or hunting?"
5. **Mirror questions,** like probes, serve to elicit more information about a certain aspect of a previous response. The question "mirrors" some part of the response.

   Interviewee: . . . and then I went to Iowa State University for about a year . . .
   Interviewer: Iowa State University?
   Interviewee: Yes, you know, in Ames. That's where . . .

6. **Hypothetical questions** are used most frequently in employment and performance appraisal interviews. They permit the interviewee to develop an extended response exploring a particular possibility. "What changes would you make if you were district manager?" "Let's assume that we could find the money for new equipment. What would you like to see installed?"

Closed Climate Questions

Closed climate questions include loaded questions, double-bind questions, forced-choice questions, and why-didn't-you questions.

1. **Loaded questions** show evidence of an assumption or a value judgment that predetermines a "correct" or "acceptable" response. "How do you feel about Melvin Crane's stupid behavior?" "What makes you think that you could run the company better?" An interviewer who hasn't done required homework may ask loaded questions inadvertently — as when a person with only a high school education is asked where he or she went to college.
2. **Double-bind questions** tend to force the interviewee to choose between two "unacceptable" answers. One classic double-bind question is, "Do you still beat your wife?" A modern version is, "Do you prefer to get drunk or get high?" Other questions that seem innocuous at first may be in effect double-bind questions: "Do you drink alcoholic beverages?" If you say no, you may be considered antisocial. If you say yes, you may be considered a lush.
3. **Forced-choice questions** are like double-bind questions in that they tend to force the interviewee to choose and defend a response. "Which is more important to you, serving humanity or making money?" "Which secretary, Susan or William, do you think should be fired?" "Would you rather read *Playboy* or *Religious Opinion* magazine?" The difference between double-

bind and forced-choice questions is one of complexity. The double-bind question has no right answer; whereas either answer to the forced-choice question may be correct if it is adequately explained.

4. **Why-didn't-you questions** accuse the interviewee of some shortcoming — usually failure to provide important information. "Why didn't you tell me about your arrest record?" "Why didn't you tell me that you failed mathematics in college?" "Why didn't you turn off the stamping press before going on coffee break?" "Why didn't you complete the report on time?"

Control of Interviews

The interviewer controls the direction and duration of the interview by asking questions, providing support, and responding to the interviewee's questions and answers.

Tightly Controlled

Tightly controlled interviews, consisting primarily of direct questions, are best when only specific, factual information is required. The interviewer usually asks all the questions; the interviewee is confined to giving the answers requested.

Moderately Controlled

Moderately controlled interviews, consisting of some direct and some open questions, are somewhat flexible. The great majority of interviews are moderately controlled, 15- to 30-minute interviews. The time span is long enough to allow the interviewer to clarify important points and to allow the interviewee to ask and receive answers to some questions as well. Moderately controlled interviews are best when time is limited but the interviewer must explore the ideas, attitudes, and beliefs of the interviewee.

Open

Open interviews, which include many open questions, are used primarily for high-level employment interviews and for problem-solving interviews. The open interview is *not* uncontrolled. The interviewer has an objective and a plan, but the interviewee is allowed to do most of the talking in a way that forces him or her to develop extended answers in a clear, logical, coherent fashion. This style of interviewing is best for discovering what someone is like, but it is time-consuming. The importance of the situation must make the investment of time worthwhile.

Being Interviewed

Most of the information presented in the foregoing discussion was from the interviewer's perspective. But in addition to understanding the interviewer's responsibilities, business communicators should also have a clear understanding of the role of the interviewee. An interview with a skilled interviewer is quite painless, but being interviewed by an unskilled person can be an awkward, uncomfortable experience. Because you will never know in advance what your interviewer may be like, be prepared. Do the following:

Understand the Purpose

1. Understand the purpose. When you can, find out *before* the interview what its purpose is. Sometimes, of course, you may be called in unexpectedly with no opportunity to discover the purpose before you are interviewed. In that case, find out early in the interview whether it has a specific purpose and, if so, what that purpose is.

Present the Right Image

2. Present the right image. In addition to dressing appropriately for the interview, make sure that you have "done your homework." If it's an employment interview, find out all you can about the company, including its policies, products, and personnel. If it's a performance appraisal interview, analyze your strengths and weaknesses before the interview takes place.

Convey the Information

3. Convey the information. As the interviewee, your main role is to provide the answers. In most interviewing situations, you'll also be expected to ask some questions. You can either work your questions in when they fit naturally or save them for the end. But make sure that you answer the questions you're asked in a clear, specific way and at a reasonable length. Make sure that you understand each question before you launch yourself on the sea of language.

   Interviewer: Tell me a bit about yourself.
   Interviewee: Do you mean my life history or what I'm like now?

Handle the Difficult Questions

4. Handle the difficult questions. If you are asked a closed climate question, deal with it as best you can. Don't get angry or attack, and don't defend yourself. Delay. If possible, ask for a clarification; you may then be able to answer a more favorable question. If the question is so clear that asking for clarification would be ridiculous, qualify your answer.

   Interviewer: Would you rather make money or serve humanity?
   Interviewee: I believe that those are compatible goals and that I can do both by . . . .

SUMMARY

Interpersonal communication is the foundation of all our human relationships. Our relationships with others are determined by the sum of our communication with them, and our communication in turn depends on our assumptions about motivation and behavior.

To achieve effective interpersonal communication, we must begin with the assumption that the actions and communication of others are meaningful to them, even if we don't understand that meaning. The reason we communicate is to increase the control we have over our own behavior and the behavior of others; all acts of communication have either a positive or a negative influence on the self-images of the sender and the receiver.

Two people in a face-to-face communication situation form a dyad. The life cycle of a dyad consists of four general stages: initial, formative, mature, and severance. Dyads have a tendency to be either open or closed to communication. Interviews differ from other dyads in that they always have a serious, specific purpose and a more definite structure than other kinds of interpersonal relationships. The six specific purposes of interviews are: employment, orientation, performance appraisal, problem-solving, counseling-grievance, and exit. An interview consists of a series of questions. Some kinds of questions — leading questions, direct questions, open questions, probes, mirror questions, and hypothetical questions — contribute to an open climate. Closed climate questions include loaded questions, double-bind questions, forced-choice questions, and why-didn't-you questions.

EXERCISES

1. Explain the importance of interpersonal communication.
2. What are the essential differences among psychoanalytic, behavioristic, and humanistic views of human motivation?
3. How does communication help us to control our environment?
4. What is conflict?
5. Which of the three ways of responding to conflict is most successful? Why?
6. Identify and explain the four stages of a dyadic life cycle.
7. How do open and closed communication climates influence organizational behavior?
8. Identify and explain the six interview types.
9. Identify and explain the five stages of interview structure.
10. Plan and conduct two moderately controlled performance appraisal interviews, one using all open questions and the other

using all closed questions. What differences do you observe in the responses of the interviewees?

SUGGESTED READINGS

Anastasi, Thomas E., Jr. *Communicating for Results.* Menlo Park, CA: Cummings, 1972.

Berkman, Harold W. *The Human Relations of Management.* Encino, CA: Dickenson, 1974.

Borden, George A., and John D. Stone. *Human Communication: The Process of Relating.* Menlo Park, CA: Cummings, 1976.

Cronkhite, Gary. *Communication and Awareness.* Menlo Park, CA: Cummings, 1976.

Huseman, Richard C., Cal M. Logue, and Dwight L. Freshley, eds. *Readings in Interpersonal and Organizational Communication.* 2d ed. Boston: Holbrook, 1974.

Jourard, Sidney M. *The Transparent Self: Self-Disclosure and Well-Being.* Princeton, NJ: Van Nostrand, 1964.

Maslow, Abraham H. *Toward a Psychology of Being.* 2d ed. New York: Van Nostrand, 1968.

McMurry, Robert N. *Tested Techniques of Personnel Selection.* Rev. ed. Chicago: Dartnell, 1975.

Stewart, John, ed. *Bridges Not Walls: A Book about Interpersonal Communication.* Menlo Park, CA: Addison-Wesley, 1973.

Stewart, John, and Gary D'Angelo. *Together: Communicating Interpersonally.* Menlo Park, CA: Addison-Wesley, 1975.

9

SMALL GROUPS

After you have read this chapter, you should be able to

1. **Explain the importance of small groups to modern business organizations.**
2. **Identify and explain the four key roles in small group behavior.**
3. **Identify and explain the five stages in the life cycle of a small group.**
4. **Explain how communication structures influence small group behavior.**
5. **List the advantages and disadvantages of small groups.**

IMPORTANCE OF SMALL GROUPS

Most Important Decisions Are Made in Small Groups

In modern organizations, almost all important decisions are made in small groups. This undoubtedly results, in part, from the increasing complexity of society and technology; but it is also because small groups produce reliably better decisions than any one person can produce. Although in some cases a highly skilled person can analyze a problem and reach a solution more efficiently than a group, the complex nature of many business problems makes it difficult to determine in advance who might have the required skills to solve a particular problem. When small groups function as they should, more information is brought to bear on the problem in question than any one individual could bring.

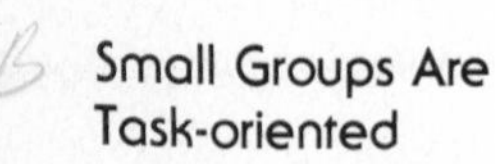

Small Groups Are Task-oriented

In this chapter we will discuss the nature of small groups. We will concentrate on the special techniques required for effective communication in the small group setting. Unlike most interpersonal communication, communication in a small group is primarily task-oriented. The participants are usually selected because they are directly concerned with the particular topic under consideration. The essential interpersonal communication skills are still required, however, for effective small group communication. You must know how to

1. Read and control nonverbal messages;
2. Listen;

3. Communicate orally; and
4. Establish an open communication climate.

In addition to these skills, you must understand group characteristics, group influences on the communication process, group dynamics, and group communication and leadership.

GROUP CHARACTERISTICS

Definition: Small Group

The number, kinds, and purposes of small groups are virtually inexhaustible. A board of directors is a small group. A jury is a small group. A committee to protect the tsetse fly would be a small group. A small group consists of any number of people from two to about twenty who have some need or purpose in common and who can communicate face-to-face with each other without the need for parliamentary procedure to control behavior. A small group may, of course, choose to use parliamentary procedure without ceasing to be a small group. But when the group becomes so large that parliamentary procedure is required to maintain order, the group is no longer small. The United States Senate is not a small group. We are concerned here with groups small enough to establish flexible procedural rules, even if the group is so formal that its behavior is in other ways just as rigid as that of the Senate.

Dyads are sometimes considered small groups. Even when dyads have a specific purpose, however, the interaction involved differs from that in groups of three or more, because the presence of other people influences the communication process. The group situation puts certain pressures on participants that do not occur in dyads; perhaps because of this, groups tend to be more formal than interpersonal relationships.

Purpose

Groups *always* have a reason for being. The almost endless variety of reasons people form small groups can be divided into three general categories:

1. Primary
2. Informal
3. Formal

Primary Groups

Primary groups consist of family and very close friends. The reason for continued existence of a primary group is essentially the self-satisfaction of the group members. Although it is possible for some individuals to form primary groups on the job, primary groups are not typical of organizations. We will not discuss them here.

Informal Groups

Informal groups are formed to foster improved interpersonal relationships rather than to accomplish any particular task or objective. Coffee-break gatherings, group lunches, and company bowling and softball teams are among the most common informal groups in organizations. The communication skills necessary in informal groups are essentially interpersonal skills. It's only when an informal group assumes a task — becoming for the moment a formal group — that other skills are required.

Formal Groups

Formal groups are those that have a specific task or objective. People may belong to formal groups either because they share a common concern or because they are assigned to the group by their organizations. The most common formal groups in organizations are the following:

1. **Informational.** Staff meetings, conferences, and briefings are examples of informational groups. These groups are useful when the group members need the same information at the same time and when management wants to insure exposure to the information and provide opportunity for questions and discussion.
2. **Education and training.** Most large organizations have entire departments whose sole purpose is to discover what employees need to know and to arrange for education and training. These departments orient employees to new programs, correct educational deficiencies, and introduce new and pertinent information. Almost any class in any school is an example of an education and training small group. Organizational in-service seminars are another example.
3. **Problem-solving.** Any group with a particular task or a specific objective is a problem-solving group. Whether the group is a relatively informal *brainstorming* session or a formal discussion of budgetary problems, its main reason for being is to solve a particular problem. The problem may range from preliminary discussions, to planning, to the carrying out of decisions.

Group Roles

Degree of Formality

Group behavior differs from interpersonal behavior primarily in the degree of formality with which participants behave. Participants in interpersonal situations have greater freedom in satisfying personal needs than group participants do. Groups can, however, help their members satisfy personal needs. For example, groups give people a sense of belonging and importance. In groups people can contribute to the accomplishment of a goal without assuming the risk of an independent decision.

Participants in groups tend to assume certain stylized roles that help them to satisfy psychological needs. These behavior patterns can either contribute to solving the group's problem or block the solution. The key roles are as follows:

1. **Leadership.** Leadership may be either *ascribed* or *earned*. Ascribed leadership results from a person's position or status in the organization, whereas earned leadership occurs when an individual assumes the responsibility for facilitating communication and goal achievement.
2. **Task specialist.** Persons performing the task specialist role are goal-oriented; their chief concern is with the facts and nature of the problem.
3. **Human relations specialists.** Human relations specialists attempt to resolve conflicts by including participants who might otherwise be left out, offering compromises, supporting the ideas of others, and testing for consensus.
4. **Self-serving.** Any dysfunctional behavior — behavior that works to prevent the group from accomplishing its goal — is essentially self-serving. Refusing to cooperate by rejecting the ideas of other participants, withdrawing from the discussion, and attempting to monopolize the discussion are typical examples.

Although these role behaviors are easy to identify and observe, most people do not fit neatly into any one pattern. Under certain circumstances, the person who normally functions as a task specialist may well engage in self-serving behavior. For a group to function well, the individuals within it must agree on roles and task achievement. Leaders, task specialists, and human relations specialists all perform necessary functions. Of course the key roles as we have described them are obviously neater (and more academic) than behavior would ever be in a real situation, but group members should recognize that the psychological roles do exist and that to a certain extent they can be controlled.

Group Influence

Norms

All group settings include certain assumptions about the behavior of participants. These assumptions, norms, may be either *explicit* (verbalized rules and regulations) or *implicit* (unspoken but agreed upon).

In a group situation, each participant feels conflicting needs to conform to and to resist the group's norms. Because participants seek prestige, acceptance, and status within the group, the situation also produces competition and conflict.

These factors — conformity, resistance, competition, and conflict — interrelate in complex ways. We all tend to conform most closely to the norms of the groups that are most important to us; we risk deviation in groups that are less important. Competition and conflict between groups tend to favor greater conformity within each group, but intragroup conflict normally reduces conformity and productivity.

Competition and Conflict

A group in which the participants adhere strictly to the norms is said to be cohesive. Cohesive groups, which are generally more productive than noncohesive groups, are marked by a greater willingness to communicate, to accept the ideas of all participants, and to work toward specific goals. A certain degree of resistance, competition, and conflict can also be productive, however. A person who is willing to deviate from the group's norms may make suggestions and raise objections that would not occur to or be expressed by group conformists.

Cohesive Groups

Another important influence is the perceived power of certain group members. Group members with high status usually send and receive more messages than members with low status, but high-status members sometimes use their power to criticize and manipulate others rather than to achieve the group's objective. High-status members also have more freedom to establish and to deviate from group norms should they choose to do so.

GROUP DYNAMICS

Groups have two definite patterns of movement: a movement through the stages of a life cycle and a decision-making pattern. Despite variations from group to group, successful groups demonstrate similar progressions through phases of interaction and through the decision-making process.

Group Life Cycle

Just as interpersonal relationships have a particular life cycle, groups — especially problem-solving groups — also undergo cyclic changes. The stages in the group life cycle are initiation, exploration and clarification, conflict, resolution, and dissolution.

Initiation

Initiation, the first stage in the life cycle of any group, consists of introductions, statement of purpose, and efforts on the part of participants to get to know one another. The group members become familiar with the expectations of the others; some basic norms are established. The length of time required for this stage depends upon the complexity of the problem; the size of the group; and the personal, social, and organizational differences among members. If the members have had previous experiences with each other, this stage may be quite short.

Exploration and Clarification

Exploration and clarification is a testing stage in which members define the problem (if there is one), discover who the leaders are, and find out how the members will relate to one another. Norms and expectations are further defined. The group decides, for example, who will introduce what ideas in what way and how decisions will be made.

Conflict

Conflict may occur because of differences between ascribed leaders and those with earned leadership. Conflict can also arise over norms, the definition of the problem or task, or proposed solutions or actions.

Resolution

Resolution is the "performing" stage. Norms and leadership have been established, most conflicts have been resolved, and the group is ready to pursue the decision-making process.

Dissolution

Dissolution brings the group to a close. The group may lose its reason for being in a number of ways. With a problem-solving group, the successful completion of the task eliminates the need for the group. An informal group may dissolve when it no longer satisfies the needs of its individual members.

From the communication standpoint, one of the most interesting features of the way the life cycle influences group behavior is in the treatment of deviant behavior. In the early stages, participants who consistently deviate from group norms receive a great deal of communication, most of it persuasive — attempts to persuade the deviant member to conform. But the deviant member who continues to refuse to cooperate into the later stages will be cut off from further communication. If a group member cooperates and conforms in the early stages, however, he or she will have much greater freedom to deviate in the later stages.

Decision-Making Patterns

One of the most important steps for any task-oriented group is decision making, which occurs during the resolution stage of the group's life cycle. Group norms, group communication structure, and group leadership determine which of the following ways of reaching a decision will be used:

1. **Consensus.** Members reach agreement by discussion of alternatives.
2. **Majority vote.** Members vote, and the plan with more than half the votes is chosen.
3. **Plurality.** Members vote, but no plan receives a majority. The plan with the most votes is selected.
4. **Authority.** The leadership insists on a particular decision.
5. **Default.** The group avoids discussion and decision making.

The decision-making process itself has five steps. The group:

1. **Defines and analyzes the problem.** This process actually begins in the initiation stage, but not until the resolution stage do the group members reach agreement on a definition of the problem and isolate its probable causes.
2. **Establishes criteria for a solution.** These criteria may be formulated explicitly or implicitly, or they may be self-evident. How the group decides on the criteria will depend on the complexity of the task, the time available for reaching a decision, and the familiarity of the group members with each other and with the problem.
3. **Proposes possible solutions.** Group norms usually determine who submits what solutions in what way. Ways in which solutions arise may range from a brainstorming session, in which all members propose as many solutions as possible regardless of their immediate practicality, to considering only solutions proposed by the official leadership.
4. **Evaluates possible solutions.** Solutions are evaluated by measuring them against the criteria established in step 2 and weighing them against each other. New criteria may be established, and parts of two or more solutions may be combined to provide the best alternative. Although the final selection of a solution should be based on objective criteria, subjective criteria (such as who made the suggestion) frequently influence the decision.
5. **Plots a course of action.** The group decides how to put the proposed solution into action. The membership must usually assume responsibility for taking some kind of action. Responsibility may be assumed voluntarily or directed by the leader.

GROUP COMMUNICATION AND LEADERSHIP

Group characteristics and group dynamics influence the communication process indirectly, depending on the reason for the group's existence and the personalities of its members. Three factors which directly influence the communication process can be selected and controlled to achieve a good flow of communication:

1. Communication structures;
2. Communication climate; and
3. Group leadership.

Communication Structures

Centralized or Decentralized

Group communication structures may be centralized or decentralized; each structure or network is particularly well suited to solving certain kinds of problems. In centralized systems, the individual members have only limited access to the ideas and opinions of others; the communication flow is controlled by a leader. In some cases the group members are actually isolated from each other, and the leader controls a flow of written messages. More frequently, the leader succeeds in establishing group norms that encourage a centralized communication network. In decentralized structures, group members have full access to the ideas and opinions of other members.

Centralized communication structures are generally referred to as the *wheel*, the *chain*, and the *Y*. Decentralized structures are all based on variations of the circle. Figure 9-1 shows diagrams of these patterns.

Structures and Leadership

The differences between centralized and decentralized structures are important. In centralized networks, the person in the central position tends to become the leader regardless of other qualifications. Leadership in decentralized groups is usually assumed by those with the proper qualifications. Centralized structures waste less time in preliminary organization, and decisions are usually reached more quickly. Decentralized structures take longer to organize, but once organized, a decentralized group can work as efficiently as a group with a centralized network.

Less flexible than decentralized groups, centralized groups are best suited to solving simple problems. For simple problems, centralized structures generally produce faster responses with fewer errors. For complex problems, however, decentralized structures usually produce higher quality answers and produce them more quickly.

The communication structure also influences group morale. In centralized groups, only the central person or persons have consistently high morale. Because a group member's morale is directly related to how valuable that person feels, the farther from the central position a person is in the structure, the lower his or her morale. The morale of all

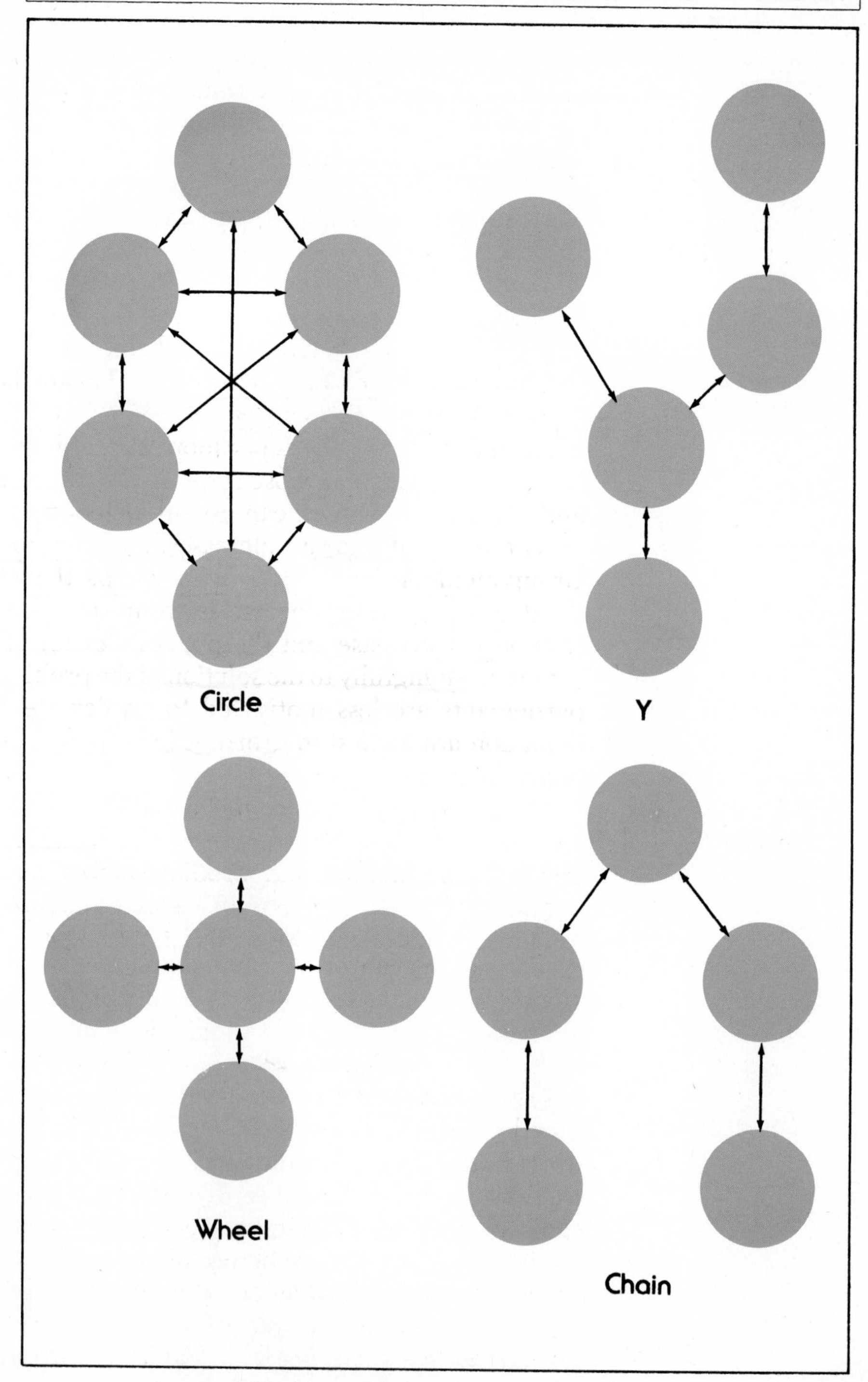

Figure 9-1. Communication structures.

members of a decentralized group tends to be about the same; it depends primarily on the nature and importance of the task.

Communication Climate

Open or Closed

The communication climate in a group situation is established in essentially the same way as it is in interpersonal communication situations. As a result we will simply remind you to review the differences between open and closed communication climates (p. 183), and we will briefly discuss motivation and participation.

Group size and diversity of membership are the two most important influences on motivation and participation. The nature and importance of the task also influence motivation, but those factors are usually beyond the control of those responsible for establishing a group. Size and diversity, however, can usually be controlled.

Group Size

As the size of a group increases, the group becomes less cohesive. Group members become less willing to participate in discussion and in the decision-making process. As group size increases, the possibilities for conflict increase and the possibilities for any individual to contribute meaningfully to the solution of the problem decrease; as a result participants are less motivated to participate. Motivation and participation are highest in groups of about five; both decline in groups larger than eight.

Group Diversity

The diversity of the group is another important influence. Groups composed of members who consider themselves equals exhibit increased participation and produce higher motivation than groups whose members perceive their status as unequals. Differences in age, intelligence, and expertise inhibit participation and group interaction.

Leadership

Ascribed or Earned

Leadership consists of facilitating group interaction, member participation, and completion of the task. As we stated earlier, leadership may be ascribed or earned. Ascribed leadership is inherent in a person's status or position, whereas earned leadership is functional. The question of leadership is usually the first problem a group considers, and until the members agree on a leader or style of leadership, the group cannot devote full attention to the task. However the selection process proceeds, leadership styles may vary from complete authoritarianism to complete permissiveness. Authoritarian or directive leadership exerts a high degree of control over other group members, whereas permissive or nondirective leadership encourages the full participation of the group membership, (see Figure 9-2).

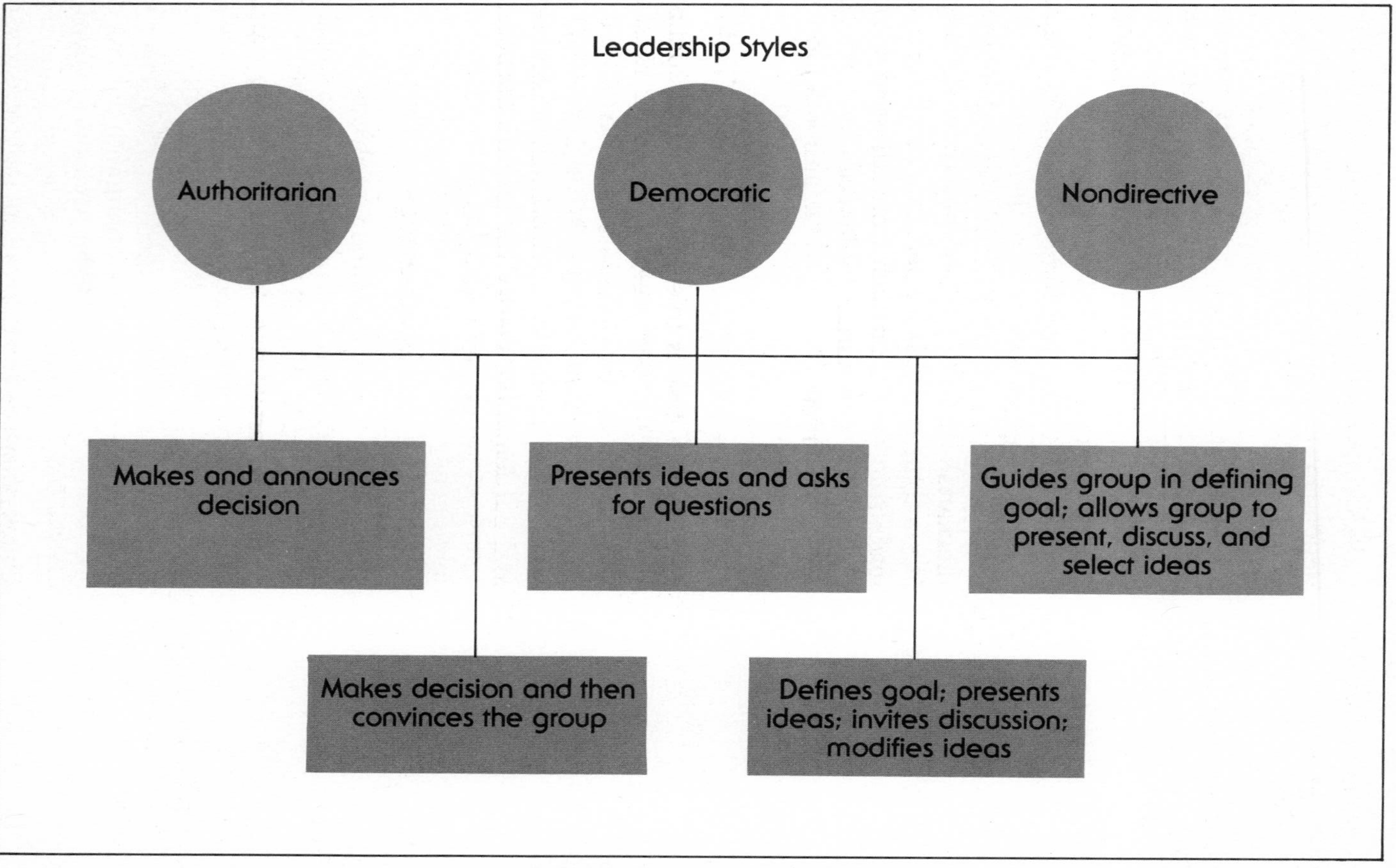

Figure 9-2. Leadership styles.

rather than to accomplish any particular task or objective; and formal groups are those that have a specific task or objective. The most common formal groups in organizations are informational, education and training, and problem-solving groups.

Groups give people a sense of belonging and importance. Group members adopt behavior patterns they think will lead to the satisfaction of needs. The key psychological roles are leadership, task specialist, human relations specialist, and self-serving.

Groups have two definite patterns of movement: a movement through the stages of a life cycle and a decision-making pattern. The five stages in the group life cycle are initiation, exploration and clarification, conflict, resolution, and dissolution.

When a group decision is called for, the leader has the responsibility of ensuring an environment favorable for group interaction and participation, clarifying the group's purpose, and providing the necessary planning and organization.

EXERCISES

1. What role do small groups play in organizations?
2. What are the differences between interpersonal communication and small group communication?
3. Explain the differences among primary, informal, and formal groups.
4. Identify and explain three objectives of formal groups.
5. Identify and explain four group roles.
6. Identify and explain the five stages in a group life cycle.
7. Explain the decision-making process and describe each of the five steps a group must go through to reach a decision.
8. What are the advantages of a centralized communication structure? of a decentralized structure?
9. How are communication structures, climate, and leadership interrelated?

SUGGESTED READINGS

Berkman, Harold W. *The Human Relations of Management.* Encino, CA: Dickenson, 1974.

Cronkhite, Gary. *Communication and Awareness.* Menlo Park, CA: Cummings, 1976.

Goldhaber, Gerald M. *Organizational Communication.* Dubuque, IA: W. C. Brown, 1974.

Hopper, Robert. *Human Message Systems*. New York: Harper & Row, 1976.

Huseman, Richard C., James M. Lahiff, and John D. Hatfield. *Interpersonal Communication in Organizations*. Boston: Holbrook, 1976.

Huseman, Richard C., Cal M. Logue, and Dwight L. Freshley. *Readings in Interpersonal and Organizational Communication*. 2d ed. Boston: Holbrook, 1974.

Koehler, Jerry W., Karl W. E. Anatol, and Ronald L. Applbaum. *Organizational Communication*. New York: Holt, Rinehart, and Winston, 1976.

Rogers, Everett M., and Rekha Agarwala-Rogers. *Communication in Organizations*. New York: The Free Press, 1976.

Sanford, Aubrey C., Gary T. Hunt, and Hyler J. Bracey. *Communication Behavior in Organizations*. Columbus, OH: Charles E. Merrill, 1976.

Schneider, Arnold E., William C. Donaghy, and Pamela Jane Newman. *Organizational Communication*. New York: McGraw-Hill, 1975.

10

FORMAL PRESENTATIONS

After you have read this chapter, you should be able to

1. **State the differences between a formal presentation and other kinds of oral communication.**
2. **State and explain the objectives of formal presentations.**
3. **Correctly analyze an audience for a presentation.**
4. **Organize material for an effective presentation.**
5. **Explain and use five special techniques for formal presentations.**

THE NATURE OF FORMAL PRESENTATIONS

A Formal Presentation Is a Fully Planned, Well-Organized, Extended Message

Formal presentations differ from other kinds of oral communication primarily because one person — the source — speaks for an extended time without receiving much oral feedback. In most other oral communication situations, the participants exchange a series of short messages until they reach an agreement of one sort or another. In a formal presentation, the source is expected to deliver a fully planned, well-organized, extended message on a topic usually announced in advance to the audience. Restricted oral feedback is a criterion of a formal presentation. Sometimes the medium used for the presentation — such as television — may make feedback virtually impossible. Other formal presentations may permit questions and answers during the presentation itself; even in these cases, however, feedback is restricted to help ensure the orderly presentation of ideas.

Degree of Formality

Planned presentation and restricted feedback are among the characteristics that make formal presentations formal. Remember that, as we stated in Chapter One, our concern is with communication for practical purposes rather than for entertainment. The serious intent of both sender and receivers, the distance maintained between the sender and the audience, and the specific time and place also contribute to the formality of any particular communication situation.

Most Formal: The Reading of a Paper

The degree of formality can vary greatly, however. The most formal kind of presentation, the reading of a paper, is rarely used in business. Academic scholars attending professional meetings, for example, *read* papers because the material is far too complex for the reader to risk deviating from the prepared text. To help ensure the accurate transfer of a complex message, the audience is often given copies of the entire text before the presentation. We are more concerned with the following common kinds of presentations, listed in order of decreasing formality.

Common Business Presentations

1. **Public speech or lecture.** Public presentations are prepared completely in advance and delivered with the aid of notes. Verbal feedback is restricted to the end of the presentation, if any is permitted at all.
2. **Sales presentation.** Sales presentations may be invited or uninvited, depending on whether the source has been specially asked to describe the product or service. In either case the source must prepare a wide variety of material in advance and select appropriate material for the situation as the presentation progresses. After the essential message is delivered, questions are encouraged.
3. **Education and training presentation.** Education and training presentations combine characteristics of the lecture and the discussion. The source must be fully prepared both to deliver a specific message and to deal with a wide range of questions about related subject matter. Verbal feedback is encouraged during and after the presentation, and sometimes even before it.
4. **Discussion sessions.** Because they permit the most interaction between the sender (or senders) and the audience, discussion sessions are the least formal of formal presentations. Time, place, and topic are still determined in advance, however; and the senders must prepare an organized message.

From your own experience with presentations of each of these types, you can probably verify that as the degree of formality decreases, the responsibility of the source decreases and the responsibility of the audience increases.

Presentation Objectives

Formal presentations may be given to inform or to persuade. The sender of the message is either trying to inform the audience or to persuade the audience to change an attitude, belief, or behavior. The organization of the message reflects its objective in the ways we've already discussed; but because the message is delivered orally, the sender must take unusual care to help the audience receive and understand the message. Preparation is the key to success.

PREPARATION

No one can give an effective formal presentation without extensive preparation. To give a successful presentation, you must know your subject, analyze your audience, and get your notes and nerves ready for your delivery.

The Subject

Informational and Persuasive Presentations

You can't give a presentation if you don't know what you're talking about. Yet for some reason, many speakers attempt to lecture an audience without doing the research necessary to guarantee current, accurate information. An informational presentation is the oral equivalent of a written report. Your information should be — *must* be — accurate, reliable, and objective. And you must have enough of it to continue presenting specific information throughout the time you've been allotted. Sales and other persuasive presentations also require complete, accurate knowledge about the product, service, or concept involved.

The Audience

A Select Group

The audience for a formal presentation is invariably a select group. Formal presentations are always announced in advance, so the audience arrives with certain expectations. These expectations depend primarily on whether attendance is required and on the nature of the subject. The degree of interest the audience has in the subject may vary from intense, enthusiastic interest to complete apathy. The audience may know a great deal — or nothing at all — about the topic. The audience may have strong current beliefs about the topic, or it may have a neutral attitude.

Because these factors are important in understanding and communicating with the audience, a speaker should do everything possible to determine the audience's interest in and current beliefs about the topic. Although the presentation must usually go on even if the audience is openly hostile, holding opinions diametrically opposed to those of the speaker, a speaker should know what reception to expect from the audience and be prepared to take advantage of it — or deal with it.

Notes

Of the kinds of formal presentations mentioned previously, only the sales presentation does not require the use of notes. To be effective, a sales presentation almost always must be prepared thoroughly in advance. The speaker may, of course, refer to notes for specific details, but the audience will expect the speaker to know about the product or service and about its competition. Formal presentations of the other types require some kind of notes so that the speaker can bring the results of planning to the presentation.

Bring the Planning to the Presentation

In Chapter Seven we said that at its simplest level, planning means thinking before you speak. Formal presentations require a written record of the research and thinking you do in advance because without notes or memorization you will not be able to remember everything.

People who do a lot of public speaking develop their own personal techniques for taking and using notes; as you gain speaking experience, you will undoubtedly develop your own technique. We suggest that you begin developing a comfortable style based on one of the two most widely used formats: 3″ x 5″ cards or 8½″ x 11″ sheets of paper.

Advantages of 3″ × 5″ Cards

Many speakers prefer to keep their notes on 3″x 5″ cards, which can be held easily and unobtrusively in the palm of the hand. Thus the speaker is free to move about in a natural manner while talking. The disadvantage of cards is that each one holds only a small amount of information, so a complex subject may require a large stack of cards.

Advantages of 8½″ × 11″ Sheets

Other speakers prefer to type their notes on regular 8½″ x 11″ sheets of paper. Because audiences expect speakers to use some notes, the visibility of the sheets need not be distracting. One disadvantage of such typed notes is that inexperienced speakers tend to rely too heavily on them, *reading* rather than *presenting* the material. Because of this heavy reliance on notes, these speakers remain fixed behind a lectern or podium, creating unnecessary distance between speaker and audience.

If you choose to keep your notes on 8½″ x 11″ sheets of paper, we recommend that you emphasize the outline rather than the specifics of your presentation. If you prepare well enough that you are not tempted to read, you can move about naturally, using your notes to keep you organized and to aid your memory with specific details that will make your presentation interesting and convincing.

Nerves

One of the greatest difficulties about making a formal presentation is dealing with your own nerves. Getting up in front of an audience the first few times is unpleasant for some, difficult for most, and nearly impossible for a few others. Stage fright can be very real. If you had a dollar for every word that has been written about the causes and cures of stage fright, you could retire right now. Yet with everything that's been written, there are only two guaranteed cures for stage fright: preparation and practice.

Stage Fright

PREPARATION: Know your material and what you intend to do with it forwards and backwards, inside and out. But, except for short sales presentations, don't attempt to memorize an entire speech. Even if your memory works perfectly, your presentation will be stilted and awkward. And you also risk having your memory fail. When that happens, you're left with nothing to say and nowhere to go. Prepare good notes; it's safer.

PRACTICE: The first presentation is the hardest; each subsequent time will get a bit easier. But regardless of how many presentations you give, you'll always have to practice. For your first presentation, practice is especially important. Try practicing your speech in front of a mirror. Pronouncing the words clearly will help you develop a smooth delivery. When you're out walking, read your notes aloud. Throughout the day and before going to bed at night, picture yourself in front of your audience. Use your imagination to picture yourself as a successful speaker, and you'll be the successful speaker you want to be.

In addition to these guaranteed cures, here are a few points that may help you deal with stage fright while you're preparing and practicing:

Focus on What You Know

1. You were asked to make your presentation because you know something about the subject that the audience does not. Focus on that aspect of the subject; give the audience something that will benefit them.

Think of Your Audience, Not Yourself

2. Your subject and your audience are more important than you are. Think about your audience and your subject rather than about yourself.

Nobody's Perfect

3. No presentation is perfect. You're bound to make a mistake or two — everyone does. Keep going forward rather than looking back.

Somebody Will Like You

4. You can't please all the people all the time. No matter how well you actually do, somebody in the audience will think you're wonderful, and somebody will think you're awful. Don't let the one who thinks you're wonderful blind you to your mistakes or let the one who thinks you're awful undermine your confidence.

MESSAGE ORGANIZATION

Help Your Audience Listen

Because we've already discussed general patterns of message organization, we'll concentrate here on the few things you must do in a formal oral presentation that aren't so vital in other forms of communication. When giving a formal presentation, remember that listening is difficult. Even when your audience has good intentions, they will find it easier to think about last night's dinner or Paris in the spring than to concentrate on your message. As a speaker, you must make listening as easy and as pleasant for your audience as possible. Message organization and clarity will help you most in holding the audience's attention, and to make them work you'll need to make your pattern of organization clear from the beginning.

Opening

We've said already that the beginning and the end of your message are the places of natural emphasis. The opening is especially critical in a formal presentation because the way you handle your opening will usually determine the audience's attitude toward you and your material. How might you begin?

1. **With a joke.** If you are good with jokes *and* you have a joke that makes an appropriate point *and* you're completely certain that no one in your audience has heard it before, a joke can be an effective icebreaker. If you can't satisfy all three criteria, avoid jokes. Your audience wants to obtain ideas and useful information, not to be entertained.
2. **With a story.** Human interest stories usually work better than jokes *if* they make an appropriate point and if that point is absolutely clear to the audience. Avoid telling your life story, however.
3. **With background information.** Merely introductory material is a waste of time. Explanations of all sorts are not interesting, and

background information is essentially explanation. If background information must be presented, interweave it with something of more interest to your audience.

4. **With a preview.** Give the audience a quick look at the main points of your presentation.
5. **With a benefit.** Tell the members of your audience how they will benefit from your presentation. Explain what information they will get from it and how they can use the information.
6. **With a good-will statement.** Express appreciation for being invited to speak and make reference to the importance of the occasion.

The first three items in this list work sometimes; the last three work all the time.

Body

Explicit Transitions

The body of your presentation consists of the facts, figures, and principles you wish to convey. Because your organizational pattern must be clear to your audience, you must use explicit transitions from one point to the next. Tell your audience how each part contributes to the whole, and how the whole is equal to the sum of the parts. From time to time refer to your purpose, showing how what you've already said and what you're about to say contribute to your overall purpose. Transitions that appear artificial in written messages are beneficial and desirable in oral presentations. You don't need to be subtle; be straightforward and say, "Now that we've seen how *X* influences *Y*, let's briefly consider how *X* influences Z."

Present Both Sides

Whenever you have resistance to overcome, or when you wish to persuade your audience to change opinions or actions, you must build your case slowly and carefully. If there are two sides to your subject, present both of them. Your audience will become aware of the other opinion sooner or later, and the fact that you neglected to mention the other side of the story will work against you.

Closing

End with a Bang

Because it is a natural point of emphasis and because it is the last impression your audience will have of you, the closing of your presentation deserves special attention. End with a bang rather than a whimper, a flourish rather than a fade-out.

1. **Don't quit before you're finished.** Continue to speak clearly, distinctly, and forcefully until the end of your very last word.

Don't let your voice fade. Don't act tired; look alert.

2. **Summarize.** Review your main points for your audience. Emphasize the benefits of doing what you've suggested, or explain why knowing about your subject will be useful.
3. **Invite questions.** If the audience has questions, answer them. When you're finished with the questions, or if there aren't any, add a brief reminder of your main point as a definite conclusion.
4. **Specify any action.** If you want your audience to act, ask for that action. Explain exactly what you want your audience to do and how you want them to do it. Make the action sound easy. Attempt to get some kind of immediate commitment from them — signing a petition, leaving names and phone numbers, or making a public statement.
5. **Be positive and forward looking.** If you end your message on a negative note, your audience will associate you with that rather than with positive elements which may have preceded it. No matter how gloomy your topic happens to be, find some hope for the future and focus on it as you conclude your presentation.
6. **Conclude when you say you will.** Your ending should be definite and emphatic: restate your main point, specify an action, and quit!

SPECIAL TECHNIQUES

When a formal presentation must include complex information, the oral message frequently needs physical communication aids to help the audience. The best and most common communication aids are boards and charts, projectors, handouts, models, and audience participation. You should remember, however, that these special techniques are only aids; they cannot substitute for a full oral presentation of the material. Prepare your complete presentation first, and then review it to see whether a special technique might clarify your material. Do you need to present a lot of statistics? Your audience won't remember a column of figures if you just read it. Do you need to clarify construction problems at an awkward building site? A visual supplement would be a great help in letting your audience "see" exactly what the problems are.

Visual Aids

Boards and Charts

The Chalkboard

The chalkboard is an old, familiar teaching device. It is such a standard communication aid that almost any place you might give an oral presentation will have a permanent or portable chalkboard available. The main advantage of the chalkboard is that it is inexpensive to use. It is a time-consuming device, however, because messages must continually be written and erased. If you have just one set of figures or concepts that will remain important throughout your presentation, you can prepare a chalkboard supplement in advance and refer to it at appropriate points in your presentation. When using the chalkboard, remember to do the following:

1. Write legibly. Make sure that everyone in the room can read the board.
2. Keep the message simple. Too much information clutters the board and confuses the audience.
3. Don't stand in the way. Make sure that the audience can see what you've written. Use a pointer to indicate appropriate parts of the message.
4. Keep the board clean. Don't clutter the board with several separate messages; it should present a single, unified message.
5. Erase the board when you're finished.

The chalkboard is most useful for spontaneous illustration of particular points your audience has questions about. When you can prepare your aids in advance, other aids are usually superior to the chalkboard.

Flip Charts

Flip charts consist of a pad of paper (usually 28″ x 34″) mounted on an easel. Like the chalkboard, the flip chart is inexpensive and can be used spontaneously. The main advantage of a flip chart is that it requires no erasing. You simply flip the used page over; if you need it again, you can flip it right back. You can also use colors much more effectively on the flip chart than on the chalkboard. The main disadvantage of flip charts is that their small size makes them inappropriate for all but the smallest conference rooms.

Display Boards

Felt or magnetic display boards are useful for displaying short messages that will remain constant throughout a presentation. They are most widely used for sales presentations to small audiences. Their main disadvantage is that they are not flexible. Display materials for these boards should be prepared in advance by someone with graphic skills so that full advantage can be taken of color, graphs, photographs, and other nonverbal aspects of communication.

Charts

Charts can display almost anything that can be put on paper. Charts are still used for some presentations when graphs, sales figures, or other supplements must be included in a presentation. In most companies, however, overhead projectors are replacing charts, display boards, and flip charts.

Models

We said in Chapter One that a model is a symbolic representation. Some presentations require models to illustrate the real thing. In fact, some presentations may require the real thing (a new-car sales presentation, for example). The use of models in presentations is largely limited to special applications familiar to those who need them — primarily certain areas of advertising, sales, architecture, and engineering.

Audience Participation

Although it's not a mechanical device as the foregoing communication aids are, audience participation serves the same functions as the other special techniques: it keeps the attention of the audience focused on your presentation and helps ensure the successful transfer of meaning. Even when your situation is very formal and feedback is severely restricted, you can keep your audience involved by continually giving them something "new" to think about.

1. Use the overhead projector and handout material to break up the "sameness" of an oral presentation. A straight lecture is hard on both speaker and audience.
2. As the speaker, you should control the audience's attention. Change the pace of your presentation from time to time to permit your audience to relax for a minute. Make the members of your audience focus their attention when you most want it focused — but give them an opportunity to relax their attention from time to time, or they will be relaxing when you want and need their full attention.
3. Ask real and rhetorical questions to force the audience to summarize the material you've just presented or anticipate the material you're about to present.

PREPARE FOR NEXT TIME

Obtain Feedback

Naturally you'll want to do a better job each time you make a formal presentation, so you should take steps to ensure that you obtain the feedback you'll need to improve.

Formal Reviews

Most formal presentations require some kind of formal-feedback system. Many public speeches and lectures, for example, are reviewed by newspapers. Sales presentations are evaluated by their success — did the audience buy.

Evaluation Sheets

Whenever formal feedback is not built into the context of your presentation, you should consider preparing an evaluation sheet, distributed as a handout, for your audience to complete. Such sheets are most frequently used to help those giving education and training presentations. Figure 10-1 illustrates an evaluation sheet used for a typical formal presentation, and Figure 10-2 illustrates an evaluation sheet used for a communication seminar.

SUMMARY

Formal presentations differ from other kinds of oral communication primarily because one person speaks for an extended time without receiving much oral feedback. The planned presentation and the restricted feedback are among the characteristics that make formal presentations formal.

No one can give an effective formal presentation without extensive preparation. To give a successful presentation, you must know your subject, analyze your audience, and get your notes and nerves ready for your delivery.

As a speaker, you must make listening as easy and as pleasant for your audience as possible. Message organization and clarity will help you most in holding the audience's attention; and to make them work, you'll need to make your pattern of organization clear from the beginning.

When a formal presentation must include complex information, the oral message frequently needs physical communication aids to help the audience. The best and most common communication aids are boards and charts, projectors, handouts, models, and audience participation.

EXERCISES

1. What are the differences between formal presentations and other kinds of oral communication?
2. Name and explain four kinds of formal presentations.
3. Name six ways to begin a formal presentation. What are the advantages and disadvantages of each?
4. What six factors does an effective closing include?
5. What physical or mechanical aids would you prefer to use for a presentation? Why?
6. Plan and deliver a formal presentation on a subject of your choice. Your presentation should be about 10 minutes long and

FORMAL PRESENTATION EVALUATION FORM

	Poor	Fair	Good	Very Good	Excellent
1. CONTENT					
Clear Transitions					
Definite Conclusions					
Explicit Facts and Opinions					
Interesting Opening					
Good Organization					
2. NONVERBAL SKILLS					
Appearance					
Eye Contact					
Gestures					
Posture					
3. GRAPHIC AIDS					
Appearance					
Coordination					
Readability					
Relevance					
4. VOICE					
Enunciation					
Modulation					
Paralanguage					
Projection					

Figure 10-1. Evaluation sheet for formal presentations.

SEMINAR EVALUATION

1. Do you think that we should repeat this seminar for others?
   ☐ Yes ☐ No

2. If yes, please indicate your topic preference in the appropriate column:

TOPIC	MORE	LESS
Nature of Communication	☐	☐
Writing Skills	☐	☐
Letters	☐	☐
Reports	☐	☐
Reading and Listening	☐	☐
Nonverbal Communication	☐	☐
Oral Communication	☐	☐
Interpersonal Communication	☐	☐
Small Groups	☐	☐
Formal Presentations	☐	☐
Organizational Communication	☐	☐
Job Application	☐	☐

3. What other topics would you like to see included?

____

4. How would you rate the instructors?

	Poor	Fair	Good	Very Good	Excellent
Knowledge of Subject	☐	☐	☐	☐	☐
Success in Stimulating Interest	☐	☐	☐	☐	☐
Clarity of Presentation	☐	☐	☐	☐	☐
Encouragement of Audience Participation	☐	☐	☐	☐	☐
Overall Effectiveness	☐	☐	☐	☐	☐

5. What did you like most about this seminar?

6. What improvements would you suggest?

7. Additional Comments:

____

____

____

Figure 10-2. Evaluation sheet for communication seminars.

should use *at least* two special techniques. Prepare an evaluation sheet and have your audience use it in rating your presentation.

SUGGESTED READINGS

Anastasi, Thomas E., Jr. *Communicating for Results.* Menlo Park, CA: Cummings, 1972.

Cronkhite, Gary. *Communication and Awareness.* Menlo Park, CA: Cummings, 1976.

Goldhaber, Gerald M. *Organizational Communication.* Dubuque, IA: W. C. Brown, 1974.

Himstreet, William C., and Wayne Murlin Baty. *Business Communications.* 5th ed. Belmont, CA: Wadsworth, 1977.

Hopper, Robert. *Human Message Systems.* New York: Harper & Row, 1976.

Huseman, Richard C., James M. Lahiff, and John D. Hatfield. *Interpersonal Communication in Organizations.* Boston: Holbrook, 1976.

Schneider, Arnold E., William C. Donaghy, and Pamela Jane Newman. *Organizational Communication.* New York: McGraw-Hill, 1975.

11 ORGANIZATIONAL COMMUNICATION

After you have read this chapter, you should be able to

1. **Explain the functions of communication within an organization.**
2. **Explain the role of communication in achieving organizational objectives.**
3. **Identify and explain formal and informal communication networks.**
4. **Explain the three broad objectives of organizational communication programs.**
5. **Coordinate general communication objectives with the specific objectives presented in Chapters One through Ten.**

THE ROLE OF ORGANIZATIONAL COMMUNICATION

In the foregoing chapters we have examined specific communication activities and discussed the ways you can use them to achieve certain specific, limited objectives. In this chapter we will discuss the ways in which these elements work together to coordinate human activity in organizations. An organization is a group of people working together to achieve a common goal. Communication structures human relationships in such a way that a group of people can work together to achieve a goal. Thus communication makes organizational life possible.

Definition: Organization

Communication Coordinates

COMMUNICATION FLOW

Even when management fully recognizes the importance of communication, the many variables in the communication process make it difficult to study and improve communication systems. Consider a common and fairly simple example of an organizational activity: the introduction of a new product. What kinds of communication flow are required at each step?

1. **The idea.** Whose idea is it? Is the product completely new or only new to the company? Does a need for the product exist, or will the company need to advertise to create a need?

2. **Research and development.** How expensive is the product? Can it meet the company's quality requirements? How long will it take to develop the product? Must the idea be changed to meet certain production requirements?
3. **Production.** Does everyone involved in production of the new product understand any new job duties? Who is responsible for quality control? Does the finished product do what it is supposed to do?
4. **Marketing.** Who wants the product? Why should the public buy it?
5. **Evaluation.** Will you be able to make a profit? Should you continue producing the product? Can you make any improvements in it? Can it be made for less? What should you tell the stockholders?

Intra- and Extra-Company Communication

A tremendous amount of intracompany communication is obviously required at each of the five steps, including proposals, interpersonal and small group discussions, formal presentations, and reports. Extracompany communication is also required to gather information about the manufacture and sales of related products, to determine the need for and interest in the product, to secure raw materials, to hire any new employees manufacturing may require, to patent key elements, to advertise the product, and to handle customers' questions and complaints.

Communication Systems Make Long-Range Goals Possible

Because organizational communication involves so many variables, we must isolate specific communication objectives before we can study systems designed to achieve those objectives. In Chapters Two through Ten we examined communication channels, the size and formality of the communication systems involved, and the specific purposes of — and audiences for — individual messages. Basically, each of those chapters is a prescription for solving a particular kind of short-range problem. However, you should also recognize how communication systems perform the general coordinating role that enables the organization to set and reach long-range goals. We have, for example, given you some practical advice on how to handle small group discussions, but we haven't said very much about why you should have small group discussions or what subjects might be appropriate for such discussions.

System Objectives

Task Objectives

In organizations, communication functions primarily to coordinate activities to achieve task, maintenance, and human objectives. Task objectives are those aimed toward achieving specific, one-time goals. The introduction of a new product is an example. The objective is set and the organization mobilizes to achieve that objective. The communication required for task objectives is the easiest to understand and control: given a specific objective, the communicators can take a practical approach to meeting it.

Maintenance Objectives

Maintenance objectives contribute to the long-range well-being of the organization. Communication to meet maintenance goals sets policies or regulates behavior. In the case of the introduction of a new product, maintenance objectives would include ensuring full use of existing resources, market research, and financial planning. Because maintenance objectives are not so clear-cut as task objectives, designing communication to achieve maintenance objectives can be difficult.

Human Objectives

Human objectives are those that help a company maintain high morale. Keeping employees informed, rewarding good efforts, and encouraging participatory management — typified by nondirective leadership — are examples. Although we know that certain communication factors must be present to achieve high morale, designing communication procedures to meet human objectives involves still more variables than maintenance communications.

What accounts for the differences between task objectives and the other two kinds? Task objectives can be accomplished by a limited number of messages. Maintenance and human objectives are accomplished primarily by an *attitude* toward communication rather than by any single message. Well-defined, specific goals are easier to achieve than abstract, general goals. We all have a reasonably good concept of what constitutes high morale, but it's still an abstract objective that cannot be accomplished by any specific message.

Attitude toward Communication

Formal Communication Networks

Organizational Hierarchy

As we pointed out in Chapter Nine, no small group can begin to achieve its task objectives until the internal matter of leadership is resolved. This is also true of larger groups. All organizations have some kind of official hierarchy to provide the necessary leadership. The official hierarchy of the organization, as represented by the company's organization chart, establishes a formal communication network for the organization: superiors tell subordinates what to do, subordinates report to superiors about what they have done, and departments ask one another for specialized help. Formal communication flows vertically downward and upward — and horizontally.

The chart in Figure 11-1 illustrates a typical organizational structure.

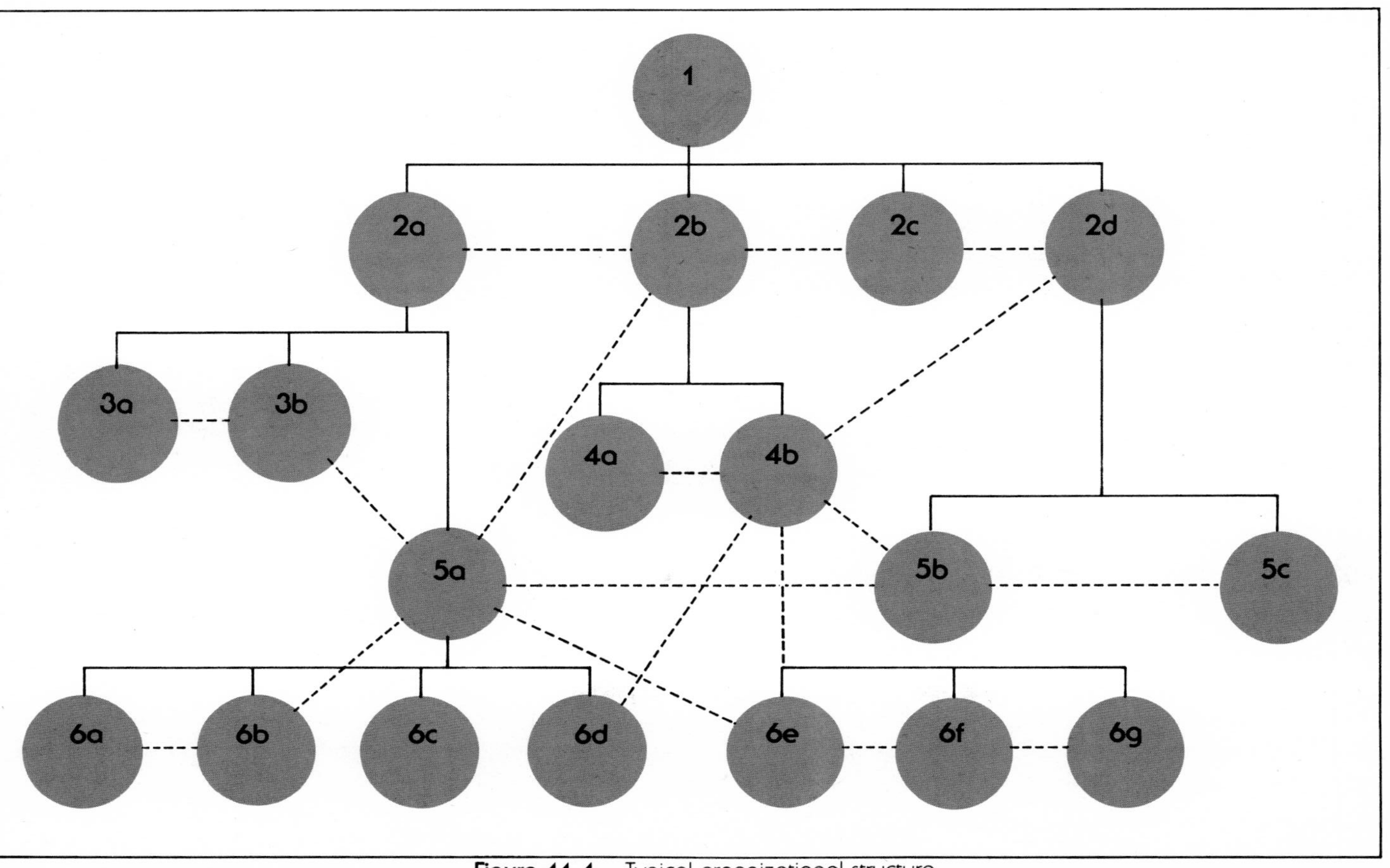

Figure 11-1. Typical organizational structure.

The number 1 indicates the person in charge, and numbers 2 through 6 indicate relative levels of organizational status. The solid lines indicate officially sanctioned lines of communication; the dotted lines represent unofficial communication networks. Note that some organizational relationships require both official and unofficial lines of communication.

Downward Communication Established Climate

Downward communication includes all official messages that go from superiors to subordinates in the organization. Downward communication establishes the communication climate in the organization and determines the quantity and quality of upward communication. Because downward communication is so important in the overall success of the organization, management must be especially careful to recognize and overcome the barriers caused by differences in attitude and perception inherent in communicating down the chain of command. Some examples of downward communication are the following:

Job description: lists and definitions of duties and responsibilities.

Job instructions: how to do it, what not to do, whom to call.

Job indoctrination: explanations of the relationship between the job and organizational goals, motivation for specific tasks.

Job performance: feedback about how well a person is doing in general or has done with a particular task.

To be successful, downward communication must:

1. **Demonstrate the "you-attitude."** Like all other communication, downward communication must take account of the receivers' values, beliefs, and problems. The fact that management wants something done may not be reason enough for an employee to do it. Management should also consider the timing of messages from the receivers' point of view because poor timing often suggests the presence of a hidden meaning.
2. **Be accurate.** Any communication that is less than truthful undermines management's credibility as an information source. Like the boy of the folk tale, a company can cry "wolf" only so often and expect a response.
3. **Be definite.** The receivers must understand the message in its context. They must understand not only their action but also the way that action fits into the company's operation as a whole.
4. **Take selective perception into account.** The farther a message has to travel, the greater the chance that it will be altered. Written messages supplemented by face-to-face discussions

provide the greatest accuracy of transmission.

5. **Provide for feedback.** Management frequently relies too heavily on written directives and other formal forms for downward communication. Manuals, newsletters, and public address systems are best when supplemented by face-to-face discussions of problems and procedures.
6. **Avoid message overload.** Ditto machines and, more recently, copiers have made it possible for companies to send countless messages at a cost that seems relatively low. But just as you can't emphasize everything in a letter, you can't emphasize all messages equally. Employees who receive too many messages tend to pay little attention to any of them. Save written communication for important messages.

Upward Communication

Upward communication includes all messages that flow from subordinates to superiors. Good communication must start at the top and proceed down; inadequate upward communication results from management's failure to provide good downward communication. Superiors who neglect downward communication invite subordinates to conceal or distort information pertinent to the well being of the company. The functions of upward communication are to accomplish the following:

1. **Keep management informed** in general, and in particular to provide management with the information required to make decisions about products, policies, and employees.
2. **Provide employees with the opportunity to submit ideas** and to participate in the decision-making process. This increases their willingness to accept decisions and downward communication.
3. **Provide management with feedback** about the effectiveness of downward communication.

Counseling, grievance systems, suggestion boxes, open-door policies, social gatherings, and staff meetings are all communication situations that encourage upward communication. All are primarily the responsibility of management. For management to obtain the accurate, reliable, and objective information it needs, a communication climate that encourages upward flow is essential. Successful upward communication requires the following:

Face-to-Face Communication

1. Frequent face-to-face contact between superiors and subordinates. Superiors who isolate themselves from their subordinates risk cutting off the flow of communication.

Recognition

2. Recognition of and rewards for accomplishment. An employee who recognizes a problem and finds a solution deserves rapid

recognition and full credit. The employee should not have to battle company red tape because someone higher in the corporate structure wants to appear more knowledgeable than the employee who originated the idea.

Ability to Listen

3. The ability to listen. Managers must take the time to listen, even to criticism. They must assume that even the least fair criticism contains a small truth and should encourage subordinates to share ideas, problems, and criticisms. Superiors must recognize that subordinates may partially withhold bad news and exaggerate good news, especially when a superior is known to be judgmental.

Appreciation of Expertise

4. The ability to treat upward communication without condescension. Employees appreciate having management recognize special, individual areas of expertise. For example, the president of an electronics company should pay close attention if a technician says that a certain capacitor in the power supply of a new solid state device won't work, even if the electronic engineers who designed the device say it will.

Follow-through

5. Action. Superiors must make good on promises made to subordinates. When a complaint cannot be resolved or an idea cannot be accepted, the employee involved deserves a reasonably full and honest explanation. Problems that can be solved should be acted on immediately.

Horizontal Communication

Horizontal communication is the flow of messages among people of equal status in the organizational hierarchy. Such messages can be exchanged for purposes of cooperation or conflict. Horizontal communication has three formal functions:

1. **Coordination.** Because organizational units must coordinate activities and share information about joint projects, regular meetings of organizational equals are necessary.
2. **Problem solving.** When the same problem faces a group of organizational equals, horizontal communication helps in discovering a solution.
3. **Conflict resolution.** When departments or organizational equals have a conflict, horizontal communication increases mutual trust and discourages rivalry between departments or groups.

Horizontal communication tends to be faster, more accurate, and less threatening than vertical communication. Organizations discourage much horizontal communication, however, because excessive horizontal communication disrupts the organizational hierarchy and results in message overload. Most organizations prefer that messages pass up the chain of command from the sender until a common superior is informed, and then back down the chain until the receiver is finally informed (see Figure 11-2).

This kind of communication structure helps *A* retain authority. If we consider this part of the organization as a small group, then the communication pattern in Figure 11-2 is a chain — the kind of pattern that is good for *A's* morale, but not very good for the morale of either S or *R*. If S and *R* need to communicate frequently, however, they will bypass the formal system and establish their own informal communication network.

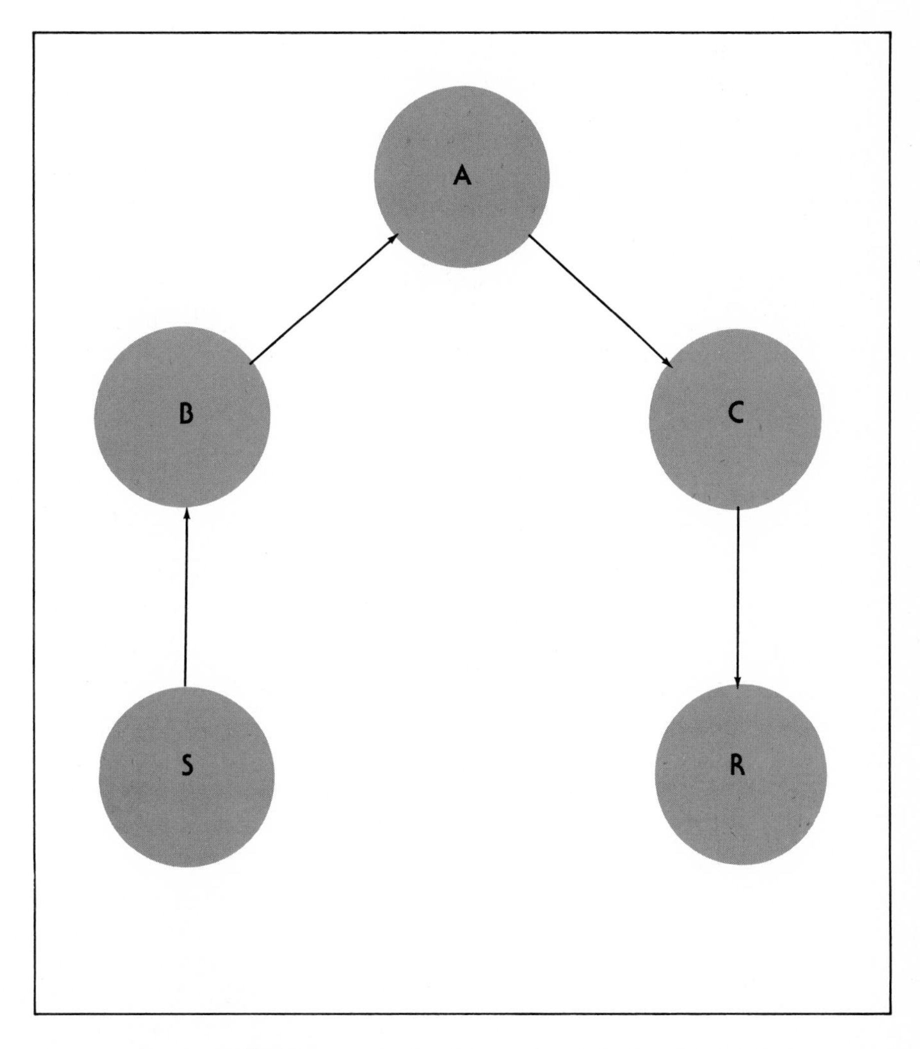

Figure 11-2. Communication flow and organizational heirarchy.

Informal Communication Networks

Even though organizations discourage horizontal communication, more communication flows horizontally than vertically. Where formal horizontal networks do not exist, employees establish an informal network, usually called the "grapevine," to provide rapid and flexible communication. Formal and informal networks are difficult to distinguish on the basis of message content. Vertical communication is formal because it's frequently written, almost always "official," and carefully controlled. Horizontal communication, official or unofficial, is almost always oral, and it is not always carefully controlled.

Grapevine

The grapevine develops out of need and the accident of special relationships. People who must talk to each other, talk to each other. People who share offices or have adjacent offices talk to each other. Some informal communication complements and substitutes for communication that might otherwise use slower, formal channels, but the informal communication system also carries a great deal of extra-organizational information.

The advantages of the grapevine are its speed and — even considering rumors — its relative accuracy. The informal communication network transmits messages by *clusters:* one person passes the message to many receivers in a short time. Not everyone receiving the information passes it on, but enough people do to make transmission quite rapid. Of course, each time the message is transmitted from a sender to a receiver, part of it is lost or distorted. Nevertheless the grapevine is a surprisingly accurate medium for noncontroversial organizational information.

Cluster Transmission

The grapevine has earned a bad reputation because a rumor — information consisting mainly of inferences based on few facts — will spread just as rapidly through the informal network as any other message. Also, because the accuracy of the grapevine is well known to those who use it, rumors are readily accepted as valid. Controversial organizational information — or any information that is important, but about which there has been little official communication — becomes the subject of speculation and rumor.

Because the grapevine is a permanent fact of organizational life, management should make use of its advantages and establish procedures to control its disadvantages. If the persons who serve as *liaisons* by transmitting information from cluster to cluster (see 5a and 4b in Figure 11-1 on page 233) can be identified, management can use the grapevine to accomplish the following:

1. Disseminate information that should not be sent over official channels.

2. Collect critical feedback that is not available through official channels.
3. Provide rapid clarification for official messages that haven't been well received or understood.

Rumor Control

Most large organizations would do well to establish an official rumor-control center to deal with the grapevine's only real disadvantage. Unless some official way of controlling rumors is established, rumors will spread unchecked to damage morale and undermine the effectiveness of the official communication network. To ensure the success of a rumor-control center, management must provide for anonymous reporting of rumors (usually by telephone) and for prompt, accurate replies. The rumor-control center must establish and maintain high source credibility.

SYSTEM GOALS

In addition to the specific objectives of individual messages and of message systems, organizations must achieve three general objectives if communication is to flow smoothly and efficiently. The entire effort of organizational communication should be directed toward establishing the following:

1. an open communication climate;
2. accurate information; and
3. competition rather than conflict.

Open Climate

Management's Responsibility

We've already discussed the major attributes of open and closed communication climates in dealing with small groups in Chapter Nine. In general, the same factors that influence the communication climate in a small group also influence the climate for the larger organization . It is management's responsibility to encourage disclosure and feedback. All employees in the organization should feel that they can express their observations and criticisms both vertically and horizontally.

In an open communication climate, employees believe that:

1. They will receive credit for their ideas and contributions.
2. Their complaints will be taken seriously, investigated, and either resolved or explained in a satisfactory manner.
3. Those higher in the organizational hierarchy are not manipulating communication flow to control them.
4. Those higher in the organizational hierarchy value them as human beings whose needs and aspirations go beyond their organizational function.

Better Coordination

An organization benefits from an open communication climate in a variety of ways. The open climate improves morale and increases employee participation in the achievement of organizational goals. It also enables superiors to discover the personal goals of subordinates; thus job assignments can be coordinated to insure maximum contribution to both personal and organizational goals.

Increased Loyalty and Efficiency

An open climate builds employee loyalty to the company; this not only increases organizational efficiency but also leads to employee efforts to establish goodwill for the organization. Employees who dislike the company can counteract quite a few advertising dollars. Finally, a company with an open climate can rely on employees to treat confidential information as confidential. In a closed communication climate, where management considers much information confidential, employees cannot distinguish what is legitimately confidential from what isn't. Under such circumstances, what is known (as well as all sorts of speculation) is widely transmitted, both inside and outside the company.

Accurate Information

One result of an open communication climate is that both vertical and horizontal information tend to be more accurate. In a nonthreatening atmosphere of trust, people tell the truth. If employees believe that management is manipulating them, they engage in countermanipulation. This can result in managers making decisions on the basis of faulty information. The only way management can ensure accurate upward communication is by providing accurate downward information and rewarding accurate upward communication, even when it involves criticism.

Reward Honest Criticism

Rewarding honest criticism is not always easy, because honest criticism is the kind that hurts the most and thus makes any of us more defensive. Even so, if management does not encourage and reward honest criticism, its best source of corrective feedback is effectively cut off. When management only welcomes good news, employees quickly learn to keep bad news to themselves. Management may not learn that a project is in trouble until too late to correct the difficulty quickly and inexpensively.

Competition Rather Than Conflict

The third goal for organizational communication systems is to encourage cooperative competition and reduce conflict within the organization. Each part of the organization depends on every other part, and the well-being of the entire organization depends on the well-being of its parts.

Opportunity to Earn Status

Because resources and status are limited in any organization, their distribution is a matter of great importance to employees. It's natural for people to want their fair share, and each person's opinion (based on perceptions) of what's fair distribution will be different. When people know what resources and status are available, know what objectives must be met to earn desired resources or status, and know that they will receive full credit for their achievements, they will compete openly by striving to meet organizational objectives.

When people are uncertain about what resources and status are available, what must be done to earn an increase in resources or status, and whether they will receive full credit for achievements, they will manipulate others in their efforts to achieve personal goals. Conflict arises when the ways of earning increased status and resources aren't sufficently clear. Conflict also arises out of differences in perception of resources, status, and their distribution.

Manipulation Leads to Conflict

Manipulation encourages countermanipulation, and countermanipulation is the first sign of *latent conflict.* Latent conflict is in some ways the most difficult kind of conflict for an organization to deal with. It reduces organizational efficiency without being recognized, acknowledged, discussed, or resolved. Again, an open communication climate is an organization's best method of reducing conflict.

COORDINATED COMMUNICATION SYSTEMS

Companies Can Control Communication Quality

Organizations have known for a long time that promotion potential and the ability to communicate are closely related. In general, the best communicators gravitate toward higher levels of management. Even so, the ability to communicate effectively has been considered primarily an individual trait — something belonging to particular individuals and not to the company as a whole. In the past few years, however, companies have begun to realize that they can control the quality of their communication systems much as they control the quality of their products.

Because communication is so important in organizational life, management should assume the responsibility for establishing a formal communication policy, complete with written objectives. No company would think to manufacture television sets without specific objectives and measurements for cost, production, and performance. No company should engage in communication without setting similar specific objectives and measurements for both intracompany and extracompany communication systems.

Intracompany Systems

To develop successful intracompany communication systems, management must make its commitment to good communication obvious, require each individual manager to practice good communication, and obtain or train individuals who can supervise intracompany communication flow. Certainly, unless management indicates full commitment to quality communication by expressing concern for good communication *and* by establishing an open communication climate, employees cannot be expected to communicate openly.

Establishing effective intracompany communication is essentially a three-step process.

1. **Write and distribute objectives for upward, downward, and horizontal communication flow.** Open communication works to everyone's advantage, so the specific objectives should be stated in terms of employees' benefits. The general goals — an open communication climate, accurate information, and competition rather than conflict — should be stressed.

2. **Establish education and training programs to insure adequate communication skills.** Good communication is not easy. If, for example, an employee said, "You sure made a rotten decision when you bought the Willard heat press," even a trained manager would tend to become defensive. Managers must really believe that it is in their long-range interest to listen to (not just *hear*, but *listen to*) whatever criticism may follow, or the training program cannot be considered successful.

3. **Practice independent communication auditing.** Because the perceptions of supervisors and subordinates differ, management has difficulty measuring the success of its own communication. The absence of observable negative feedback may not be an indication of a successful communication program. Independent communication auditing would permit employees to complete questionnaires anonymously and to communicate face-to-face with someone who would protect the confidentiality of their statements.

Extracompany Systems

In many ways a company can achieve high-quality communication with the outside world more easily than with and among its own employees. Most extracompany communication has specific, identifiable goals. Companies want to sell products or services, to be well thought of, and to make a profit. Companies have long recognized that each contact with the public should contribute to the company's advertising and public relations programs.

If organization policies concerning extracompany communication have a failing, it is that they make little or no provision for measuring the communication efforts of specific individuals. The company's efforts as a whole — advertising and formal public relations efforts — tend to be well planned, coordinated, and evaluated. Companies hire experts to write letters for mass mailings. But it's a rare company that monitors the letter-writing efforts of employees who routinely correspond in the company's name.

As with intracompany communication, education and training and a formal means of measuring communication performance are the keys to effective extracompany communication. Any communication education and training program should teach both the specific objectives of messages and channels and the general goals of effective communication. Whatever the communication situation, the key factors for success of the program are credibility, clarity, and empathy. To communicate effectively you must be believed, be clear, and see things from your receiver's point of view.

SUMMARY

An organization is a group of people working together to achieve a common goal. Communication structures human relationships in such a way that a group of people can work together to achieve a goal.

In organizations, communication functions primarily to coordinate activities to achieve task, maintenance, and human objectives. Task objectives can be accomplished by a limited number of messages. Maintenance and human objectives are accomplished primarily by an attitude toward communication rather than by any single message.

The official hierarchy of the organization, as represented by the company's organization chart, establishes a formal communication network for the organization. The informal communication network is known as the "grapevine."

Organizations must achieve three general objectives if communication is to flow smoothly and efficiently. The entire effort of organizational communication should be directed toward establishing an open communication climate, accurate information, and competition rather than conflict.

Promotion potential and the ability to communicate are closely related: the best communicators gravitate toward higher levels of management. Because communication is so important in organizational life, management should assume the responsibility for establishing a formal communication policy, complete with written objectives.

EXERCISES

1. How does communication make organizational life possible?
2. What is the function of communication in achieving organizational objectives?
3. Identify and explain the three broad objectives of organizational communication programs.
4. What are the differences between formal and informal communication networks?
5. Name and explain the factors involved in successful downward communication and in successful upward communication.
6. What are the advantages and disadvantages of horizontal communication?
7. How can a company improve its internal communication flow?
8. How do the objectives of specific messages relate to the general objectives of organizational communication systems?
9. Visit with a member of top management at an organization of your choice to discuss the objectives of the company's communication systems. Write a short report analyzing your findings.
10. Visit with lower-ranking members of the organization used in Exercise 9. Are their perceptions of the communication flow in the organization the same as those of top management? If not, why not? Write a short report analyzing your findings. Do you have any recommendations for the company?

SUGGESTED READINGS

Berkman, Harold W. *The Human Relations of Management.* Encino, CA: Dickenson, 1974.

Goldhaber, Gerald M. *Organizational Communication.* Dubuque, IA: W. C. Brown, 1974.

Haney, William V. *Communication and Organizational Behavior.* 3d ed. Homewood, IL: Richard D. Irwin, 1973.

Huseman, Richard C., Cal M. Logue, and Dwight L. Freshley. *Readings in Interpersonal and Organizational Communication.* 2d ed. Boston: Holbrook, 1973.

Katz, Daniel, and Robert Kahn. *The Social Psychology of Organizations.* New York: J. Wiley, 1966.

Koehler, Jerry W., Karl W. E. Anatol, and Ronald L. Applbaum. *Organizational Communication.* New York: Holt, Rinehart and Winston, 1976.

Likert, Rensis. *New Patterns of Management.* New York: McGraw-Hill, 1961.

Likert, Rensis. *The Human Organization.* New York: McGraw-Hill, 1967.

McGregor, Douglas. *Human Side of Enterprise.* New York: McGraw-Hill, 1960.

McGregor, Douglas. *Professional Manager.* New York: McGraw-Hill, 1967.

Sanford, Aubrey C., Gary T. Hunt, and Hyler J. Bracey. *Communication Behavior in Organizations.* Columbus, OH: Charles E. Merrill, 1976.

Schneider, Arnold E., William C. Donaghy, and Pamela Jane Newman. *Organizational Communication.* New York: McGraw-Hill, 1975.

Thayer, Lee. *Communication and Communication Systems.* Homewood, IL: Richard D. Irwin, 1968.

12

JOB APPLICATIONS

After you have read this chapter, you should be able to

1. **List and analyze your work qualifications.**
2. **List and analyze job opportunities.**
3. **Prepare an effective resume and write an effective letter of application.**
4. **Explain the special techniques of job interviews.**
5. **Write an effective follow-up letter.**

WRITTEN JOB APPLICATIONS

Job Application Package

A job application package is a persuasive message consisting of a resume and a cover letter, usually called a letter of transmittal or letter of application. We have saved this discussion of job applications until last because you will use many of the skills presented in the previous chapters to prepare your application package and to handle the job interview. The written application, for example, relies heavily on the "conviction" aspect of the persuasive structure discussed in Chapters Two and Three; the interview will develop along the lines discussed in Chapter Eight. You'll also need nonverbal communication skills to present the right image. In this chapter we focus on ways you can use these various skills for the purpose of obtaining a job.

Written applications for jobs have been around for a long time, and they are still widely used because they work. Your job application package may be the most important piece of business correspondence you undertake. The finished product should show that you took its preparation seriously. The best application package in the world can't guarantee you a job, but a poorly prepared application can certainly prevent you from being selected for an interview.

What Do Employers Want?

Willingness to Work

Job Skills

Potential

All employers want persons with a history of willingness to work, the ability to perform the required task, the ability to get along well with others, and sufficient potential to merit promotion. Your application package should support your claim that you satisfy each of these requirements.

The readers of your applications will be in one of two categories: either they will have asked for your application (and perhaps hundreds of others at the same time) or they will not have asked for it. Your application, then, will be either *invited* or *uninvited*. In many ways these two cases are quite similar.

Invited Application
Uninvited Application

In both cases you should apply for one particular job. In an invited application you have a want ad, job description, or specific request to go by; in an uninvited application, you should apply for the job you can do best. With invited applications, job descriptions usually ask for far more qualifications than any one applicant could reasonably be expected to have. For example, a job description may say, "five years' experience desired." This doesn't mean that the employer won't settle for less, however, if you show that you can do the job.

What Can
You Do Best?

With uninvited applications, you may fear that if you apply for a particular job, the person hiring or the personnel department won't consider you for other jobs that happen to be open. This is usually not true. Most people responsible for hiring attempt to match applicants and their qualifications to the jobs that are open, and the strong applications will be given consideration.

Nothing sounds weaker in an application than, "If you've got a vacancy, I'll take it." Job applicants — especially college graduates — should be mature enough to have some idea of what they want to do with their lives, and the application package should reflect this sense of purpose. Also, your package should reflect the you-attitude by showing a willingness to do work useful to your prospective employer. Your package should show self-confidence and competence (don't misspell any words). All the tricks (such as singeing the edges of your resume to show that you are a hot prospect) have been tried; most employers want a conventional presentation. But a job application package that is within the convention can — and should — reflect your individuality.

You-Attitude

Self-confidence
Competence

The Basics

The package itself has two basic parts:

Resume

1. The resume, data sheet, or vita. You write this part first. Authorities can't agree on which term to use for this part, but whatever one calls it, it performs essentially the same function. In our opinion, the terms generally attempt to differentiate varying degrees of sophistication. The *data sheet* is the least sophisticated, usually presenting only the most fundamental facts without *any* accompanying interpretation. The *resume* (from the French, *résumé*, "a summary") offers more inter-

pretation of the bare facts. The *vita* (Latin for "life") is much longer than either a data sheet or a resume, usually including a lengthy summary of professional accomplishments, publications, and the like. Vitas are appropriate only for important positions requiring that applicants have many professional accomplishments.

Letter of Application

2. The letter. This is usually called a letter of application, but it may be referred to as a letter of transmittal or a cover letter when used with a resume or vita. Even though the letter is the most persuasive part of the package, you should not try to write it until you have completed your data sheet or resume.

You can consider the resume as an informative enclosure to accompany the letter, if you wish. It is a critical informative enclosure, however, because it indicates your ability to select important information, organize it in a useful way, and present it in an attractive, readable manner.

The data sheet or resume will usually be printed or mechanically reproduced from a typewritten original — by offset or high-quality photocopy — not dittoed, **and not a carbon!** Your prospective employers will know that you will be using your printed resume for more than one application. Your resume should be specific enough to show your sense of purpose, but avoid limiting yourself any more than you have to. Every now and then a person is qualified for work in two completely unrelated fields, such as banking and food processing. Such an individual should go to the effort of preparing separate resumes. Usually, however, the kinds of jobs for which an applicant would be qualified are sufficiently related that one job objective — and one resume — can be made to work.

ANALYZING BEFORE YOU WRITE

Before you can begin preparing your resume and letter of application you must determine your goals, analyze your qualifications for achieving those goals, and develop a strategy for selling yourself to prospective employers.

Assessing Your Qualifications

Answer the following questions as honestly as you can:

1. **Professional objectives.** What occupational goals have you set for yourself? Why do you wish to pursue these goals? Are your goals realistic? Are they flexible?

2. **Education.** What has your education prepared you to do? How do your major and minor fields of study relate to one another? How do your major and minor relate to your professional objectives? Can you do what your education suggests that you can without a great deal of in-service training?
3. **Experience.** Do you have work experience related to the kind of work for which you are applying? Have any of your jobs taught you specific skills required for the kind of work you want to do? Do you have a well-developed work history? Does your previous experience show a willingness to work hard?
4. **Personal qualities.** Do you have any special personal attributes that make you especially well suited for the kind of work you are seeking? Do you enjoy working with people? with numbers? with books? Have any of your hobbies taught you something about the kind of work you're applying for? Did you work to finance your college education? Can you cooperate, follow instructions, and work as a member of a team? Have you demonstrated initiative in the past?

Assessing Job Opportunities

Once you have clarified what you want and what you can do, you must locate companies that may not only need your skills but also give you the opportunity to achieve your professional goals.

1. **What kind of company would you like to work for?** You should consider size, location, opportunities for travel (or for staying put), the product or service, and the company's history, operations, and policies. If you want further education, will the company support your efforts to obtain it?
2. **How do you find job openings?** Use your college placement office; use classified ads (*Help Wanted* and *Situations Wanted*) in newspapers and professional journals; check the yellow pages in the telephone book; make direct application to the companies of your choice; ask your friends and relatives; and file with public (state) and private employment agencies.
3. **How do you select the best possibilities?** Once you have found job openings in companies that appeal to you, consider what each of those companies offers you. What is the company's position in the industry? Has the company's growth rate been stable? Does the company have good prospects for the future? Does the company promote from within?

Marketing Your Qualifications

After you know what you can and would like to do and for whom you would like to do it, you must market yourself to your selected audience. A company will hire you because someone there decides that you can do useful work for the company and that the company will be better off for adding you to the payroll.

Before you can persuade someone to hire you, you must convince the person that your education and experience qualify you to do certain work and that your attitude toward work will ensure that you will actually do the work for which you are hired.

Education

1. What aspects of your education contribute most directly to your ability to do the work required? Make a list of the job duties you'll have, and make a separate list of the course work that applies to each. Subject matter learned is more important than course titles. Concentrate on the advanced work in your area of study — beginning and intermediate courses and work are generally assumed.

Experience

2. What aspects of your work experience contribute most directly to your ability to do the work you'll be required to do? Even if your experience is limited, you can find important qualities to stress: sense of responsibility, ability to work well with people, and ability to make decisions.

Personal Qualities

3. In spite of pertinent education and experience, companies will not hire you unless you demonstrate the kind of personal qualities that will make you useful to the firm. Have you demonstrated a willingness to work hard? Do you have a well-developed work history?

Remember that the person who hires you is thinking primarily about what you can do for the company. Keep in mind that what counts is your audience's view of your skills, and that you control that view to a certain extent. You-attitude and positive tone will help you create the kind of favorable impression that will get you hired.

Purposes of Job Application Package, Interview, and Follow-up Letter

You have three basic tools to work with in making your presentation: your job application package, the interview, and follow-up correspondence. Each of these tools has a specific use. The job application package is designed to get you the interview; the purpose of the interview is to persuade the interviewer that you are the right person for the job; and the follow-up letter should remind the interviewer, after seeing your competition, that you are the best person.

THE RESUME

Your resume must cover four broad categories: personal details, education, experience, and references. Most personnel directors prefer resumes two typewritten pages long. You probably can't give a full picture of yourself in one page, and employers dislike reading more than two pages of resume. Make intelligent use of space in covering the four categories. Limit printed resumes to one page.

Personal Details

In addition to your name and address, most basic personal details — height, weight, date of birth, and marital status — should be given first even though they don't say much about your qualifications for a job. Now that it is illegal for companies to request photographs of applicants, some firms will disqualify you for sending one. A recent trend is to move personal details out of the emphatic first position and subordinate them by placing them toward the end, just before the list of references.

A more conservative approach is to keep the personal details first, but to allow them only a little space and to subordinate them by omitting any heading. Another way to subordinate the personal details is to put the essential facts into one neat line of typewritten copy. To make it brief, omit redundancies: if you say 175 pounds, you don't need to explain that the figure is your weight.

Education

Education will probably be your most important division. It deserves a major heading and several subheads. Some categories you might use include schools attended, honors earned, grade-point average (if noteworthy), major and minor fields, and activities.

Give special emphasis to those courses that make you exceptionally well qualified. All accounting majors take introductory accounting, wherever they go to school and whatever the specific title of the course may be. So it doesn't help much to list introductory courses. Concentrate on upper-division work that indicates the range and depth of your educational background.

Concentrate on Advanced Courses

If you earned at least part of your college expenses, be sure to say so. Working your way through school demonstrates your willingness to work.

Experience

Work History Is Important

Experience is the other important area. Even if none of your working experience is job-related, showing that you have worked is important. Be sure to tell where and when you worked and what you did. List your job duties in a way that will have meaning for your reader, but don't state the obvious: if you worked as a waiter, you don't need to specify that you carried food to tables, took orders, and so forth. Mention any special responsibilities, such as closing up at night. If your work was part-time, say so. Full-time summer work should be listed as such. Prospective employers frequently expect to see your reasons for having left previous jobs.

References

Listing References Helps

A few years back, when the job market was not so tight, it was sufficient to say, "References will be furnished upon request." Today you are generally better off if you list your references on your resume. Most employers give serious consideration to applications without references. Even so, listing references gives you a slight edge when competing with other applicants; that edge may prove important in getting you the interview. Be sure to get each person's permission before listing him or her as a reference — no one likes to be taken by surprise. You may also find that your reference's opinion of you is not what you thought it was.

In listing your references, give the person's courtesy title (Mr., Mrs., Miss, Ms., Dr.); full name; professional title (personnel director, office manager, department chairperson); business mailing address; business telephone number; *and* connection to you. In some cases the person's title will make the connection clear: "Dr. Harvey Hallister, Professor, Department of Accountancy, University of Florida . . ." should be sufficient to show that Harvey Hallister was your teacher. If Dr. Hallister also was the director of your senior independent study, you should add that detail.

The best references are academic and employment references. Personal references, such as friends, relatives, church leaders, and family physicians cannot usually give employers the information they seek.

Special Interests and Other Optional Entries

Should you mention special interests that are not job-related? Yes, if you have room *after* covering the more important details. The personnel director reviewing your resume may share a hobby with you, which certainly won't hurt. If you list your interests, be specific. Don't just list "music"; do you sing, play, collect, or listen? What kind of music? If you have had military experience, hold special licenses (private pilot's, FCC, real estate), have received special honors or awards, you should mention them at least briefly.

Date

Dating resumes is optional. The date can show a prospective employer that the information is recent, but the date may also force you to prepare a new resume before the details of your circumstances have changed. We prefer — and recommend — dated resumes because they suggest greater care and authority. Figure 12-1 is a sample of a typewritten resume.

THE LETTER OF APPLICATION

Type Letters Individually

Once you have prepared your resume, your next step is to write the accompanying letter of application. Each application letter should be individually typed and prepared for a particular audience.

Ask for an Interview

The letter is a persuasive message; it uses the delayed structure, *Attention, Interest, Conviction, Action.* The purpose of the letter, the "action" you are seeking, is for you to obtain an interview. Do *not* ask for the job; ask for an interview. As with all sales letters, you must attract your reader's attention to succeed. With uninvited applications, or when the job market is especially tight, consider using an oversized envelope so that your application will be more visible than most of the others coming in. Even when the secretary opens the mail and passes the material to someone else, your presentation will stand out because it will be unfolded. The extra neatness may give you a small but important edge. Do not use other tricks or gimmicks to attract attention — your letter should be neat, nicely typed, and conservative in appearance.

Use Oversized Envelope

In general, you should use the words "job" and "work." The words "vacancy" and "opportunity" suggest either you don't care what you do or that you are concerned only with getting ahead. The word "position" also has special connotations — it implies high status in the business world. The person to whom you are writing may well want you to start with a *job* and work your way up to a *position.*

Your first paragraph must catch your reader's "attention." Do something for your reader — talk work — at the same time you are

NADIA L. TSUKAHARA

467 Lovers Lane New Lenox, IL 60441 (815) 485-3048	After 15 May 1977: 99 Lincoln Highway Frankfort, IL 60351 (815) 476-3942

Single 5'5" 115 pounds Born 16 November 1954

Professional Objective	To pursue a career in the advertising phase of marketing. I am especially interested in copy writing.

EDUCATION

Sep 1973 to Apr 1977	College of Business, Department of Marketing, Illinois State University, Normal, IL 61761. BBA Degree April 1977.
Major	Advertising. Advanced courses include Copy and Layout, Consumer Behavior, and Advertising Media/Campaigns/Strategies. Projects for Copy and Layout included two full-page magazine layouts and corresponding copy. Term project for Advertising Media/Campaigns/Strategies involved analysis of image problem of University Placement Services. Portfolio available.
Minor	Business Communication, Department of Business Education and Administrative Services. Advanced courses include Business Communication, Organizational Communication, Report Writing, Persuasive Communication, Broadcast Communication, Television Production, and Journalism. All courses contributed to a broad background in written and oral communication. College courses financed through part-time and summer employment.

EXPERIENCE

Sep 1976 to Jan 1977	Internship at Corn Belt Advertising Company, 405 Larkin Road, Normal, IL 61761. Worked 14 hours a week on media advertising for 6 units of credit in marketing. Prepared copy for television, radio, and newspaper advertising for the Golden Seed Company.

Figure 12-1. A typewritten resume.

Nadia L. Tsukahara 2

EXPERIENCE (Continued)

Jun 1976 to Sep 1976	Clerical worker for Star Chemical Company, 1156 Brandon Road, Joliet, IL 60436. Worked full time during the summer performing a variety of clerical duties. Quit job to return to school.

ACTIVITIES AND INTERESTS

Sep 1974 to Apr 1976	Marketing Club. Offices held: Secretary-treasurer, vice-president. Advertising Club. Offices held: Secretary (two terms), vice-president, president (current office).

Hobbies include tennis, skiing, sailing, sewing, and reading.

HONORS, AWARDS, AND PUBLICATIONS

Dean's List seven out of eight semesters.
Copy Cat award for excellence in advertising, January 1975
"Undergraduate Advertising Curriculum," Ageless Advertising, 20 No. 5 (1976), pp. 4-6
"Why I Chose Advertising," Money Marketing, 3 No. 2 (1976), pp. 19-47.

REFERENCES

Dr. John R. Edwards, Chairman, Department of Marketing, Illinois State University, Normal, IL 61761. (309) 438-2111.

Dr. Cathleen M. VanDyke, Professor, Department of Management, Illinois State University, Normal, IL 61761. (309) 438-2112.

Dr. Eugene Q. Lina, Assistant Professor, Department of Business Education and Administrative Services, Illinois State University, Normal, IL 61761. (309) 438-2113.

Mr. Samuel DeHans, President, Corn Belt Advertising Company, 405 Larkin Road, Normal, IL 61761. (309) 726-5678.

Mrs. Doris L. Gans, Vice-President of Personnel, Star Chemical Company, 1156 Brandon Road, Joliet, IL 60436. (815) 726-3894.

Mr. James R. Sokol, President, Golden Seed Company, 1303 Jefferson Street, Normal, IL 61761. (309) 726-9021.

1 March 1977

Figure 12-1. Continued.

showing that you are in fact writing about a job. Don't be cute. Your letter and resume are obviously a job application package, so let your reader know right away what job you're applying for and how you found out about the job. The employer wishes to have the work done that you are offering to do, so you're beginning with a benefit for your reader.

Your first paragraph should introduce your most important selling point for the job in question. You have three things to consider: your education, your experience, and personal qualities that make you uniquely suitable for the job in question (or for the one particular job for which you are best qualified).

The "interest" section of your letter should reflect your knowledge of the company and its work in general — or of the particular job, if you know that a particular job exists. Even though you are discussing yourself, keep your reader in the picture. What does your employer want?

Show Rather Than Tell

Rather than *telling* your reader what you think he or she wants or needs, *show* your reader that you can fill those needs because of your education, experience, and personal qualities. Don't say, "You need a person who . . . ." Instead, subordinate specific references to the company's needs by commenting on your own qualifications: "Because I am a person who . . . I could make a valuable contribution to . . . ."

The main part of your letter will be the "conviction" part. In this section of the letter, you must *prove* that your education, experience, and personal qualities have prepared you to do the work in question. Consider writing a separate paragraph on each of those elements, though you can interweave the highlights of your personal qualities with the educational and experience information.

Stress the aspects of your background most appropriate for the job and company addressed. Do not merely repeat facts listed on your resume; rather, give details about courses, jobs, and extracurricular activities that show your full abilities. Make sure that you say something about each requirement listed in the ad for the job (or each requirement that you know applies to the kind of work if you're writing an uninvited application letter).

Omit negative factors that your reader will have no way of knowing about. Negative factors that will be obvious to a reader who looks at your resume should be subordinated: put strong points before and after, use positive language, and if possible, attach a reader benefit to the negative aspect. If you're older than the average college graduate, for example, talk about maturity, stability, and good judgment.

At the same time that you are overcoming your deficiencies, do not suggest deficiencies where none exist. You are probably more qualified than you think, and your job experience has been more valuable than you think. The negative thought, "My only work experience was dishwashing part-time while I was going to school," should be expressed in positive terms: "I earned half of my college expenses working part-time as a dishwasher while attending school full time."

Ask for a Specific Action: An Interview

When you ask for action, be careful to find a middle ground between begging and demanding. Your letter and resume should show that you have something to offer. Begging for an interview will undermine the conviction you have established. At the same time, your reader is under no obligation to see you at all, much less to see you at your convenience.

If one particular time would be better for you than another, then suggest it, but give your reader the opportunity to arrange things according to his or her schedule. Make it easy for your reader to reply by giving your telephone number. Providing a reply card is sometimes helpful, especially in those aspects of business that are concerned with aggressiveness — sales, marketing, and advertising.

The Package Is You

In preparing your resume and letter of application, remember that to your reader, that package *is* you. Until the interview, your reader will see only that package and will compare it to perhaps hundreds of other packages. If your package doesn't look sharp and full of promise, someone else's will.

If you don't type well, hire someone to type your letters. Use 25 percent rag-content paper. Mention your reader's name, company, product, or service two or three times in the body of the letter so your reader will be certain that the same letter isn't going to hundreds of firms. If you get no response from your first letter, send a second one about three weeks later. If you receive a negative response — and if you really want the job and haven't found something else — send a second application letter in about eight weeks.

Compare the following letters of application. Both letters were actually written by students who were in the process of applying for jobs. The first letter shows the kinds of things students do wrong most frequently. The applicant says too many things the reader already knows and says almost nothing about himself. We have left the grammatical errors unchanged. The letter was not successful.

The second example says a great deal about the applicant. Note the student's use of the word *opportunity* in the first sentence. The applicant is *not* looking for the opportunity to make a career for himself; he is looking for the opportunity to show his reader that he can do useful work. This letter was quite successful.

Poor

1078 Notting Avenue
Joliet, IL 60432

1 March 1977

Mr. Angelo Casten
Spartan Stores Inc.
2435 Hillcrest Road
Joliet, IL 60436

Dear Mr. Casten:

Spartan Stores have been the fastest growing and surely the most dynamic food retailer in the Joliet area. I have read many impressive articles about Spartan Stores and their growth.

While reading the March issue of Progressive Grocer, I noticed your advertisement for a college graduate with food retailing experience. I would like to inform you about my qualifications.

I am a graduate of Illinois State University's Food Distribution Program with a minor in General Business. ISU's program is a combination of theory and practical experience. In my four years at ISU, I have been trained in every department. Presently I am the night manager at the Larkin Avenue Country Store.

Interaction through communication has always been my theory towards successful customer and employee relationships. Communication is the key to success in the management field.

Spartan Stores have proved that being a customer and employee orientated company is the answer to loyalty and success. Becoming affiliated with your company is my goal. Write and tell me when we can talk about Spartan Stores.

Respectfully,

Homer Williams

Better

851 Valley Lane
Joliet, IL 60436

1 March 1977

Mr. William R. Roddenberg
Heritage Accounting Inc.
7 South Dearborn Street
Chicago, IL 60603

Dear Mr. Roddenberg:

I am enthusiastically seeking the opportunity to show you how an eager "almost-graduate" in accounting can perform as a responsible assistant.

This summer, the last before my graduation in December 1977, gives me more than two months to do just that. I am prepared to accept the challenge a junior accountant's work presents. Most of all, I want to tackle assignments using the knowledge my education and experience have given me.

The base of my education has been the accounting curriculum at Illinois State University in Normal, IL. In these courses I learned the patience and attention to detail which are essential to accuracy. Cost accounting gave me an in-depth picture of accounting operations. In tax, I related both the individual and the business entity to the legal environment. Advanced accounting and auditing provided an overview of the business world and its reliance on the skills of the certified public accountant. The practice audit case, a semester-long project, introduced what future accountants will have to know about government regulations to meet firms' needs.

Through work experience I have developed the ability to work well with others and to adapt to new environments. Retail sales work in a photo store allowed me to deal with many types of customers. I learned to adapt to the requirements of each new situation and to communicate my ideas readily. My present work in the Air National Guard calls for satisfying the needs of superiors as well as subordinates. I have demonstrated my ability to work well within the organizational structure. Effective communication is a priority for me as part of both my managerial and operations duties in the Guard.

I have the initiative to combine my knowledge with determined work to make accounting a successful career. I want to prove it this summer by accepting the challenge and responsibility your firm would offer me.

I want to demonstrate my enthusiasm for professionalism to you now, and so I am eager for a chance to discuss my goals, education, and other qualifications in an interview arranged at your convenience.

Sincerely yours,

Stephen Barker

THE JOB INTERVIEW

A successful interview depends as much on what is done *before* the interview as what happens *in* the interview. An interviewee who is well prepared has much more control over the interview than the poorly prepared person.

Preparation

After you have assessed your qualifications and the job opportunities, your next step is to arrange for an interview with the company of your choice. If your letter of application and resume have been successful, you will probably receive a letter inviting you to an interview; but the chances are that your appointment for the interview will be arranged by telephone. You will receive either a call or an invitation to call and arrange for an appointment.

If you are asked to call:

1. Before you call for the appointment, safeguard against possible memory loss by having a pen and note pad handy. Jot down the name, address, and phone number of the company you're about to call. On the same sheet of paper, write *who, when,* and *where,* so you can fill in this information as you talk on the phone.
2. After you dial the number, ask for the person in charge of hiring. When the operator gives you the name, jot it on your sheet of paper. Be sure to get the correct spelling and pronunciation. Ask the operator for the person's title as well.

3. When you are connected to your party, introduce yourself and request a specific time, date, and place for the interview. Be flexible. Repeat and record the information. Express appreciation.

If you are called:

1. Be prepared. Keep a copy of your resume and a list of the companies to which you've sent applications near your phone. The list should include the name and title of the person, the name and address of the company, and the specific job for which you've applied.
2. Take notes during the conversation. Make sure that you record the information correctly. More than one qualified job applicant has shown up at the wrong company at the wrong time.

Research

After making the appointment, do some research. Get information about the company from the library, school placement office, company employees, or the company's annual report. Find out the location of the company's main plants and offices and its branch offices. Does the company have subsidiaries? What type of product does it manufacture? What kind of service does it offer? What are the company's growth patterns and its prospects for the future? Knowing something about the company will give you the confidence and security you need to relax during the interview.

Getting Ready

Prepare yourself for the day of the interview. Get a good night's sleep. Allow yourself plenty of time in the morning to get ready. Appearance counts — be neat and clean.

The Meeting

Be punctual. To be on the safe side, arrive 10 to 15 minutes early. When you arrive at the office, introduce yourself to the receptionist. Observe the physical surroundings and the office environment while you wait. Is it a place where you would enjoy working?

When the interviewer is ready for you, the receptionist may direct you to the appropriate office, or the interviewer may come directly to you. In either case, when you first meet with the interviewer, greet him or her by name and extend your hand for a handshake. Your grasp shouldn't be too strong, nor should it be limp. Wait until you're asked to be seated. Sit up in your chair, looking alert and interested. Don't smoke or chew gum. Look your interviewer in the eye. Smile.

Most job interviews take less than 30 minutes. Be alert to terminating signs from the interviewer; take the hint and prepare to leave. Make sure that the interviewer has a good copy of your resume. Thank the interviewer and leave graciously.

Interview Hints

In addition to the general interviewing procedures presented in Chapter Eight, the following suggestions are particularly important in job interviews:

1. Go to the interview alone.
2. Be patient while waiting in the reception area.
3. Be pleasant and poised. Smile. Watch your posture and control nervous mannerisms.
4. Watch your grammar, pronunciation, and nonverbal behavior.
5. Don't beg or boast. Don't try to bribe.
6. Express appreciation for the interview.
7. Thank the receptionist as you leave the main office.
8. Follow up with a letter of appreciation.

Questions Frequently Asked in Job Interviews

The following questions are asked often enough that you should determine in advance how you will answer them:

1. Tell me a bit about yourself.
2. What are your goals?
3. Why do you want to work for our company?
4. Would you rather work with others or by yourself?
5. Have you ever had any problems with your parents, fellow students, or faculty members?
6. Would you rather make money or serve humanity?
7. When did you become self-supporting?
8. How important is salary to you?
9. What have you learned on your previous jobs?
10. Are you in good physical condition?
11. What are your plans to further your education?
12. What books do you read for pleasure?
13. How was your education financed?

14. What do you think will determine your progress in our company?

FOLLOWING THROUGH

The job application process is not complete until you have been hired, have been rejected by the company, or have refused the job offer. If you still want the job after the interview, you must write at least one follow-up letter to (1) thank the person for the interview, (2) overcome any deficiencies that the interviewer brought up during your interview, and (3) express continued interest.

Follow-up Letters

The nature of the follow-up letter will depend on your evaluation of the interview, where the interview was conducted, and how many other applicants were being interviewed for the job. If the interview took place on your campus and the interviewer was interviewing many applicants for several different jobs on many different campuses, for example, you should write a reasonably long letter and enclose another copy of your resume. If only one or two people are being interviewed at the company, a short thank-you note would be more appropriate.

Simple Follow-up Letter

A simple follow-up letter could be as brief as this:

```
I certainly enjoyed talking with you about the job of
Assistant Manager for B & B Enterprises.

After the interview, I was more convinced than ever
that I could make a valuable contribution to
B & B's management program, and I'm looking forward
to hearing your decision about my application.
```

Complex Follow-up Letter

Write a complex follow-up letter when you need to accomplish more. If your interviewer raised some objection to hiring you, use the follow-up letter as a means to overcome that deficiency. Or take advantage of the follow-up letter to show that you learned something from the interview. The two objectives can frequently be combined:

```
Thank you very much for the time you spent with me
when you visited Illinois State University last
```

week. I enjoyed talking with you about the possibility of working as the Assistant Manager for B & B Enterprises.

Since we talked, I've given further thought to the questions you asked about my lack of formal training in communication. As you stated in the interview, your main concern is to hire someone who can handle the correspondence and face-to-face communication the job of Assistant Manager entails; and though my formal training is limited to the three basic courses offered at Illinois State, those courses were thorough and demanding.

In addition to my formal training, my extracurricular activities have called for well-developed communication skills. In my role of President of Alpha Pi Phi, I wrote many letters--including the most successful fund-raising letter in the history of the fraternity--and chaired many meetings. I would be able to bring this on-the-job experience with me to B & B. I am also following your suggestion and reading several of the communication books you mentioned.

I believe that I can make a valuable contribution to B & B Enterprises, and I would appreciate it if you would let me know if there is anything else I can do or tell you about myself to help you decide about my application.

Job Acceptance Letters

The Letters Are a Contract

Job acceptance letters are easy to write. They are immediate messages, beginning with the good news. But don't forget that the letter offering the job and the letter accepting it constitute a contract — make sure that you understand exactly what's being offered before you accept. Your letter of acceptance should include those aspects of the job, its responsibilities, and rewards that you consider essential.

I accept the job of Assistant Manager for B & B Enterprises with pleasure.

The salary of $15,000 for an 11-month year, the duties specified in your letter of 20 April 1977, and the fringe benefits are all agreeable to me. I also understand that my passing the six-month probationary period is contingent upon my successfully completing at least one additional communication course at Illinois State University; I agree to enroll in an evening class in report writing during the Spring Term.

As we agreed by phone, I will take two weeks off after my graduation on 23 April; and I will report for work at 8:00 a.m. on Monday, 9 May 1977.

See you then.

Job Refusals

Don't Burn Bridges

Letters refusing job offers are more difficult to write. As with all negative messages, you are much better off avoiding a direct and absolute "no." Express continued interest in the firm, basing your refusal on considerations that leave the door open to future employment with the company. You must not, however, imply that you'll be leaving the company whose offer you are accepting.

I certainly enjoyed talking with you about the job of Assistant Manager for B & B Enterprises, and the opportunity you offer is indeed a good one.

As you pointed out in my interview, most of my managerial training and experience are with resources other than people; and for this reason I have decided that for my first job I should accept employment with a company* that will let me work with the resources I know best. Of course I fully intend to develop my communication skills further, and I'm grateful for the reading list you provided.

I'm still convinced that B & B Enterprises is the finest company of its type, and you can be sure that when I need communication products or services, B & B will be the first name I think of.

*It's okay to be specific and name the company.

SUMMARY

A job application package is a persuasive message consisting of a resume and a letter of application. The written application relies heavily on the conviction aspect of the *attention, interest, conviction, action* structure.

Whether the readers of your letter and resume have invited your application or not, they will want to see evidence of willingness to work, ability to perform a given task, ability to get along well with others, and sufficient potential to merit promotion.

After you have analyzed your own qualifications and desires, analyze companies, jobs, and opportunities. Prepare your resume first, focusing on a specific job category. Write your letter after you have prepared the resume. Each letter should be as specific as you can make it. Your resume will be printed, and copies will go to several companies. You should write each letter for a specific company, however, and preferably for a specific person in a specific company.

Prepare for your interview by researching the company, its products, plant locations, policies, and clientele. The more you know about the company, the better off you'll be. Always express appreciation for the interview, and always write a follow-up letter.

Letters accepting jobs should be specific; make sure that you agree to all the terms in the letter offering you the job. Letters refusing jobs are negative messages, so you should subordinate the negative aspect as much as possible. Make sure that you don't cut yourself off from future employment with the firm.

EXERCISES

1. Assuming that you are a graduating senior or using your present qualifications, apply for an appropriate job (full time after graduation, part-time during the school year, or full-time summer work) with a resume and a letter of application.
2. Give your letter and resume to your instructor, a classmate, or a friend who can be objective. Have that person interview you for the job of your choice.
3. Write a follow-up letter to that person, expressing appreciation for the interview and overcoming any deficiencies that became apparent during the interview.
4. Assume that you have been offered the job. Write letters:
   a. Accepting the job.
   b. Refusing the job.

SUGGESTED READINGS

Bonner, William H. *Better Business Writing*. Homewood, IL: Richard D. Irwin, 1974.

Bolles, Richard Nelson. *What Color Is Your Parachute? A Practical Manual for Job-Hunters and Career Changes*. Berkeley, CA: Ten Speed Press, 1975.

Brown, Leland. *Communicating Facts and Ideas in Business*. 2d ed. Englewood Cliffs, NJ: Prentice-Hall, 1970.

Himstreet, William C., and Wayne Murlin Baty. *Business Communications*. 5th ed. Belmont, CA: Wadsworth, 1977.

Lesikar, Raymond V. *Business Communication: Theory and Application*. Rev. ed. Homewood, IL: Richard D. Irwin, 1972.

Menning, J. H., C. W. Wilkinson, and Peter B. Clarke. *Communicating through Letters and Reports*. 6th ed. Homewood, IL: Richard D. Irwin, 1976.

Murphy, Herta A., and Charles E. Peck. *Effective Business Communications*. 2d ed. New York: McGraw-Hill, 1976.

Sigband, Norman B. *Communicating for Management and Business*. 2d ed. Glenview, IL: Scott, Forsman, 1976.

Stewart, Marie M., Frank W. Lanham, and Kenneth Zimmer. *College English and Communication*. 3d ed. New York: McGraw-Hill, 1975.

Wolf, Morris Philip, and Robert R. Aurner. *Effective Communication in Business*. 6th ed. Cincinnati: South-Western, 1974.

INDEX